SURPRISED
BY
CHRIST

MY JOURNEY *from* JUDAISM

to ORTHODOX CHRISTIANITY

By V. Rev. A. James Bernstein

Conciliar Press Ministries
Ben Lomond, California

Surprised by Christ:
My Journey from Judaism to Orthodox Christianity
© Copyright 2008 by A. James Bernstein

All Rights Reserved

Published by   Conciliar Press Ministries, Inc.
P.O. Box 76
Ben Lomond, California 95005-0076

Printed in the United States of America

ISBN 10: 1-888212-95-0
ISBN 13: 978-888212-95-2

Unless otherwise noted, all Scripture quotations are from the New King James
Version of the Bible, © 1982 by Thomas Nelson, Inc., Nashville, Tennessee
and are used by permission.

On the front cover: Father James Bernstein's mother, Belle, is the young girl in the
center of the old family photo.

Second printing, 2009.

Manufactured under the direction of Double Eagle Industries.
For manufacturing details, call 888-824-4344

Contents

Foreword ⌒ 9
Acknowledgements ⌒ 13

Part I ⌒ *Not the Messiah I Expected*
Chapter 1 ⌒ *Raised in the Shadow of the Holocaust* 17
Our Roots in Jerusalem ⌒ 18
Living among the Gentiles ⌒ 19
Ike's Candy Store ⌒ 20
Sounds of the City ⌒ 22
Let's Play Ball! ⌒ 23
A Sense of Evil Lurking ⌒ 25
A Champion at Chess ⌒ 28
The Divine Destiny of the Jews ⌒ 29
Chapter 2 ⌒ *My Conversion* *31*
The First Possibility ⌒ 32
The Second Possibility ⌒ 36
The Third Possibility ⌒ 37
The Turning Point ⌒ 38
Holy Books in the Garbage ⌒ 40
The Hunger Strike ⌒ 41
A Visit to a Wall Street Lawyer ⌒ 41
Chapter 3 ⌒ *Is Christ Divine?* *45*
Jesus Forgives Sins ⌒ 46
Jesus Accepts Worship ⌒ 47
Christ Raised Himself from the Dead ⌒ 50
Christ the "I AM" ⌒ 51
My First Church ⌒ 53
The Gift of Tongues ⌒ 54
Public Preaching ⌒ 55
Chapter 4 ⌒ *Discovering the Prophecies of Christ* *57*
What the Scriptures Reveal about Prophecy ⌒ 58
A Chosen Lineage and the Formation of a People ⌒ 60
A Titanic Struggle ⌒ 62
Embryonic Prophecies That Grew ⌒ 63
When Is the Messiah to Come? ⌒ 65
The "Weeks" of the Prophet Daniel ⌒ 66
Messiah, Son of David ⌒ 68

A Second-Century Book on Prophecy ⌣ 70
The Suffering Servant ⌣ 71
Isaiah 53 ⌣ 72
Psalm 22 ⌣ 77
Chapter 5 ⌣ *College Years*...*81*
The World's Fair ⌣ 82
The Civil Rights Movement ⌣ 83
The Great Blackout of 1965 ⌣ 85
Chapter 6 ⌣ *In the Holy Land* *89*
A Traitor among My People ⌣ 89
Meeting Grandmother ⌣ 90
The Six-Day War ⌣ 91
Suicide! ⌣ 93
Old Jerusalem ⌣ 94
What of Old Israel? ⌣ 95
Are the Jews Still Chosen of God? ⌣ 96
The Mystery of Israel's Blindness ⌣ 96
Returning to America ⌣ 99

Part II ⌣ *Discovering the Church*
Chapter 7 ⌣ *Evangelical Protestant Ministries*...................*103*
The Vietnam War ⌣ 106
InterVarsity Christian Fellowship ⌣ 109
Jews for Jesus ⌣ 111
Love Not Lust ⌣ 113
The Jesus Movement ⌣ 115
Christian Street Theater ⌣ 117
Chapter 8 ⌣ *Why the Scriptures Are Not Enough* *121*
A Maelstrom of Confused Doctrines ⌣ 122
A Struggle for Understanding ⌣ 126
The Bible of the Apostles ⌣ 127
Early Christian Writings ⌣ 128
Who Decided? ⌣ 130
Human and Divine ⌣ 131
A Question of Authority ⌣ 132
The Church of the New Testament ⌣ 133
The Word of God in Oral Tradition ⌣ 134
Which Came First? ⌣ 136
Chapter 9 ⌣ *Worship in the Ancient Church*.....................*139*
A Deep Distrust of Roman Catholicism ⌣ 140
Ancient Worship Was Liturgical and Sacramental ⌣ 142

How the Earliest Christians Worshiped ⌒ 144
Does Ancient Worship Matter? ⌒ 147
The Centrality of the Eucharist ⌒ 148

Chapter 10 ⌒ *A New Commitment*.................................*155*
Our Wedding ⌒ 158

Chapter 11 ⌒ *Finding the Original Church*....................*161*
Fencing the Table ⌒ 163
Orthodox Christian Doctrine ⌒ 164
Orthodox Christian Morality ⌒ 167
Orthodox Christian Obedience ⌒ 170
A Broken Unity ⌒ 171
Communion in the Orthodox Church ⌒ 176

Chapter 12 ⌒ *Orthodoxy: Jewish and Christian*...............*179*
Worship in Scripture ⌒ 179
Discovering Christian Roots ⌒ 182
The Church of the Holy Land ⌒ 185
Rediscovering the God of the Jews ⌒ 186
Rediscovering Our True Sacrifice ⌒ 188
Rediscovering Jewish Mysticism ⌒ 189
Rediscovering the Joy of the Lord ⌒ 191
Coming Home ⌒ 193

Chapter 13 ⌒ *What Became of the Apostolic Jewish Christian Church?*..............................*197*
The Nazarenes ⌒ 198
Two Movements of Jewish Christians ⌒ 199
The Great Escape ⌒ 200
A Gentilized Christianity ⌒ 201
Into the Abyss ⌒ 202
Further North ⌒ 204
The Turning Point ⌒ 206
Where Are the Descendants of the Nazarenes? ⌒ 207

Part III ⌒ *Discovering Salvation with Depth*

Chapter 14 ⌒ *How Fallen Are We?*...............................*211*
Back to New York ⌒ 212
Is Death from God? ⌒ 214
How Fallen *Are* We? ⌒ 219
What Is Inherited from Original Sin? ⌒ 221
Lasting Repercussions of Augustine's Theology ⌒ 224
Our EOC Friends Become Orthodox ⌒ 227
My Ordinations ⌒ 228

Chapter 15 ᕔ *What Salvation Is Not:*
Solutions to Problems That Don't Exist............................*231*
Will There Be the Devil to Pay? ᕔ 232
A Payment to Appease an Angry God? ᕔ 233
Indulgences: Punitive or Remedial? ᕔ 238
The Penal Substitutionary Theory of Atonement ᕔ 240
Sinners in the Hands of an Angry God ᕔ 241
Too Hard to Bear: The Moral Exemplar Theory
of Atonement ᕔ 245
The Purpose of the Sacrificial System ᕔ 246
Propitiation or Expiation? ᕔ 251

Chapter 16 ᕔ *What Is Salvation?* *255*
God as "The Lover of Mankind" ᕔ 256
Diagnosing the Disease of Sin ᕔ 258
The Language of Salvation in the New Testament ᕔ 260
The Language of Salvation in St. Athanasius ᕔ 267
What Is Not Assumed Is Not Healed ᕔ 268

Chapter 17 ᕔ *God Became Man So That Man*
Might Become God *275*
Returning to the Holy Land ᕔ 275
Beyond Forgiveness ᕔ 277
"I said, 'You are gods'" (John 10:34) ᕔ 279
Eucharist: Divine and Human ᕔ 282
To Be Filled One Must Be Emptied ᕔ 284
Knowing God Is Progressive ᕔ 285

Chapter 18 ᕔ *Is God Humble?* *289*
God: Composite Unity or Absolute Unity? ᕔ 290
God's Condescension: In His Incarnation ᕔ 291
One of the Trinity Suffered in the Flesh ᕔ 293
Humility: Strength or Weakness? ᕔ 296
Tools with Which to Gain Humility ᕔ 299

Chapter 19 ᕔ *The Divine Fire of God's Love* *305*
Is Hellfire Physical or Spiritual? ᕔ 306
What Makes Heaven, Heaven and Hell, Hell? ᕔ 309
The River of Fire ᕔ 312
Hearts of Wax or of Clay? ᕔ 313
Divine Fire Purifies ᕔ 316
God Never Stops Loving All ᕔ 319
Understanding Scripture on the Judgment ᕔ 321
The Doors of Hell Are Locked on the Inside ᕔ 324
From Glory to Glory: Perfection that Grows ᕔ 326
Within the Divine Fire of God's Love ᕔ 328
Endnotes ᕔ 331

This book is dedicated
to the greatest Jew,
Jesus Christ,
and to the greatest Jewess,
the Virgin Mary.
And also
to the "people of their flesh,"
the Jews.

"He who does not love does not know God,
for God is Love." (1 John 4:8)

Foreword ໑

Surprised by Christ is an autobiography, an intellectual history, and a conversion story, and more than these, conveys a spiritual and theological vision in a message that touches people from many different backgrounds. That vision is of the Living God revealed in Jesus Christ, who is the fulfillment of the Old Covenant, the life of the Faithful, the hope of the despairing, and the motivation for those who strive to preach the Gospel in all its integrity.

Fr. James's own life and struggle to know God led him from Judaism to Christianity, through the evangelical world, the Jews for Jesus movement, and the strivings of a community of evangelicals for the historic Christian Church. His experience bridges a fascinating spectrum of the cultural and religious trends of the last half of the twentieth century. Born in the shadow of the Holocaust, he grew up in New York, attended college in Queens, lived in Israel during the Six Day War, and experienced the Jesus Movement and hippie culture of the San Francisco Bay Area in the early seventies. He later became involved with the group springing from Campus Crusade that became the Evangelical Orthodox Church, which gradually discovered the Orthodox Tradition. He was received several years before that group into the Orthodox Church in America, and then entered St. Vladimir's Seminary. It was here, first in the Bay Area and then at St. Vladimir's, that our lives crossed. After seminary, he transferred to the Antiochian Archdiocese and was ordained in order to resume work with his old friends from the Evangelical Orthodox movement. He continues to work in that context as it has developed over the past twenty years.

More than an autobiography, though, Fr. James gives us an outline of his intellectual and spiritual development. His broad experience and education give this book a unique perspective. His Jewish heritage grounds his vision in the Semitic roots of Christianity and provides a contrast to the very Western Christian set of cultural presuppositions with which most of us were raised. This is revealed not only in the development of his thought regarding the prophecies of the Old Testament and the realization that Orthodox Christianity is truly the fulfillment of Orthodox Judaism; he also keeps the consciousness of the Old Covenant as it is fulfilled spiritually in Christ, the deep continuity and spiritual vision in the experience of the Living God who is revealed by Jesus Christ.

I know of no other book that deals so thoroughly with the intellectual and spiritual process of conversion from Judaism to Orthodox Christianity. This is significant not only for Jews who are considering Orthodoxy. It is also important for the many contemporary evangelicals who have a strong orientation either towards Judaism or towards Zionism. The point is that Orthodox Christianity is the fulfillment of Orthodox Judaism and thus its true successor, whereas a Judaizing of Protestantism does violence to both.

This book also contains an excellent presentation of the spiritual and intellectual movement from evangelicalism, with its cultural roots deep in the Western tradition, to Orthodox Christianity. Over and above the usual evangelical questions of liturgy, sacraments, saints, and the like, Fr. James deals with the underlying presuppositions of the cultural Christianity which is common to almost all Americans: the Augustinian and Anselmian ideas that differentiated, and later divided, the West from the broader Orthodox Catholic Church. These include the ideas of original sin, the atonement, and the concepts of salvation, as well as the nature of hell and divine punishment—the divine fire of God's love.

Theologically addressing these basic presuppositions, Fr. James shows that Orthodox Christianity has a vision of God and salvation radically different, and far more healthy, than the culturally conditioned presuppositions of American popular religion. To become an Orthodox Christian is not a matter of accepting a few additional doctrines, like the veneration of Mary and calling salvation "theosis." Conversion demands a radical shift, not only in which church one attends, but in the very ways we think about God. How we think about God conditions our experience of Him. Conversion to Orthodox Christianity means that we have to change our basic presuppositions in order to open ourselves more fully to the great mystery of God's Presence, love, and mercy. We have to discard the old ways of thinking about God and salvation, which, insofar as they are erroneous, block the experience of God and present obstacles on the path to salvation.

One of the strengths of this book is that this theological challenge is presented not so much in terms of polemics or apologetics (though these are not absent!), but primarily in terms of personal realizations along the path of intellectual and spiritual growth. Nevertheless, this book presents a strong challenge to us to examine our own theological and spiritual assumptions, and thus to tread the path of repentance, the renewal of our minds and hearts, in order that we may more faithfully ascend to the divine vision embraced by the uncreated fire of God's love.

by His Eminence, Jonah,
Metropolitan of All America and Canada
(Orthodox Church in America)

Acknowledgements ᘒ

I EXTEND MY HEARTFELT GRATITUDE TO THOSE WHO FIRST told me of the love of Christ, especially my brother Solomon and my childhood neighbors in Queens, New York, George Linkus and Tom Carrubba and his family; and to Moishe Rosen, who first challenged me to maintain Jewish identity as a Christian. My deepest appreciation to those who introduced me to Orthodox Christianity while living in Berkeley, California, especially Deacon Jeremiah Crawford and Father Jack Sparks.

I am indebted to those who encouraged me to write this book and enabled it to happen: the editors Fr. Peter Gillquist, Mary Vaughn Armstrong, and Katherine Hyde; Carla Zell and all the members of the Conciliar Press book team; as well as Abbot Jonah Paffhausen, Gary McGinnis, and Peter Chopelas.

My fervent thanks to those who inspired me not to deny my Jewish heritage after becoming an Orthodox Christian: Fr. John Meyendorff (of blessed memory), Fr. Thomas Hopko, Professor Veselin Kesich, and His Eminence Metropolitan Kallistos (Ware).

My profound gratitude for those in Israel who are Orthodox Christians of Jewish heritage, who have preserved within me hope that a contemporary Jewish expression of the Orthodox Christian Faith will come to fruition, especially Fr. Alexander Winogradsky in Jerusalem.

My thanks to my church family of St. Paul Antiochian Orthodox Church in Brier, Washington, which for seventeen years has been my family indeed; to the Most Reverend Metropolitan PHILIP (Saliba) and the Right Reverend Bishop JOSEPH (Al-Zehlaoui); and the Antiochian Orthodox Christian Archdiocese,

13

which though having Arabic roots has accepted me with open arms and love.

Last of all, thanksgiving for my wife Bonnie and our four children, Heather and her husband Reverend Fr. David Sommer, Holly, Peter, and Mary and her husband James D. Curry, who have encouraged me in my life and the writing of this book—I couldn't have done it without you.

Archpriest A. James Bernstein
Lynnwood, Washington
July 5, 2007

Part I

Not the Messiah I Expected

Chapter 1

Raised in the Shadow of the Holocaust

I AWOKE SUDDENLY TO THE SOUND OF A BRICK CRASHING through our huge storefront window. My parents, Isaac and Belle, and I had been sound asleep in our bedrooms immediately behind the candy store we owned in Queens, New York. A flimsy wooden door was all that separated my bedroom from the storefront where the family worked during the day.

I heard shouts coming from the store, and Dad, whom everyone called Ike, ran in that direction while Mom screamed, "Ike, watch out! Ike, watch out!" Then came the profanity, voices shouting, "Jew bastards!" "Kikes, get out!" "We're going to kill you!"

It seemed like a nightmare. Where was I? Was this Nazi Germany? Wasn't I in the urbane Jewish stronghold of New York City? As I got out of bed and cautiously approached the door, I saw a number of young men struggling to restrain the man who had committed the villainous deed. Evidently he had drunk too much at the tavern across the street and decided to vent his fury on us.

As they dragged the man away, my dad, whose native language was Yiddish, yelled "*Meshuggener!*" ("Crazy!").

Mom and Dad often spoke to one another with great animation, hand gestures and all. To ensure that I couldn't understand, they alternated between Yiddish and Hebrew. It was important to them that I be sheltered from the dark dread clouds of the sinister past, so they were determined to speak only English to me, as if somehow that would keep me from knowing about these things. But try as they would, they couldn't keep everything from me, because the curses I understood. And at times like this, it seemed as if curses comprised much of their speech.

A few weeks later a picture of the man who had assaulted us was plastered on the front page of the major New York City newspapers. After smashing our window, he killed a man, and the police were called to apprehend him. He tried to escape but was caught by a single policeman, who happened to be his brother. This special interest news item became the talk of the city.

Our Roots in Jerusalem ∽

IN SPITE OF INCIDENTS LIKE THIS, MY FAMILY LOVED AMERICA, especially New York City. Dad had been born in the Old City of Jerusalem when Israel was still known as Palestine, and had been raised to be an ultra-Orthodox Hasidic Jewish rabbi. He received his ordination certificate from the chief rabbi of the Ashkenazi Jewish community in Palestine, Rabbi Chaim Joseph Sonnenfeld himself, who is considered to be a Jewish sage. The Hasidic movement grew up in Eastern Europe in the eighteenth century in reaction to the excessive academic emphasis prevalent in much of Judaism. The Hasidic Orthodox emphasized mysticism, a joyful, exuberant spirituality, and the sage as miracle-worker.

Mom's parents were also Orthodox. They had their origins in Latvia within the Hasidim's opposing camp called the *Mitnagdim*, Hebrew for "opposers." Mom was born in Pittsburgh, Pennsylvania. Her parents and Dad's parents had known one another in Jerusalem and arranged for Mom and Dad to marry. That's how it was done in the old days. I'm not complaining, because their union produced me, Arnold NMN Bernstein. (The NMN on my government-issued Selective Service card stood for "No Middle Name." Most Jewish men did not have middle names.)

In 1932, while traveling to the United States by ship from the Holy Land, Mom took a train from Italy to Bremen, Germany, passing through Berlin. While there she heard and saw vicious things said and done to Jews. This put her on high alert.

That same year, she married Dad in Minnesota, where a year later my brother Sol was born. In 1935 all three moved to Palestine, where they lived for six years. Prior to the outbreak of World War II, Mom said that Nazi planes were heard over Jerusalem and that the Muslim Grand Mufti of Palestine was rousing Arabs against the Jews. Feeling it too dangerous to continue living in the Holy Land, she persuaded Dad to move back to America.

So in 1941 she, Dad, and my brother Sol, who is thirteen years older than I, took the last ship leaving Palestine for America. At that time it was too dangerous to go through the Mediterranean Sea and the North Atlantic, so they took an Egyptian ship from the Red Sea that went all the way around southern Africa, across the South Atlantic to South America, and then north to New York. It was then that Mom gained expertise in removing nits (head lice eggs) from Sol's and her own hair with very fine-toothed combs and cracking them between her two thumbnails. This was an art that somehow carried over to life in the New World, where she would nonchalantly smash endless hordes of New York cockroaches with her bare hands.

Living among the Gentiles ❧

THOUGH RAISED IN NEW YORK CITY, I WAS ACTUALLY BORN AT the Sparrow Hospital in Lansing, Michigan, on May 6, 1946.

When I was a few months old, we moved to New York, our new "promised land."

The war and its accompanying Holocaust had done terrible things to Dad. It caused him not only to cease being an Orthodox Jew, but also to lose all faith in God. He could no longer serve in good conscience as a rabbi. While in this disillusioned state, he bought what became Ike's Candy Store in a predominantly Gentile neighborhood in Woodhaven, Queens.

Our neighbors were mostly first- and second-generation immigrants from Italy, Ireland, Germany, and Eastern Europe—a true melting pot. Across the street was Franklin K. Lane High School with about 5,000 students. One-third were African American from Brooklyn, one-third were of Puerto Rican descent, and one-third were whites from the local neighborhood. What a mix!

Ike's Candy Store ∾

THE CANDY STORE WAS NOT MY SECOND HOME; IT WAS MY FIRST. I spent most of my waking hours there when I wasn't in school. The store had a long counter with tall round swivel chairs.

The first of three waves of customers would arrive between six and nine o'clock each morning. On their way to trains and buses, they purchased their morning papers and coffee. We could tell what their political and social leanings were by the newspapers they bought. The *Wall Street Journal* for those working in the financial district, who tended to be conservative Republicans; the *New York Times* for the more sophisticated, who wanted in-depth analysis of international news and tended to be more liberal; the *Mirror Journal-American* and *Herald Tribune* for those desiring more local news in a less sophisticated style, who tended to be more middle-of-the-road in their political leanings.

The *New York Daily News* was a sensational, popularist

∾ SURPRISED BY CHRIST

conservative newspaper written in a very simple style. This was the paper of choice for our neighbors, as it was believed to present the truth, no holds barred. Foreign-language newspapers served the numerous European immigrants, primarily Italians. Dad read two Yiddish newspapers—*The Forward* and *The Day*. We had more newspapers than we had baseball teams.

Cigarettes were also a big seller as the local commuters stocked up for the day's work. People smoked everywhere—in the candy store, on trains and buses, in workplaces and offices, in restaurants, in restrooms, even on planes.

The second wave of customers arrived at lunchtime, from eleven A.M. to one P.M. At times it seemed as if all the five thousand students from the high school across the street were attempting to cram into the store at the same time. The items of choice were bottled soda pop, potato chips, and various candy bars—the standard student lunch. We also sold a lot of school supplies, as well as magazines and the ever-popular comic books and baseball cards. Alas, if I had saved my constant and abundant supply of comic books and baseball cards, I would be a rich man today.

Lunchtime was when we had to be most on guard, as that was when kids, if given the chance, would steal us blind. Once, during a fistfight staged at the rear of the store to divert Dad and my brother Sol, two young men in the front of the store picked up the huge cash register, ran out, and laboriously carried it down the street. This was no ordinary cash register. It was as big as they came, gold-colored, covered with manual keys and levers, with pop-up signs that made jingling sounds when the keys were pressed. The register was so heavy the thieves could not get far. When Dad caught up with them, they dropped it and fled. After that the register was securely attached to the wall by a large metal chain.

The cash register's weight was due in part to the pure silver coins in it. Customers disposed of all sorts of old silver coins, many of which found their way from Ike's cash register into my coin collection. We received old silver dollars, two- and three-cent pieces, half-dimes, old quarters, and half-dollars—even an 1838 silver half-dollar in terrific condition.

The third wave of customers arrived on their way home from work. Often they purchased the evening *Daily News* along with antacids. We offered a number of kinds of antacids, including Alka-Seltzer, the tablet that fizzled when it was placed in water; Bromo-Seltzer, a powdered equivalent; Tums-like tablets; and "two-cent plain," which was simply a glass of seltzer water. These concoctions provided relief from the stress of the day's work.

Some families would arrive after dinner for our locally famous ice cream sundaes, banana splits, malts, and milkshakes, or Italian sodas offered in various flavors. Often ice cream orders were covered with abundant amounts of homemade whipped cream, squeezed out of a large flexible tubelike container.

Other neighbors came just to socialize and talk about the news events of the day. My friend Louie's father frequently came to scrutinize the dry, gnarled, Italian cigars, making sure they were perfect and without cracks.

Sounds of the City ❧

LOUD NOISES WERE AN EVER-PRESENT PART OF MY LIFE IN NEW York City: the clattering of jackhammers and droning of power generators as concrete was chiseled; the wailing of fire engines and police car sirens throughout the day; the daily noon-hour testing of nuclear warning sirens with their high, oscillating pitch, and the steady all-clear wail that followed; the sporadic gunfire that would erupt at night as both lone criminals and gangs fought in the streets. In pleasant contrast, I also remember the bells chiming from the local Catholic church on Sunday mornings.

But the sound that most characterized my youth was that of the elevated trains screeching to a halt a few yards from us at the Elderts Lane elevated train stop on the Jamaica Avenue BMT line. Hundreds of tons' load on bare steel wheels scraping on bare metal rails painfully pierced my ears. This high-pitched sound of screeching brakes was the New York "Sound of Music" that I heard every half-hour, twenty-four hours a day, three-hundred-sixty-five days a year for twenty-five years. Was this perhaps the cause of my thirty-percent hearing loss? Unfortunately, that loss was not great enough to prevent my hearing the nightly sounds of vicious profanities that our "friendly" neighbors spewed.

Years later, when I moved to a more country-like environment on the West Coast, it took months for me to experience normal sleep because it was too quiet to bear. I went through noise withdrawal. To make the transition smoother, I put the radio on every night in order to go to sleep.

The most memorable sound of all occurred the night when thousands of people in the neighborhood awoke to the piercing, horrific wailing sound of the oscillating sirens that warned of incoming nuclear weapons. The sirens had somehow accidentally gone off, causing the entire neighborhood to think that we had only a few minutes to live before being collectively incinerated. The next day we kids at the high school shared the fascinating stories of how our families prepared to die. Most of my friends' parents got out their Bibles and prayed.

Let's Play Ball! ⌁

MY EDUCATION INCLUDED THE BEST THE STREETS OF NEW YORK had to offer. On top of that, what better learning could be found than that offered in the New York grade schools? I attended Public

Schools (P.S.) #60, #65, and #97. Whatever creativity was lacking in the names of the schools was more than made up for by the distinct advantage of being in what New Yorkers proclaimed was the cultural center of the universe. And what other city had three, yes three, baseball teams: the New York Yankees, the Brooklyn Dodgers, and the New York Giants? As a kid, that was all I cared about.

Playing ball on the streets of New York was as exciting as it comes, as we had to maintain total focus while avoiding getting hit by passing cars. Without peripheral vision, you were dead. We played as many types of ball as there were ethnic backgrounds in our group—stickball, punch ball, slap ball, handball, kings, points, hit-the-stick, and last but not least, war. These were all played with a unique ball called a Spaulding, or affectionately a "pinky," as the ball was like a tennis ball minus the fuzz with a pink smooth surface. My father sold these balls and provided an endless free supply for my friends and me. This explains why I was every ball-playing kid's best friend. And having a candy store that offered free candy, soda, ice cream, and whipped cream to my buddies didn't hurt!

The high school across the street provided huge fields in which to play baseball and football, and courts for basketball, softball, handball, and stickball. A few blocks away was Forest Park, which stretched for miles with parks, lakes, golf courses, horseback riding, even an outdoor band shell where weekly musical events were held. We would often go there to play.

As a kid I had the best of both worlds—an unlimited number of friends from the densely populated neighborhood in which we lived, and wide-open fields, parks, and forests within walking distance in which to play. And it was safe. Everyone watched out for everyone else, and if there was any trouble, our local Irish Catholic cop was always accessible, walking his beat. In New York we had an easily identifiable division of labor. The cops were Irish Catholic, the teachers were Jews, the union leaders and organizers were Italian.

A Sense of Evil Lurking ∽

RELIGION WAS A SIGNIFICANT PART OF LIFE IN OUR COMMUNITY. I often woke to the sounds of ringing bells from the local Roman Catholic churches. When I was a student in the public grade schools, my classes became virtually empty on Friday afternoons as kids left a couple of hours early to attend Catholic catechism.

Mom kept kosher. She had two sets of dishes, one for meat products and one for dairy products. Jewish law prohibits the mingling of the two. When preparing meat, we had three choices of how it could be cooked: well-done, well-done, or well-done. To "kosher" meat, Mom salted it heavily the night before, not with regular salt, but with special koshering salt consisting of gigantic crystals. It reminded me of the Epsom salts she put into her bathwater to make it like ocean water. Koshering salt drained every drop of blood out of the meat during the night, so that when cooked the following day it tasted like bloodless cardboard.

I joined the glee club in grade school. My favorite time of the year was the Christmas season, because I could sing Christmas carols without being a Christian. In those days Christmas carols sung in the public schools were still about Christ. I loved the carols. They were so bright, so joyful. I am convinced that somehow they worked their way into me, preparing the soil of my heart to receive the seed of the Gospel.

At Christmas I felt jealous of my Gentile friends. They received so many fine gifts, like electric train sets, gas-powered plane sets, and tons of silly games to play. I got Chanukah *gelt* (money). The joke we had was that while Santa came down the chimney to give the Gentiles Christmas presents, Charlie Chanukah came down the incinerator to put Chanukah *gelt* on our Chanukah bush. I liked *gelt*, but I really liked silly presents more.

Along with the carefree joy of being raised in a kid's paradise and living behind a candy store, there was a dark side to my life. The brick shattering the candy store window jarringly reminded me of that. Jewish history has more than its fair share of terror and suffering.

The Cypress Hills Jewish cemetery was within walking distance of our home and stretched for miles. It was right next to the high school on the Brooklyn side of the Queens/Brooklyn border. At times we would wander over, sneak through the chain link fence, and play hide-and-seek. It was a strange place to play; it wasn't like a modern-day cemetery with every tombstone identically small, often lying flat on the ground. This one had many high tombstones and large stone mausoleums, as well as endless rows of tall hedges. We had innumerable places to hide, even to get lost.

Sometimes we had so much fun we would delay going home. As the day gave way to dusk, a certain terror would arise within me. What if I got left behind? Would I become trapped like the unliving? Sometimes when going to sleep, I would think of the endless numbers buried in the vast cemetery. It lurked nearby like a doorway to a dark, hidden abyss. At times I woke up with an overwhelming sense of dread, of a dark presence. I would be paralyzed—unable to move—for some minutes. These horrific experiences reinforced my belief in the existence of an invisible world of evil.

My bed was in the room next to the door that led down into the basement. In that area were many rooms, but I most dreaded one in particular: the coal furnace room, with its chute and large pile of coal. At times I dreamed that the basement door opened and I was drawn, as if by a magnetic force, through the doorway, down the long flight of stairs, through the various rooms to *the* room that I most feared. Something drew me there, to the evil that dwelt beneath the rear corner of the coal bin. I struggled in my dream to resist, to hold onto the bed, the table, the door, the stairs, anything that would prevent me from being drawn to the evil that wanted to consume me.

My brother Sol knew about evil. Sol was a terrific brother, very gentle and kind. He told me that he once awoke in the dead of night with a strong sense of an evil presence in his room and saw a huge face on the ceiling staring down at him. He froze. For some time it would not go away. He felt as if he were going mad and did not know what to do. So he prayed. As he prayed, the face diminished in size and slowly disappeared. What he most remembered were the fierce eyes.

Sol told me that he thought such an experience might cause insanity if the person did not pray to God for help. That seemed reasonable to me. After that I prepared my prayers so that if I awoke at night, paralyzed with a hideous face staring down at me, I would know what to do.

Some people see the best in others and do not live with a sense of dread. But I was raised in the shadow of the Holocaust. The dark cloud of six million Jewish souls hovered about me, pressing upon me, their murder revealing the reality of evil, sin, and demonic existence. I had no problem believing in the existence of evil. Often I asked myself, why six million others and not me? If my parents had been killed, I would never have been born.

As a child of three or so I had a brush with death. My nose was congested, and Mom made a boiling hot tub of water containing a nasal clearing solution. I was supposed to lean over it while sitting on the couch and inhale the healing fumes. One day my mother left and my brother took charge. Somehow I fell into the steaming hot tub of water. My brother immediately wrapped me in some towels that had been placed in cool water and got me to the hospital. Fortunately my burns were not severe enough to kill me, but they did take over a year to heal. My back is still scarred. Such events damage the interior as well as the exterior.

A Champion at Chess ～

WHEN I WAS ABOUT TEN YEARS OLD, A NEIGHBOR WHO LIVED down the street offered to teach me how to play chess. Why not, I thought. I really took to it, and in a short time was beating him. I advanced and soon played a much more serious chess player, Don, who frequented the store. He lived for chess. Sometimes we walked to Forest Park, where many concrete chess tables were available. Amazing games were played there on weekend afternoons by amazing people. They were all eccentrics; that was the one thing they seemed to have in common. In that context my playing skills took off as I fell in love with the game.

Don had a friend who was our next-door neighbor. He played even better than Don and introduced me to tournament chess. His name was Frank Brady, and he later became famous as a chess tournament organizer and also as the biographer of the world chess champion Bobby Fischer. Soon I joined the Marshall Chess Club in Greenwich Village and played a lot of tournament chess. By the time I was thirteen, I was the U.S. Junior Chess Champion in the under-sixteen category. Subsequently, during my four years in high school, I won the New York City High School Chess Championship three out of four times. I also won the Marshall Chess Club Amateur Chess Championship twice.

Such was my life. It was a happy life, with many friends, loving parents, and unlimited opportunities. Yet not all was well. An underground river of dread undermined the foundations of my peaceful existence. The ghosts of six million Jews would not leave me. I feared that at the core of the universe was a meaningless void—a spiritual black hole—that the beauty called life had no artist. Doubt took hold of me, causing my youthful joy to sour. I began to consider what purpose, if any, life might have.

The Divine Destiny of the Jews ◟

WE LIVED WITHIN WALKING DISTANCE OF OUR LOCAL CONSERVATIVE Jewish synagogue. I attended services sporadically and went to Hebrew school once a week after public school. Mom and I attended annual High Holy Day services. During this time I began seriously to read the Bible (Old Testament). Much of it seemed compelling to me, especially its description of fallen humanity, corruption, and sin. The account of Israel's ongoing relationship and struggle with God deeply impressed me. I accepted the biblical accounts of Israel's unique calling to be the chosen people of God.

Within history's flow, there seemed to be a Jewish destiny. Although we were dispersed throughout the world and fiercely persecuted, our preservation as a people seemed to be part of a greater drama that was still in process. The return to the land of our origin somehow seemed more than a quirk of history. After all, what other people had been dispersed without a country for two thousand years, or received as intense a persecution for as long as the Jews and yet survived? And not just any persecution, but one culminating in what is universally held to be the most systematic and sophisticated attempt at genocide in history at the hands of Nazi Germany. Has any other people retained their unique religion, culture, and identity through centuries of dispersion, and then returned against impossible odds to the land of their origin? What other people revived the ancient language of their forefathers that had not been spoken for two millennia, thereby making it—Hebrew—the living language of an entire nation?

The number of Jews worldwide, I have been told, consists of less than 0.0001 percent of the world population. Yet Jewish impact on the fields of science, economics, and the arts is astronomical. Approximately twenty-five percent of Nobel Laureates to date have been Jews. Many have said that the three men who had the greatest impact on the modern world, for better or worse, were Albert Einstein in science, Sigmund Freud in psychology, and Karl Marx in politics—all Jews. *Time* Magazine named Einstein "the Person of the Twentieth Century." Was this Jewish prominence accidental, or the result of cultural and social forces alone, or was there in addition some mysterious providential force at work, somehow channeling events and our people towards some divinely directed destiny?

As I pondered the biblical accounts, it became ever clearer that God's love and man's resistance to His love, which are dramatically and graphically presented in the Bible, apply not only to a specific people, the Jewish people, but to all people. We all tend to be egocentric, self-serving, self-absorbed, faithless, unloving, and rebellious. Thus, God's love is often ignored, resisted, diverted, and misrepresented. I certainly had no difficulty recognizing myself as being what the Bible describes as hardhearted. Yet in spite of my authentic love of the Scripture and prayer, God seemed very distant, the King of the Universe—to be talked about, but not known personally.

Chapter 2

My Conversion

AMONG MY BEST FRIENDS WERE TOM AND FRANK. BOTH loved classical music, were Christians, and had parents who were from Sicily. Frank, who had been raised Roman Catholic, had recently become interested in the Jehovah's Witnesses. I asked him to give me a New Testament to read, as we did not have one, and he gave me the Jehovah's Witness version. I was about sixteen years old, and for me, receiving the New Testament—which I had always viewed as "the enemy's book" and absolutely forbidden—was scary. I read it with fear and trembling, feeling that I was committing a great, unpardonable sin, fully expecting to uncover great evil in it. I studied it in secret under the covers in my bedroom at night, with a flashlight.

I was mesmerized by the New Testament's description of Jesus Christ. This was not at all the person I expected to find as the central figure of Christianity. I thought I would discover someone who was ruthless, intolerant, prejudiced, and even militant—a lot like a few of the Christians I knew. Instead I found a model of faith, love, wisdom, and restraint. Under intense attack, He conducted Himself with what appeared to be truly supernatural grace, wisdom, and love. In the accounts of His life contained in the Gospels, I could not find a single event in which He behaved in any way less than exemplary. Then I came to the accounts of His week of passion, betrayal, and crucifixion. Of this I was certain—no one ever lived as did Jesus. I was confronted with a major decision: what to do with Christ.

The First Possibility ⤚

I DECIDED TO APPROACH THE ISSUE AS LOGICALLY AS I COULD. The first possibility I considered was that Christ's life could have been made up or grossly exaggerated—a concocted story written and expanded on by others. I soon dismissed this theory on the grounds that the apostolic eyewitnesses to the events clearly believed them to be authentic. They lived their lives based on Christ's life, as they in turn were wholly dedicated to love and serve Him. Why would they all be willing to suffer, be tortured, and be hideously martyred for something they knew to be a lie? This explanation just didn't make sense.

Additionally, the Gospel accounts indicate that the apostles were greatly resistant to believing, even after witnessing numerous miracles and hearing of Christ's Resurrection from Mary Magdalene and the myrrhbearing women. The Scripture says:

> Now when *He* rose early on the first *day* of the week, He appeared first to Mary Magdalene, out of whom He had cast seven demons. She went and told those who had been with Him, as they mourned and wept. And when they heard that He was alive and had been seen by her, they did not believe. After that, He appeared in another form to two of them as they walked and went into the country. And they went and told *it* to the rest, *but* they did not believe them either. Later He appeared to the eleven as they sat at the table; and He rebuked their unbelief and hardness of heart, because they did not believe those who had seen Him after He had risen. (Mark 16:9–14)

⤚ SURPRISED BY CHRIST

A parallel account is found in the Gospel of Luke:

Then they returned from the tomb and told all these things
to the eleven and to all the rest. It was Mary Magdalene,
Joanna, Mary *the mother* of James, and the other *women*
with them, who told these things to the apostles. And
their words seemed to them like idle tales, and they did
not believe them. . . . Now as they said these things, Jesus
Himself stood in the midst of them, and said to them,
"Peace to you." But they were terrified and frightened, and
supposed they had seen a spirit. And He said to them,
"Why are you troubled? And why do doubts arise in your
hearts? Behold My hands and My feet, that it is I Myself.
Handle Me and see, for a spirit does not have flesh and
bones as you see I have." When He had said this, He
showed them His hands and His feet. But while they still
did not believe for joy, and marveled, He said to them,
"Have you any food here?" . . . And He took *it* and ate in
their presence. (Luke 24:9–11, 36–41, 43)

In these accounts we see the disillusionment, despair, and grief
of the disciples following the crucifixion and death of Christ. They
were in hiding in fear of Christ's persecutors and did not believe
at all the reports of His Resurrection. Finally Christ Himself appeared to them and conversed with them, but they "still did not
believe for joy, and marveled."

Jesus explained to His disciples how what had transpired
fulfilled the Old Testament scripture:

Then He said to them, "These *are* the words which I spoke
to you while I was still with you, that all things must be
fulfilled which were written in the Law of Moses and *the*

Prophets and *the* Psalms concerning Me." And He opened their understanding, that they might comprehend the Scriptures. Then He said to them, "Thus it is written, and thus it was necessary for the Christ to suffer and to rise from the dead the third day, and that repentance and remission of sins should be preached in His name to all nations, beginning at Jerusalem. And you are witnesses of these things." (Luke 24:44–48)

His challenge to the two disciples traveling the road to Emmaus was even more forthright:

Then He said to them, "O foolish ones, and slow of heart to believe in all that the prophets have spoken! Ought not the Christ to have suffered these things and to enter into His glory?" And beginning at Moses and all the Prophets, He expounded to them in all the Scriptures the things concerning Himself. (Luke 24:25–27)

Of all the accounts of the resurrected Christ revealing Himself to the disciples, the most graphic I discovered was in the Gospel of John. Christ had presented Himself to the apostles, but the apostle Thomas was absent. When the apostles told Thomas what had happened, he did not believe.

Then, the same day at evening, being the first *day* of the week, when the doors were shut where the disciples were assembled, for fear of the Jews, Jesus came and stood in the midst, and said to them, "Peace *be* with you." . . . Now Thomas, called the Twin, one of the twelve, was not with them when Jesus came. The other disciples therefore said to him, "We have seen the Lord." So he said to them,

"Unless I see in His hands the print of the nails, and put my finger into the print of the nails, and put my hand into His side, I will not believe." And after eight days His disciples were again inside, and Thomas with them. Jesus came, the doors being shut, and stood in the midst, and said, "Peace to you!" Then He said to Thomas, "Reach your finger here, and look at My hands; and reach your hand *here*, and put *it* into My side. Do not be unbelieving, but believing." And Thomas answered and said to Him, "My Lord and my God!" Jesus said to him, "Thomas, because you have seen Me, you have believed. Blessed *are* those who have not seen and *yet* have believed." (John 20:19, 24–29)

The apostles and disciples of Christ were more than hesitant to believe that Christ had risen from the dead—they were outright disbelieving. The apostle Thomas, known as Doubting Thomas, would not accept that Christ had arisen until he touched Him. The fact that the followers of Christ were so reluctant to believe made their accounts more credible to me. These disciples were not gullible—rather they were skeptics who were confronted with the risen Christ face-to-face in the flesh.

After His Resurrection, the Scripture states, Christ was seen not by a select few for a short time, but by many over a prolonged period. Luke writes regarding the apostles, ". . . to whom He also presented Himself alive after His suffering by many infallible proofs, being seen by them during forty days and speaking of the things pertaining to the kingdom of God" (Acts 1:3).

Later in the same book he quotes St. Paul as saying, "But God raised Him from the dead. He was seen for many days by those who came up with Him from Galilee to Jerusalem, who are His witnesses to the people" (Acts 13:30–31).

The apostle Paul writes in his own account that the risen Christ was seen by over five hundred disciples, as well as by the apostles and finally by himself:

> . . . and that He rose again the third day according to the Scriptures, and that He was seen by Cephas, then by the twelve. After that He was seen by over five hundred brethren at once, of whom the greater part remain to the present, but some have fallen asleep. After that He was seen by James, then by all the apostles. Then last of all He was seen by me also, as by one born out of due time. For I am the least of the apostles, who am not worthy to be called an apostle, because I persecuted the church of God. (1 Corinthians 15:4–9)

The apostle Paul had a unique direct encounter with Christ while in the process of vigorously persecuting the Christians. I read the account of Paul's conversion in Acts 9 and once again was impressed at his dramatic change of attitude—from being the fiercest opponent he became the leading proponent of Christ. Certainly nothing less than an encounter with the risen Christ could effect such a change.

These accounts of the conversions of innumerable skeptics and opponents of Christ into disciples willing to be martyred—often hideously—for their belief in the reality of His Resurrection from the dead, I found extremely compelling.

The Second Possibility ❧

IN ADDITION TO THE FIRST POSSIBILITY I CONSIDERED AND THEN dismissed—that the accounts of Christ's life could have been made up or grossly exaggerated—I considered a second possibility:

that Jesus and His disciples were all deluded. That is, though they lived exemplary lives, they had no supernatural or divine empowerment or significance. Their lives were beautiful, but the claims were false.

If His apostles truly exhibited superior love, honesty, and humility, of which I had no doubt, how could so many be so deluded about something as basic as the foundation on which everything was built? Innumerable eyewitnesses attested to the essential reality of God, of the supernatural, and of the miraculous. I understood that a number of religions existed whose founders similarly claimed to proclaim truth, and whose disciples to some degree lived lives consistent with that "truth." Yet the limited exposure I had—and it was limited—caused me to believe that the level of love, faith, and holiness was greater, deeper, in the early Christians than in any other religious group I knew of.

At my young age, I determined that any investigation of other religions would need to be a slow and protracted effort taking many years. At this stage I was focused on examining in depth what was before me—Christ and the Christian faith.

The Third Possibility ⌁

THE THIRD POSSIBILITY I CONSIDERED WAS THAT THE TEACHINGS of Christ and His disciples held some degree of truth and validity, but that truth was only partial. That is, though Christ and His disciples did in fact live lives that reflected their claims, nevertheless, the Gospels should not be taken at face value.

The problem I had with this explanation was that the claims presented in the New Testament are very clear and forthright. Either Christ was the Messiah or He was not; either His teachings were true or they weren't; either Christ was sinless or He sinned; either He performed great miracles, such as raising Lazarus after he had been dead four days, or He did not; either He prayed from the Cross, "Forgive them, for they know not what they do," or He did not; either He rose from the dead or He did not; either He ascended into heaven or He did not. These events were historical in nature and not just metaphorical. The answers to these questions are clear-cut: either yes or no, either true or false.

The claims of the Gospel were compelling. Yet I was in a quandary as to how to proceed in my quest for truth, for God.

The Turning Point ❧

Wrestling with the issues of truth is no simple matter. The more I struggled, the more frustrated I became. I was entangled in a web of conflicting ideologies, and I realized that regardless of my effort, I might not be capable of discovering ultimate truth, of knowing God.

This led to serious discouragement and a sense of futility. As a young man of sixteen, I was idealistic enough not to surrender to despair—but it was not easy. Often, in exasperation, I would wonder: If life has no ultimate design or purpose, why continue living? I arrived at a point of crisis when my need to discover the truth of God became all-consuming. I continued to study and win chess tournaments, and superficially appeared "normal," but beneath it all was an unseen maelstrom.

Then a glimmer of hope appeared. I became aware that though my desire for God was praiseworthy, my efforts to discover or experience Him were futile: it was not possible for me as a finite creature, through my efforts alone, to discover the eternal God. The only way I could find Him was if He first found me. My only hope was that if I desired God enough, God in His love and mercy might reveal Himself to me.

So I began praying, "God, if You exist, I beg of You, reveal Yourself to me." Because I was so impressed with the Gospels and the life of Christ, I also pleaded with most desperate intensity, "Enable me to know whether Christ is true or not." For a few days I continued, in private and with an abundance of tears, to beseech the Creator to rescue me.

Then the totally unexpected happened. One day when I was alone in my bedroom, I very suddenly, as if from nowhere and yet also from everywhere, experienced a dramatic sense of the presence of God. It was much more than an inner warmth gradually building to a point of culmination. It was more like a flash of lightning coming from the pitch-black darkness of night. It was sudden and overwhelming, and I felt it at the core of my being. It is not possible to adequately describe the essence of this encounter. It was the living light of the presence of God. I did not merely think, *I knew* that it was God. I knew it as clearly as I knew my own existence and the existence of the world.

The Presence communicated to me directly in an indescribable way, "I AM, I exist, and I am always here with you, at all times and in all places. Do not fear; I love you and always will." These were not words that I heard, but rather the sense of what was communicated. Also revealed was that Jesus Christ and the Gospels are true.

What especially made this encounter with God real for me was that I can remember a specific point in time before which I walked, as it were, in a darkness. Whatever thoughts, words, emotions, or prayers I said prior to this encounter were expressed in an atmosphere of darkness in which God was a distant possibility, not a presence. Following this dramatic encounter, the inner light went on and God became ever-present. The sense of His presence never departed and in fact remains with me to this day.

I consider this to be my personal conversion to Christ. I understand that many have not had such encounters. I don't think that everyone has to have such an experience. Some are raised within the Christian Faith and at some point claim it as their own; others convert from other faiths. In both cases, often the transition is gradual and not sudden. God in His wisdom chose this particular way to reveal Himself to me. For this I will be forever grateful. But I do not expect that everyone who desires it will have the same encounter. God deals with each of us uniquely.

Holy Books in the Garbage ᴄ∾

FOLLOWING MY CONVERSION, NOTHING WAS THE SAME. I BECAME much more confident in my belief in the existence of God and the truth of the Christian faith, and also had a sense of inner peace. At the same time, in my youthful exuberance and zeal, I became somewhat obnoxious. In short order I purchased and hid a number of books about Christ and Christianity.

One day, on returning home, I noticed a pile of books next to the garbage can in front of our house. Dad was out front with a few neighbors, who saw my shocked expression when I discovered them there. Included were some Bibles, which I reminded Dad contained the Old Testament as well as the New. The "Christian" neighbors, as well as Dad, thought the whole matter entertaining and laughed.

I was quite upset, not so much at Dad, whose actions were not surprising, but at the Gentile neighbors who professed Christianity. Fortunately, my friend Tom's parents permitted me to store my books in their house down the street. This couple provided me great comfort as Dad, and to a much lesser degree Mom, became increasingly hostile to my newly adopted faith.

The Hunger Strike ⌒

ABOUT THIS TIME, MY COUSIN WAS DETERMINED TO MARRY A Gentile man with whom she was deeply in love. This caused no little disturbance in her family. My uncle was so upset that he went on a hunger strike. He determined to eat nothing unless the Gentile young man would agree to convert to Judaism. It was a pathetic situation, as my uncle's fast continued for so many days that the family had to have him taken to the hospital. As the family tumult increased to the breaking point, the poor young fellow succumbed, agreed to convert, and eventually was circumcised. Now converting to Judaism for a young, uncircumcised man involved no small effort and sacrifice. Typically for an adult male, the painful prospect of being circumcised is enough to deter all but the very hearty few. It did not deter him!

When the decision was made, my uncle ceased his fast, to the great relief and joy of all—including my dad, who was quite close to him. The two brothers then turned their attention to me and discussed a strategy to return me to the Jewish fold. Dad told me that his brother had almost persuaded him to engage in a similar fast. In the end, Dad decided against it. When I asked him why, his response was, "I didn't want to starve to death."

A Visit to a Wall Street Lawyer ⌒

DAD RECEIVED COUNSEL FROM OTHERS WITHIN THE JEWISH community to take another tack in seeking my return to Judaism. It was decided that we would visit a Jewish Wall Street lawyer who specialized in bringing wayward Jews "back home." Off Dad and I went on the forty-minute train ride to Lower Manhattan's Wall Street.

In my youthful zeal, I was excited about discussing the life of Christ with a Jewish kinsman. In reality, it was more like going to a dentist to have a tooth removed. There were few niceties. The lawyer immediately proceeded to list a number of apparent contradictions within the four Gospels in order to prove their falsity. Indeed, some of these I did not have a clue how to resolve. I looked and felt silly. I quickly realized that if I discussed the Scriptures with him on his grounds of dates, figures, timing of events, and data, I would lose. I did appreciate what I was told, but I also had some questions to ask him.

My approach was to deal with the overall theme of the Scriptures and to show the essential continuity between the Old and New Testaments. That is, to deal with the big picture—with the obvious rather than the obscure. The question I posed to him was, "When in the Old Testament was there a substantial period in which the people of Israel and Judea did not resist God's rule, His law, and His chosen leaders and prophets?"

We discussed this at length. The point I sought to make was that, if the essential struggle presented in the Old Testament consists of an unbelieving, hardhearted, stiff-necked people resisting God and His direction, then why should we believe that the situation would be any different when the Messiah was revealed to His people? My contention was that in both Testaments there is continuity and a common theme of God reaching out in love and judgment, and His people resisting and rebelling. It seemed to me that it was much more consistent with the Old Testament that the Messiah would be rejected by His people than that He would be accepted. In this I also stressed that our people, the Jewish people, acted as representatives of the whole human race and were not any more rebellious or hardened than the rest of humanity.

It became evident to me that my understanding of the Old

Testament differed from the lawyer's, as well as my dad's, in a very significant way. Whereas I saw Jewish history as consisting of an ongoing resistance against God's love and will, they took pride in Jewish faithfulness. I was convinced that an honest reading of the Old Testament supported my position. As we returned home, my father expressed anger both at the lawyer's inability to convince me and at my stubbornness.

Chapter 3

Is Christ Divine?

THE FIRST NEW TESTAMENT I HAD WAS GREEN-COLORED and published by the Jehovah's Witnesses. At the time, I thought all New Testaments were the same; I didn't realize that the Jehovah's Witness movement had its own unique translation, which was rejected by all other Christians. What separated the Jehovah's Witnesses from mainstream Christianity was their teaching that Jesus Christ was not divine, but rather created by God; He did not eternally exist. Being sixteen and having little exposure to Christian teaching, I was quite ignorant about these things.

It was through reading the New Testament that I had decided to believe in Jesus. The uniqueness of His life and teachings was compelling. But who was He? For me, He was the Messiah, the perfect man, but not divine—certainly not God. For some reason, I thought only Catholics believed that He was divine. When my close friend Joey Bellomo (whose parents had immigrated from Italy) told me Protestants also taught that He was divine, I was shocked! Joey told me that the Jehovah's Witnesses were considered to be a sect, a heresy.

This led to the first major theological hurdle I was confronted with as a new Christian: Is Jesus divine? The idea that a man could be divine, be God, was considered blasphemy in Judaism. How could an individual be both a man and God? How could God die? It just didn't make sense to me. On the other hand, the fact that mainstream Christianity taught that Jesus is divine meant I had to seriously research and pray about this. I began a systematic study of the issue, using literature provided by both camps.

Jesus Forgives Sins ᴄᴡ

IN ALL OF ISRAEL'S SACRED HISTORY, NO MAN CLAIMED THE authority to forgive sin—not Moses, not Elijah, not King David, not any of the other prophets. Yet Jesus did. Three of the Gospels present the account of the healing of a paralytic and record Jesus forgiving his sins. Matthew records Jesus' saying, "Son, be of good cheer; your sins are forgiven you" (Matthew 9:2; see also Mark 2:5; Luke 5:20).

In the Gospel of Luke's account (5:17–28) the scribes and Pharisees present say, "'Who is this who speaks blasphemies? Who can forgive sins but God alone?'" Jesus responds, "'But that you may know that the Son of Man has power on earth to forgive sins,'—He said to the man who was paralyzed, 'I say to you, arise, take up your bed, and go to your house.'" The religious leaders' reaction indicates that the authority Jesus claimed—to forgive sins—was understood within Israel to be God's authority alone.

Similarly, an encounter is described in which Jesus forgives the sin of a woman of ill repute. The account says that as Jesus ate in the house of a Pharisee,

> . . . a woman in the city who was a sinner . . . brought an alabaster flask of fragrant oil, and stood at His feet behind *Him* weeping; and she began to wash His feet with her tears, and wiped *them* with the hair of her head; and she kissed His feet and anointed *them* with the fragrant oil. Now when the Pharisee who had invited Him saw *this*, he

spoke to himself, saying, "This man, if He were a prophet, would know who and what manner of woman *this is* who is touching Him, for she is a sinner." (Luke 7:37–39)

Jesus, knowing his host's thoughts, then relates a parable about forgiveness and concludes by saying, "'Therefore I say to you, her sins, *which are* many, are forgiven, for she loved much. But to whom little is forgiven, *the same* loves little.' Then He said to her, 'Your sins are forgiven.' And those who sat at the table with Him began to say to themselves, 'Who is this who even forgives sins?'" (Luke 7:47–50).

Jesus Accepts Worship ﹏

FROM MY EARLIEST YEARS I WAS TAUGHT THE TEN COMMANDMENTS. The first two include the statement, "You shall have no other gods before Me . . . you shall not bow down to them nor serve [worship] them" (Exodus 20:3–5). God alone is worthy of worship.

Yet the four Gospels describe a number of instances in which Jesus accepted worship. One such account is of a man who is given his sight after having been born blind. Jesus asks the man, "'Do you believe in the Son of God?' He answered and said, 'Who is He, Lord, that I may believe in Him?' And Jesus said to him, 'You have both seen Him and it is He who is talking with you.' Then he said, 'Lord, I believe!' And he *worshiped* Him" (John 9:35–38, emphasis added).

In addition, at least three instances following the Resurrection are described in which Jesus accepted worship. Of the women who came to the tomb to anoint Jesus' body, the Gospel says, "Jesus met them saying, 'Rejoice!' So they came and held Him by the feet and *worshiped* Him" (Matthew 28:9, emphasis added). Another account relates the disciples' encounter with the risen Christ just prior to His ascension into heaven: "And they *worshiped* Him, and returned to Jerusalem with great joy" (Luke 24:52, emphasis added).

The most dramatic and definitive occurrence takes place when "doubting" Thomas tells the other disciples, "Unless I see in His hands the print of the nails, and put my finger into the print of the nails, and put my hand into His side, I will not believe" (John 20:25). Subsequently Jesus appears to the disciples, and after Thomas has opportunity to see and touch Christ's wounds, he worships Christ, exclaiming, "My Lord and my God!"

With this in mind, I recalled that when He was tempted by Satan in the wilderness, Jesus exclaimed, "Away with you, Satan! For it is written, 'You shall worship the LORD your God, and Him only you shall serve'" (Matthew 4:10). Thus Jesus vehemently confirms that *God only* is to be worshipped. When Thomas exclaims to Jesus, "My Lord and my God," Jesus accepts his worship and does not correct him.

The Jehovah's Witnesses claimed that the Greek word *proskuneo* (translated "worship" in non-Jehovah's Witness Bibles) only means "to honor" or "to make obeisance" and should be translated as such. Yet the word is used extensively throughout the New Testament and obviously refers to worship, as it is often used with regard to God. The word is used when Satan demands that Jesus worship him, and also in Jesus' response, "You shall worship the LORD your God."

In the Book of Revelation, the apostle John is described as being overwhelmed by what he is shown by an angel: "And I fell at his feet to worship him. But he said to me, 'See *that you do* not *do that*! I am your fellow servant, and of your brethren who have the testimony of Jesus. Worship God!'" (Revelation 19:10). The word translated as "worship" here is the same Greek word used in the other passages in which "worship" occurs. Here the angel would not permit John to either fall before his feet or worship him, yet Christ permitted His disciples to do both.

Another significant Scripture is found in the Book of Hebrews: "For to which of the angels did He ever say: 'You are My Son, / Today I have begotten You'?" (Hebrews 1:5a). The implication is that the statement was not made to any of the angels, but only to the incarnate Son of God. Yet the Jehovah's Witnesses told me that Jesus preexisted before His Incarnation as the angel Michael, and that therefore this does refer to an angel.

This passage continues, "'I will be to Him a Father, / And He shall be to Me a Son.' But when He again brings the firstborn into the world, He says: 'Let all the angels of God worship Him'" (Hebrews 1:5b–6). The angels are to worship the Son! The Son therefore cannot be a created angel.

The passage concludes, "And of the angels He says: 'Who makes His angels spirits / And His ministers a flame of fire.' But to the Son *He says*: 'Your throne, O God, is forever and ever; / A scepter of righteousness is the scepter of Your Kingdom. / You have loved righteousness and hated lawlessness; / Therefore God, Your God, has anointed You / With the oil of gladness more than Your companions'" (Hebrews 1:7–9). God says one thing to the angels, but then says something different to the Son. He also speaks to the Son, addressing him as God! To the Son, God says, "Your throne, O God," and "Therefore God, Your God, has anointed You."

The phrase, "Let all the angels of God worship Him" (6b), as well as all the other passages in which Christ accepts worship, seemed compelling proof that Jesus is more than an angel—that in fact He is divine.

Christic Raised Himself from the Dead ᐤ

WHEN ASKED BY THOSE HOSTILE TO HIM:

"What sign do You show to us . . . ?" Jesus answered and said to them, "Destroy this temple, and in three days I will raise it up." Then the Jews said, "It has taken forty-six years to build this temple, and will You raise it up in three days?" But He was speaking of the temple of His body. Therefore, when He had risen from the dead, His disciples remembered that He had said this to them; and they believed the Scripture and the word which Jesus had said. (John 2:18–22)

Subsequently, Jesus explains how this is possible:

"Therefore My Father loves Me, because I lay down My life that I may take it again. No one takes it from Me, but I lay it down of Myself. I have power to lay it down, and I have power to take it again. This command I have received from My Father." (John 10:17, 18)

According to mainstream Christianity, Jesus was raised with the same body with which He was crucified. Following the Resurrection, Jesus said to the shocked disciples, "'Behold My hands and My feet, that it is I Myself. Handle Me and see, for a spirit does not have flesh and bones as you see I have.' When He had said this, He showed them His hands and His feet" (Luke 24:39, 40). His body was transformed, glorified, but still retained the physical wounds of His crucifixion. It was not another body—a "spiritual body" as the Jehovah's Witnesses claim. Jesus wanted the disciples to touch Him—to "handle" Him in order to prove that

He was *not* a "spirit" or a ghost. These Scriptures convinced me that Jesus was risen in the body in which He was crucified.

But how could He raise Himself? The traditional Christian understanding, I discovered, says that Christ has both a human nature and a divine nature. In His human nature He is united to us, and in His divine nature He is united with God the Father and the Holy Spirit. The Son of God died in the flesh, yet in His divine nature He is eternal and cannot die. That is why He could raise Himself.

Christt the "I AM" ∿

I WAS RAISED BELIEVING THAT AMONG THE MOST SIGNIFICANT events described in the Old Testament is the revelation of God's name to Moses. The account says:

> Then Moses said to God, "Indeed, *when* I come to the children of Israel and say to them, 'The God of your fathers has sent me to you,' and they say to me, 'What *is* His name?' what shall I say to them?" And God said to Moses, "I AM WHO I AM." And He said, "Thus you shall say to the children of Israel, 'I AM has sent me to you.'" (Exodus 3:13, 14)

This name is significant in that it is uniquely God's name.

During an encounter with those accusing Him of being demon-possessed, Jesus claims God's name for Himself. He says to the hostile crowd:

> "Your father Abraham rejoiced to see My day, and he saw *it* and was glad." Then the Jews said to Him, "You are not

yet fifty years old, and have You seen Abraham?" Jesus said to them, "Most assuredly, I say to you, before Abraham was, I AM." Then they took up stones to throw at Him. (John 8:56–59)

Jesus' application of God's name to Himself caused great consternation. The Jews considered this to be blasphemy, which was punishable by death.

Understanding that the Jehovah's Witness Bible, the New World version, tends to translate significant passages dealing with the question of Christ's divinity differently from *all* other Bibles, I compared their translation to others. In this process I actually gave greater weight to the Jehovah's Witness translation, believing that if Christ were divine, it should be apparent even if their Scriptures are at times deceptive. So it proved to be. Ironically, it was in the reading of the New World version of the New Testament that I was convinced of Jesus' divinity.

To give an example, the New King James Version says, "For in Him [Christ] dwells all the fullness of the Godhead bodily" (Colossians 2:9). This passage could not be clearer in presenting the Christian understanding of the Incarnation—that is, of God becoming enfleshed as a man. The New World version renders this verse, ". . . all the fullness of the divine quality dwells bodily." This adjustment in terminology failed in its attempt to cloud the issue, as the essential meaning remains clear. Furthermore, the Greek word *theotes* used here actually means "deity" or "Godhead." If "divine quality" is in fact a mistranslation of the word, it still seemed to me to convey essentially the same understanding.

Additional passages that impressed me include:

He [Christ] is the image [icon] of the invisible God, the firstborn over all creation. . . . All things were created through Him and for Him. And He is before all things, and in Him all things consist. (Colossians 1:15–17)

In the beginning was the Word [Christ], and the Word was with God, and the Word was God. He was in the beginning with God. All things were made through Him, and without Him nothing was made that was made. . . . And the Word became flesh and dwelt among us. (John 1:1–3, 14)

The more I examined the Scripture passages relating to Christ's divinity, the more convinced I became that Christ is truly divine—God incarnate. At the same time, I sought a rationale that would explain why God would not simply send a creation of His—perhaps an angel—to fulfill what needed to be accomplished. A pivotal point in my thinking came when I concluded that superior love would be demonstrated in the Creator's manifesting Himself as a creature and speaking to us directly, rather than in sending a creature of His to do the "dirty work" for Him. The Incarnation became for me the expression and manifestation of God's perfect and unfathomable Love.

My First Church ᕦ

ONCE I HAD ACCEPTED THE MAINSTREAM CHRISTIAN VIEW OF Christ, I began looking for a church in which to worship Him. The first Christian church I visited was housed in a storefront on Ocean Parkway in Brooklyn. It was a Pentecostal Assemblies of God church led by an energetic Jewish woman who had converted to Christianity. I entered the small, brightly lit hall as she strummed her guitar and enthusiastically sang, "We're Marching to Zion." The few others present—a motley group—sang loudly off-key with hands raised. Between songs, individual congregants made exclamations of praise and gave "exhortations." Often two or more would speak at the same time or overlap. Everyone seemed to be participating fully and spontaneously in worshipping God.

To say the least, it was very different from my experience of worship in the synagogue. Though I admired everyone's enthusiasm, I really felt out of place. Either you were a full participant, moving and speaking like everyone else, or you stood awkwardly like me. I felt my silence and stillness had become the center of everyone's attention. It was as if I had on my chest a huge neon sign that flashed, "SAVE ME."

The Gift of Tongues ᴄᴠ

FOLLOWING THE SERVICE I DISCOVERED THE PEOPLE TO BE MOST friendly, but also intimidating. It seemed that everyone was on a mission from God to be certain that I personally believed in Jesus, was born again, and had been baptized in the Holy Spirit. I told them that I was born again. But then they wanted to know if I spoke in tongues. Of this I knew nothing. It wasn't long before I found out—for when I indicated my ignorance there were a few who were more than ready to help me discover this "gift."

The term "speaking in tongues" is the English translation of the Greek word *glossolalia*. The New Testament refers to this phenomenon in a number of places, in particular when the Holy Spirit descended on the apostles at Pentecost in the form of fiery tongues and caused them to speak to those gathered from many lands. The Scripture says, "And they were all filled with the Holy Spirit and began to speak with other tongues, as the Spirit gave them utterance. . . . And when this sound occurred, the multitude came together, and were confused, because everyone heard them speak in his own language. Then they were all amazed and marveled" (Acts 2:4, 6–7).

The gift of tongues is understood to be the God-given ability to speak an earthly language that one does not know, or to speak and worship in what is called the angelic language. In practice, those who believe they have this gift speak in what they consider to be an angelic language during both worship and private prayer. Because this gift was given at Pentecost, those who claim to have it are often called Pentecostals. Their belief is that the gift was given to the apostolic Church but then died out as the Church grew cold and corrupt. They believe one of the signs of our being in the last days is the fulfillment of the prophecy that says, "And it shall come to pass in the last days, says God, / That I will pour out of My Spirit on all flesh" (Acts 2:17, quoting Joel 2:28–32).

I felt deficient because I did not speak in tongues. My charismatic friends pitied me for being only half a Christian. For Pentecostals, this gift was more than an extra benefit received at conversion: it was *the sign* and proof of being authentically converted. My not speaking in tongues meant that my conversion was suspect. Some fellow Jewish converts encouraged me to pray harder to get the "gift." They laid their hands on me in prayer. Try as they did, I never got it. My brother Sol, who had become a Christian before I did, while living in Chicago, never got it either. I always thought him to be more authentically spiritual than I. In fact, I didn't know anyone more spiritual than Sol. So if he didn't get it, I assumed I didn't have much to worry about.

Public Preaching ᵔ

MY NOT HAVING BEEN BAPTIZED IN WATER AND NOT SPEAKING IN tongues didn't prevent the pastor from asking me to witness for

Christ with her and a few others. For us as Jewish Christians, this meant going to a street corner in a Jewish neighborhood, standing on a makeshift platform, and with the aid of a loudspeaker telling others why I, as a Jew, believed in Jesus.

I was young, naïve, innocent, and without guile. Those nearby didn't appreciate our being there, especially the Orthodox Jews. Before long, I felt threatened. I also wondered what I was doing. The pastor liked my preaching and encouraged me, but I stopped when I realized that a little old woman was not much defense against a mob. We soon cleared out.

As we drove back to the church, she said, "Praise God—that was your baptism of fire!" I thought to myself, "Does that mean I won't have to speak in tongues after all to be a full-fledged Christian?"

Sometime later, I read the scripture that refers to speaking in the tongues of angels: "Though I speak with the tongues of men and of angels, but have not love, I have become sounding brass or a clanging cymbal" (1 Corinthians 13:1). I decided that it was far more important for me to learn how to speak the language of love than to speak an unknown language. After that, I didn't feel badly about not having the gift of tongues.

Chapter 4

Discovering the Prophecies of Christ

As a child, I thought biblical prophecy was the province of religious fanatics, nuts, and weirdoes. You know—the guys in Times Square who wear placards with scripture quotes and shout, "Repent! The end is at hand!" I viewed the study of prophecy as an esoteric exercise subject to manipulation and falsification. Prophecy buffs, I believed, saw in predictions and their alleged fulfillment what they were preconditioned to see. In short, I was a skeptic.

Yet on the other hand I believed in God, in Christ, and in the Scriptures, and I was fully aware that the Bible contained many divinely inspired prophecies. This presented a dilemma. I wanted to believe in the legitimacy of prophecy and its fulfillment without becoming a wacko!

I found a vast range of prophecies in the Bible encompassing the future of individuals and tribes, the states of Israel, Judea, and their surrounding peoples, the world, indeed the universe. But the centerpiece of all biblical prophecy is that which concerns the coming of the Messiah. This is because the Messiah is not just a man; He is *the* Man, the prototype Man, the Savior, the Deliverer, the Teacher, as well as the Prophet, Priest, and King. For the Jew, the Messiah is one who will usher in the unending era of peace on earth.

The Old Testament provides many prophecies regarding the coming Messiah; the New Testament explains how the messianic prophecies are fulfilled in Christ.

What the Scriptures Reveal about Prophecy ∾

JESUS OFTEN REFERS TO PROPHECIES FULFILLED IN HIMSELF. FOR example, while I was living at home in Queens and struggling with whether Jesus was the Messiah or not, I read that at the outset of His ministry He read the Scriptures aloud in the synagogue and concluded by saying, "Today this Scripture is fulfilled in your hearing" (see Luke 4:16–21).

Jesus often predicted His own suffering, death, and Resurrection, and while doing so referred to specific Old Testament prophecies. In the Gospel of John, Jesus says to the Jewish people, "You search the Scriptures, for in them you think you have eternal life; and these are they which testify of Me. . . . For if you believed Moses, you would believe Me; for he wrote about Me" (John 5:39, 46).

What did Moses write about Jesus? In a number of passages, Moses states what the Messiah will be and do. In one of the more forthright prophecies, Moses said to the children of Israel some 1300 years before Jesus' birth:

> "The LORD your God will raise up for you a Prophet like me from your midst, from your brethren. Him you shall hear, according to all you desired of the LORD your God in Horeb in the day of the assembly, saying, 'Let me not hear again the voice of the LORD my God, nor let me see this great fire anymore, lest I die.' And the LORD said to me: 'What they have spoken is good. I will raise up for them a Prophet like you from among their brethren, and will

put My words in His mouth, and He shall speak to them all that I command Him. And it shall be *that* whoever will not hear My words, which He speaks in My name, I will require *it* of him.'" (Deuteronomy 18:15–19)

According to rabbinic Judaism, there has never been a prophet like Moses. Christians hold that the above prophecy was fulfilled in Christ and implies that the Messiah is to be more than human. This is shown by God's response to His people's complaint that they could not endure the Lord communicating to them on Mt. Horeb in fire and dramatic wonders. Instead, He says, He will speak to them in a gentle way, in and through the Prophet/Messiah.

The foremost of the apostles, Peter, said, "To Him all the prophets witness" (Acts 10:43a). He also wrote:

For we did not follow cunningly devised fables when we made known to you the power and coming of our Lord Jesus Christ, but were eyewitnesses of His majesty. . . . And so we have the prophetic word confirmed, which you do well to heed as a light that shines in a dark place . . . knowing this first, that no prophecy of Scripture is of any private interpretation, for prophecy never came by the will of man, but holy men of God spoke *as they were* moved by the Holy Spirit (2 Peter 1:16, 19–21).

Peter here refers to the Old Testament, the only Scripture the earliest Christians knew, since the New Testament was still in the process of being written and compiled (canonized). The central theme of the prophecies in the Old Testament pertains to the coming Messiah. These prophecies cover every aspect of the Messiah's life, including of what lineage He would be born, at what time, in what place, and under what circumstances; how He would live His life, what He would teach, how people would react to Him, and how He would suffer and die. Along with these prophecies come predictions of miracles He would perform, including the most astounding of all—His Resurrection from the dead.

A Chosen Lineage and the Formation of a People ～

THE RAISING UP OF THE PEOPLE AND RELIGIOUS CULTURE INTO which the Messiah would be born is especially prominent in the earlier messianic prophecies. The uniqueness of this people consists in God's revealing Himself to them in an astoundingly direct way: He showed them spiritual truth, His moral code, and how to worship Him. He also reveals what *not* to believe and do. Much of the Old Testament concerns the nature of this revelation and the struggle to maintain its purity among this people—the Jews—who are always in danger of falling away. Furthermore, God preserves the Jews against surrounding peoples and pagan cultures that would dilute and even destroy what God has entrusted to them.

The Old Testament describes the birth and development of a chosen lineage and of the Jewish people. Noah is said to have had three sons—Ham, Shem, and Japheth. Of the three, Shem, who is considered the father of the Semitic people, is presented with this prophecy given by Noah: "Blessed *be* the LORD, / The God of Shem, / And may Canaan be his servant. / May God enlarge Japheth, / And may he dwell in the tents of Shem" (Genesis 9:26, 27).

Subsequently, Abraham, the patriarch of both the Jewish and Arabic peoples, is described as having been called by God out of Ur to establish a chosen lineage. He is told, "In your seed all the nations of the earth shall be blessed, because you have obeyed My voice" (Genesis 22:18; see also Genesis 12; 17).

Abraham's sons included Ishmael, who is considered the father of the Arabic peoples, and Isaac, to whom the Jewish people trace their descent. Isaac is given this prophecy: "in your seed all the nations of the earth shall be blessed" (Genesis 26:4).

Isaac in turn had two sons, Esau and Jacob. To Jacob also God said, "in you and in your seed all the families of the earth shall be blessed" (Genesis 28:14). Another scripture says of Jacob's descendants, "A Star shall come out of Jacob; / A Scepter shall rise out of Israel . . . Out of Jacob One shall have dominion" (Numbers 24:17, 19).

During Jacob's lifetime, an event transpired that resulted in his name being changed to Israel. Israel had twelve sons, who became fathers of what are known as the twelve tribes of Israel. Of one of his sons, Judah, it is said, "Moreover He [God] rejected the tent of Joseph, / And did not choose the tribe of Ephraim, / But chose the tribe of Judah" (Psalm 78:67, 68). As the people of Israel grew in numbers, God revealed to them through Moses the Ten Commandments, the Law, and a specific form of worship. Subsequently, prophets arose who would reaffirm this revelation and call the people back to its adherence.

Within the context of an extremely decadent surrounding pagan culture, an oasis of truth, virtue, and true worship was formed. Neighboring Gentiles, not only in the Middle East but throughout the world, included within their religious systems elements of idolatry, emperor worship, human sacrifice, witchcraft, magic, temple prostitution, sexual perversion, cannibalism, and general gross immorality. Though within heathen cultures there existed, and still exists, some authentic virtue and spiritual values, it seemed to me that moral confusion and ignorance prevailed. Within this worldwide fog of spiritual darkness, God chose what is described as "the least of all peoples" to build this unique oasis of spirituality in which to reveal the Christ. Moses had proclaimed to his people:

> "For you *are* a holy people to the LORD your God; the LORD your God has chosen you to be a people for Himself, a special treasure above all the peoples on the face of the earth. The LORD did not set His love on you nor choose you because you were more in number than any other people, for you were the least of all peoples." (Deuteronomy 7:6, 7)

Additionally, the Scripture records God as saying to Moses:

> "'Now therefore, if you will indeed obey My voice and keep My covenant, then you shall be a special treasure to Me above all people; for all the earth *is* Mine. And you shall be to Me a kingdom of priests and a holy nation.' These *are* the words which you shall speak to the children of Israel." (Exodus 19:5, 6)

A Titanic Struggle ❧

MUCH OF THE OLD TESTAMENT PRESENTS A CRITICAL ONGOING struggle in which huge and mighty empires and pagan religious cultures seek to obliterate the tiny oasis of ancient Israel and Judah; but they do not succeed. The Scriptures speak of purifying the Jewish people as a metal is purified within a fiery furnace: "But the LORD has taken you and brought you out of the iron furnace, out of Egypt, to be His people, an inheritance, as you are this day" (Deuteronomy 4:20); and "He will sit as a refiner and a purifier of silver; / He will purify the sons of Levi, / And purge them as gold and silver, / That they may offer to the LORD / An offering in righteousness" (Malachi 3:3).

A long succession of persecutions arose, beginning with slavery in Egypt under Pharaoh, followed by the destruction of the northern ten tribes of Israel by the Assyrians, followed by the captivity of the tribes known as Judah under the Babylonian Empire. Subsequently, an abortive attempt at genocide took place under the Persian Empire, and then an attempt at cultural/religious assimilation under the Grecian Empire. This was followed by a further attempt to paganize the Jews under the Roman Empire, culminating in AD 70 with the total military conquest of Judea and the destruction of Jerusalem by the Romans.

Throughout this process of purification, the ancient Jews suffered greatly at the hands of surrounding empires. At the same time they were challenged by their own Jewish prophets to return to God and to the spiritual and moral purity of the Law. In this way what is called "a remnant" of faithful was preserved. It is as if rocky and hardened soil were being tilled, broken, aired, softened, and fertilized so as to provide the proper conditions in which the tree of life, Christ, could be planted and grow.

Another aspect of this divinely revealed spiritual and moral system, I came to realize, was that it provided the means by which the Messiah could be recognized as the Messiah. In a pagan context, nothing would be in place by which to assess and recognize Him. Jesus said that He came "to fulfill" the Law (Matthew 5:17). This He could not do if there were no divinely revealed Law to fulfill.

Embryonic Prophecies That Grew ∾

IT IS THOUGHT THAT THE OLD TESTAMENT WAS COMPILED OVER a period of a thousand years (1500–400 BC). During this period many prophets foretold the coming of the Messiah. There were no prophets between 400 BC and the time of Christ's appearing. The intertestamental book of 1 Maccabees confirms this: "There was great perplexity in Israel, such as had not been seen since the days when the prophets ceased to be seen in their midst" (1 Maccabees 9:27).

Some say there are 333 prophecies of the Messiah in the Old Testament. That may be, but one does not have to read all of them in order to be convinced that Christ is the promised Messiah. Only a few select ones helped to convince me.

As I read the Old Testament, I began to see a progression from the first books, which contain embryonic prophecies, to later books, which contain more detailed and fuller predictions. As a seed sprouts and grows, so do the prophecies. In the very first book of the Bible, Genesis, following the fall of Adam and Eve, an embryonic prophecy is given which grows over time. God confronts the devil, represented as a serpent, who has been the instrument of man's fall into sin. At the same time God provides Eve, the mother of the human race, with hope. God says to the devil:

> "And I will put enmity
> Between you and the woman,
> And between your seed and her Seed;
> He shall bruise your head,
> And you shall bruise His heel." (Genesis 3:15)

This prophecy is interpreted to mean that Mary, who is often called "the second Eve," would bring forth a Seed—the Messiah/Christ, whose heel would be bruised. This wound is understood to be fulfilled in His suffering and death. His death is not permanent, for in His Resurrection death is overcome. The bruising of the serpent's head is far more severe, in that it destroys forever the power of the devil. Indeed, it is the Christian belief that the crucifixion, death, and Resurrection of Christ brought about the destruction of the devil's power.

And note that the Messiah who bruises the serpent's head is the Seed of the woman and not of a man. Perhaps this indicates the uniqueness of the Messiah's conception, being the seed of the woman alone—as fulfilled in the miraculous conception of the Son of God by the Holy Spirit in the womb of the Virgin Mary (see Luke 1:31–35).

When Is the Messiah to Come? ∽

IN READING ABOUT THE TRIBE OF JUDAH, I ENCOUNTERED ANOTHER prophecy that gives an indication of *when* the Messiah is to come: "The scepter shall not depart from Judah, / Nor a lawgiver from between his feet, / Until Shiloh comes; / And to Him *shall be* the obedience of the people" (Genesis 49:10).

The word "scepter" refers to the tribal staff or tribal identity of Judah, which will not pass away "until Shiloh comes." Both Jewish and Christian commentators agree that Shiloh is a name of the Messiah. The prophecy reveals that the Messiah would have to come before the tribe of Judah lost its identity. In AD 70 the Roman legions destroyed the Jewish temple in Jerusalem, in which tribal records were kept. Soon after, all tribal identity was lost, except for those of the tribe of Levi. This prophecy therefore tells us that the Messiah had to come before AD 70.

Being of Jewish descent, I desired to know what Jewish rabbis had to say about this scripture—as well as others. At times, I would go to the New York Public Library on Fifth Avenue near Times Square. Back then it had a terrific Judaic section with many writings of the rabbis translated into English. I would often take my visits to the library as an opportunity to walk down Fifth Avenue, see the sights, and perhaps play a game of chess at the Chess and Checker Club of New York on 42nd Street in Times Square. On the way I could drop by Nathan's Jewish Deli to buy a kosher hot dog, a potato knish, and a Dr. Brown soda pop. It was always exciting to visit midtown Manhattan, as it overflowed with energy and never slept.

At the library I discovered that Rashi, one of the most renowned rabbis, clearly taught that Shiloh refers to the Messiah. He said, "'Until Shiloh comes,' this indicates that all nations will bring a gift to Messiah the son of David" (Midrash Rabbah 97). Additionally, the Targum of Onqelos—an ancient translation of the Hebrew text into Aramaic—states, "The transmission of dominion shall not cease from the house of Judah . . . until the Messiah comes to whom the kingdom belongs and whom nations shall obey."

The more I examined the commentaries, the more convinced I became that this scripture pertained to the coming of the Messiah before the destruction of the Temple in AD 70. The passage also said that "the people" (Hebrew *ahmeem,* "nations" or "Gentiles") will come and obey the Messiah. This impressed me because it predicted that Gentiles would accept Christ.

The "Weeks" of the Prophet Daniel ᴄ⁓

A MORE DETAILED CHRONOLOGY OF CHRIST'S COMING IS FOUND in the Old Testament Book of Daniel. It is believed this book was written about 540 BC, following King Nebuchadnezzar of Babylon's conquest of Judah and the subsequent deportation of its inhabitants to Babylon. The scripture foretelling the time of the Messiah's coming reads:

"Know therefore and understand,
That from the going forth of the command
To restore and build Jerusalem
Until Messiah the Prince,
There shall be seven weeks and sixty-two weeks;
The street shall be built again, and the wall,
Even in troublesome times.
And after the sixty-two weeks
Messiah shall be cut off, but not for Himself;
And the people of the prince who is to come
Shall destroy the city and the sanctuary.
The end of it *shall be* with a flood,
And till the end of the war desolations are determined."
(Daniel 9:25, 26)

This prophecy sets forth a timetable for the Messiah's appearance. In reading the prophecy, it was helpful to know that the Hebrew word *shavuim* does not literally mean "weeks"; it means "sevens." The equivalent Greek word *heptads* also means "sevens." (Another Hebrew word, *shavuot*, means "weeks.") So "seven weeks" should actually be translated "seven heptads" of years, or forty-nine years. (In biblical symbolism, a day equals a year.)

The passage says that seven sevens of years, or forty-nine years, are given for those returning to Jerusalem to rebuild the temple that had been destroyed. Under the prophets Nehemiah and Ezra, this was done (see their books in the Old Testament). This scripture also tells us that following the forty-nine years there will be sixty-two "weeks," or heptads of years: sixty-two times seven equals four hundred thirty-four years "until Messiah the Prince." The countdown begins at the time of the issuing of the decree to restore and rebuild Jerusalem.

Two of the most significant decrees regarding the rebuilding of Jerusalem were given by Cyrus in 538 BC (2 Chronicles 36:22, 23; Ezra 1:1–4; 6:1–5), and by Artaxerxes I in 445 BC (Nehemiah 2:1–8). Using either of these dates as starting points, we arrive at the general time in which Jesus Christ was born. Exact dates vary from scholar to scholar. Some attempt a more detailed calculation of events in order to show that the dating is precise to the very year. Whether the figures work out to the exact year was not as important to me as knowing that all the calculations agree that the Messiah would appear at the approximate time Christ was born.

The second half of the prophecy explicitly says the Messiah will be "cut off," which is the biblical term for being executed. It also says "but not for Himself"—that is, not because of His own sins, for He had none, but for the sins of others.

The prophecy concludes by saying the city of Jerusalem and the sanctuary, the rebuilt temple, are to be destroyed following the "cutting off" of the Messiah. This, as we have noted, happened in AD 70, when the Roman legions under Titus destroyed Jerusalem and the temple—approximately forty years after the "cutting off" or crucifixion of Christ. The "weeks" of the Daniel prophecy seemed to me to provide a clear time frame in which the Messiah was to come, and its fulfillment in Christ was for me self-evident.

Messiah, Son of David ❧

HAVING DISCOVERED IN SCRIPTURE THE MESSIAH'S LINEAGE AND the approximate time of His birth, I also was struck by the central position King David held in messianic prophecies. The Scriptures, in further narrowing down the Messiah's lineage, state of David's father Jesse, who lived in about 1000 BC, "There shall come forth a Rod from the stem of Jesse, / And a Branch shall grow out of his roots. / The Spirit of the LORD shall rest upon Him" (Isaiah 11:1, 2). There follows a prolonged description of the attributes of this descendant of Jesse that clearly reveals Him to be the Messiah.

Jesse had eight sons, his youngest being David, who became king of Israel. Of King David, the Scripture says:

"Behold, *the* days are coming," says the LORD,
"That I will raise to David a Branch of righteousness;
A King shall reign and prosper,
And execute judgment and righteousness in the earth.
In His days Judah will be saved,
And Israel will dwell safely;
Now this *is* His name by which He will be called:
THE LORD OUR RIGHTEOUSNESS."
(Jeremiah 23:5, 6)

A prominent title used of Jesus throughout the New Testament is "Son of David." Not only is the Messiah to be a descendant of David, but He is to be born in the area that David was from:

"But you, Bethlehem Ephrathah,
Though you are little among the thousands of Judah,
Yet out of you shall come forth to Me
The One to be Ruler in Israel,
Whose goings forth *are* from of old,
From everlasting." (Micah 5:2)

This prophecy, believed to have been written in the fifth century BC, says that the Messiah is to be born in Bethlehem, the city

David was from. The Davidic family were called Ephrathites—that is, they resided in Ephrath, a suburb of Bethlehem (see Ruth 1:2; 1 Samuel 17:12). The New Testament tells us that because of the census ordered by Caesar Augustus, Joseph and Mary, who was heavy with child, had to travel from Nazareth, where they lived, to Bethlehem, where their lineage was, to be registered (see Luke 2:1–7). While they were there, Christ was born. That this prophecy, written over 400 years before the birth of Christ, would name the very village in which Jesus Christ would be born was to me absolutely astounding.

The Micah prophecy, though brief, also indicates this Messiah would be more than a mortal man. The expression "from of old, from everlasting" in the original Hebrew can be said to be the strongest expression used in Scripture for eternity. It is used for God Himself in Psalm 90:2 and for divine wisdom in Proverbs 8:22, 23.

A Second-Century Book on Prophecy ∿

IN TIME I CAME UPON ANOTHER BOOK THAT AIDED MY JOURNEY through the world of messianic prophecy. This ancient book, written in the mid-second century, is entitled *St. Justin Martyr's Dialogue with Trypho*. It consists of a conversation between the Christian Justin, who explains why he believes Jesus to be the Messiah, and Trypho the Jew, who explains why he doesn't.

A most significant fact surfaced as I read this book. Prophecy fulfilled in Christ was presented by early Christians not as just one proof among many demonstrating the validity of His claims; rather it was presented as proof positive. Along with Christ's life, teaching, death, and Resurrection, fulfilled prophecy was held by the ancients to be conclusive evidence of the authenticity of

Jesus' identity as Messiah. Fulfilled prophecy was clearly much more important to the apostles, the New Testament writers, and the Christians of the first few centuries than it is to Christians today.

The Suffering Servant ⌒

OF ALL THE PROPHECIES I ENCOUNTERED, THE ONES DESCRIBING the life the Messiah would live were the most impressive. Knowing what His lineage would be and where and when He would be born got my attention, but reading about how He would live, how He would suffer and die for others, was awesome.

The Old Testament prophetic descriptions of the suffering Messiah are so extensive and detailed that many rabbis (before recent times) believed the Scriptures presented a Messiah who would come, suffer, and die for His people. Unwilling to accept Jesus Christ as that Messiah, rabbinic Judaism devised an alternative view which taught that two separate Messiahs would come. The first was called "the suffering Messiah," also known as "Messiah Son of Joseph." The other was called "the glorious Messiah," known as "Messiah Son of David." In this scheme, the second Messiah comes to vindicate the execution of the first by raising him from the dead and establishing the messianic kingdom of peace on earth.

Orthodox Judaism has historically held there would be two separate Messiahs, but in reaction to Christianity has increasingly emphasized the role of the glorious Messiah and deemphasized that of the suffering Messiah. In more recent times, Judaism presents the whole people of Israel as being the suffering Messiah who suffers at the hands of the Gentile world! This view has in fact become a dominant Jewish position.

Isaiah 53 ∿

ONE OF MY FAVORITE OLD TESTAMENT WRITERS IS THE PROPHET
Isaiah. I love his passion for justice and his dramatic flair. His book
contains many prophecies, along with straightforward proclama-
tions in which God is presented as challenging false prophets and
gods to foretell the future as He does (see Isaiah 41:21–23; 42:8,
9; 46:9–11).

The single most impressive passage detailing the Messiah's life
is found in Isaiah 53, written some seven hundred years before
the birth of Christ. All the earliest Jewish sources, such as the
Mishnah, the Gemara (the Talmud), and the Midrashim, interpret this scripture as referring to the coming Messiah. The first
rabbi to give an alternative explanation was Rabbi Rashi (around
AD 1050), who said that Isaiah 53 referred to Israel. His statement
provoked an intense debate with his contemporaries, particularly
Rabbi Rambam, also known as Maimonides.

Maimonides says this passage describes "what is to be the
manner of Messiah's advent. . . . Isaiah speaks of the time when he
will appear . . . the unique phenomenon attending his manifesta-
tions is that all the kings of the earth will be thrown into terror
at the fame of him . . . in the words of Isaiah—at him kings will
shut their mouth."[1]

In stating this, Maimonides drew upon ancient texts such
as the Babylonian Talmud, which says in Midrash Thanhumi,
"Rabbi Nahman says, the word 'man' in the passage . . . refers to
the Messiah, the son of David . . . where Yonathan interprets it
as, 'Behold the man Messiah.'"[2]

In the long Isaiah passage, the tense at times changes from
future to past. This grammatical technique is used to affirm the
surety of the future events by describing them as having already
occurred. The full passage follows:

✦ SURPRISED BY CHRIST

Behold, My Servant shall deal prudently;
He shall be exalted and extolled and be very high.
Just as many were astonished at you,
So His visage was marred more than any man,
And His form more than the sons of men;
So shall He sprinkle many nations.
Kings shall shut their mouths at Him;
For what had not been told them they shall see,
And what they had not heard they shall consider.

Who has believed our report?
And to whom has the arm of the LORD been revealed?
For He shall grow up before Him as a tender plant,
And as a root out of dry ground.
He has no form or comeliness;
And when we see Him,
There is no beauty that we should desire Him.
He is despised and rejected by men,
A Man of sorrows and acquainted with grief.
And we hid, as it were, *our* faces from Him;
He was despised, and we did not esteem Him.

Surely He has borne our griefs
And carried our sorrows;
Yet we esteemed Him stricken,
Smitten by God, and afflicted.
But He *was* wounded for our transgressions,
He was bruised for our iniquities;
The chastisement for our peace *was* upon Him,
And by His stripes we are healed.
All we like sheep have gone astray;
We have turned, every one, to his own way;

And the LORD has laid on Him the iniquity of us all.
He was oppressed and He was afflicted,
Yet He opened not His mouth;
He was led as a lamb to the slaughter,
And as a sheep before its shearers is silent,
So He opened not His mouth.
He was taken from prison and from judgment,
And who will declare His generation?
For He was cut off from the land of the living;
For the transgressions of My people He was stricken.
And they made His grave with the wicked—
But with the rich at His death,
Because He had done no violence,
Nor *was any* deceit in His mouth.

Yet it pleased the LORD to bruise Him;
He has put *Him* to grief.
When You make His soul an offering for sin,
He shall see *His* seed,
He shall prolong *His* days,
And the pleasure of the LORD shall prosper in His hand.
He shall see the labor of His soul, *and* be satisfied.
By His knowledge My righteous Servant shall justify
    many,
For He shall bear their iniquities.
Therefore I will divide Him a portion with the great,
And He shall divide the spoil with the strong,
Because He poured out His soul unto death,
And He was numbered with the transgressors,
And He bore the sin of many,
And made intercession for the transgressors.
(Isaiah 52:13—53:12)

This passage clearly seems to be speaking of an individual who is the Messiah. Certainly it is not a collective person—the people of Israel. Throughout the passage, the individual is presented as suffering *for* the nation of Israel. The writer, who is a Jew, uses terms such as "our report," "when we see Him," "we hid," "He has borne our griefs and carried our sorrows." The pronouns used—"we" and "our"—indicate that the individual suffers for the Jewish people. It is a person suffering—not a people.

The passage contains many specific points fulfilled by Christ:

"Who has believed our report?"	The accounts of Christ's life are so astounding they are difficult to believe.
He is "despised and rejected" and "we hid . . . from Him."	This is how most of His kinsmen reacted to His life and ministry.
He has "borne our griefs and carried our sorrows," was "wounded for our transgressions" and "bruised for our iniquities."	Christ suffered and died not for Himself, but for us.
"By His stripes we are healed."	His life and suffering enable us to experience healing.
"He opened not His mouth . . . He was led as a lamb to the slaughter."	He was taken to judgment before the civil authorities and presented to the people. He refused to offer any self-defense.

"He was taken from prison and from judgment."	Christ was presented before the people with His fellow prisoner Barabbas, who was chosen by them to be released.
"He was cut off from the land of the living."	He was executed.
"For the transgressions of my people."	Not for Himself, but for others—specifically Isaiah's people, the Jewish people.
"And they made His grave with the wicked."	He was crucified between two thieves and died along with them.
"But with the rich at His death."	He was buried in the tomb of a rich man, Joseph of Arimathea.

Isaiah 53 speaks for itself. It shook me to the core. An honest reading of the Scripture compelled me to believe that it spoke of Christ. How could the prophecy be fulfilled in more obvious terms than it was by Christ? My entire Jewish upbringing taught me Jesus could not be the Messiah because He died an accursed death, did not bring peace on earth, and did not exalt Israel among the nations. Yet this prophecy could not be clearer—the Messiah was to be rejected and despised by His own people and put to death. And His death was no ordinary death. The Messiah's death was to be the most gruesome imaginable.

Psalm 22 ～

PSALM 22 IS A POWERFUL DESCRIPTION OF CHRIST'S HORRIFIC death. Jesus actually quoted portions of this prophecy from the Cross.

My God, My God, why have You forsaken Me?
Why are You so far from helping Me,
And from the words of My groaning?
O My God, I cry in the daytime, but You do not hear;
And in the night season, and am not silent.
But You *are* holy,
Enthroned in the praises of Israel.
Our fathers trusted in You;
They trusted, and You delivered them.
They cried to You, and were delivered;
They trusted in You, and were not ashamed.
But I *am* a worm, and no man;
A reproach of men, and despised by the people.
All those who see Me ridicule Me;
They shoot out the lip, they shake the head, *saying*,
"He trusted in the LORD, let Him rescue Him;
Let Him deliver Him, since He delights in Him!"
But You *are* He who took Me out of the womb;
You made Me trust *while* on My mother's breasts.
I was cast upon You from birth.
From My mother's womb
You *have been* My God.
Be not far from Me,
For trouble *is* near;
For *there is* none to help.

Many bulls have surrounded Me;
Strong *bulls* of Bashan have encircled Me.
They gape at Me *with* their mouths,
Like a raging and roaring lion.
I am poured out like water,
And all My bones are out of joint;
My heart is like wax;
It has melted within Me.
My strength is dried up like a potsherd,
And My tongue clings to My jaws;
You have brought Me to the dust of death.
For dogs have surrounded Me;
The congregation of the wicked has enclosed Me.
They pierced My hands and My feet;
I can count all My bones.
They look *and* stare at Me.
They divide My garments among them,
And for My clothing they cast lots. (Psalm 22:1–18)

Statements from this psalm fulfilled in Christ's crucifixion include:

"My God, My God, why have You forsaken Me?"	These are the words Christ cried out while upon the cross.
"O My God, I cry in the daytime, but You do not hear; and in the night season, and am not silent."	His crucifixion began at 9:00 A.M., when the sun shone brightly. But from noon until his death at 3:00 P.M., "there was darkness over all the land" (Matthew 27:45).

"All those who see Me ridicule Me; they shoot out the lip, they shake the head, saying, 'He trusted in the LORD, let Him rescue Him; let Him deliver Him, since He delights in Him!'"

Nearly identical words were used by those present at Jesus' crucifixion: "And those who passed by blasphemed Him, wagging their heads" (Mark 15:29a); and "Likewise the chief priests also, mocking with the scribes and elders, said, 'He saved others; Himself He cannot save. If He is the King of Israel, let Him now come down from the cross, and we will believe Him. He trusted in God; let Him deliver Him now if He will have Him'" (Matthew 27:41–43)

"They divide My garments among them, and for My clothing they cast lots."

John 19:23, 24 tells us, "Then the soldiers, when they had crucified Jesus, took His garments and made four parts, to each soldier a part, and also the tunic. Now the tunic was without seam, woven from the top in one piece. They said therefore among themselves, 'Let us not tear it, but cast lots for it, whose it shall be,' that the Scripture might be fulfilled which says: 'They divided My garments among them, / And for My clothing they cast lots.' Therefore the soldiers did these things."

"They pierced My hands and My feet." *   This verse describes the act of crucifixion.

The details in this psalm are far too vivid and specific to be anything but a prophecy of the death of Jesus Christ.

These prophetic scriptures taken all together convinced me beyond any doubt that our Lord Jesus Christ is the long-awaited Messiah of my people, Israel.

---

* Rabbinic Judaism has translated this last verse from the Masoretic text as "like a lion my hands and feet," which really makes no sense. Therefore they insert "they are gnawing at" into the verse. The ancient Septuagint version—a Greek translation of the Hebrew text done by the Jews 250 years before Christ—says "pierced," as above. The Septuagint translators had access to Hebrew manuscripts that were at least a thousand years older than the Hebrew Masoretic text used by modern rabbinic translators. The Septuagint proves that the ancient Jews understood the word to be "pierced" and not "lions." Given the intense controversy about Christ among the Jews at the time of His life, it is reasonable that the translations that predate Christ would be less biased than those that postdate Him. Regardless, whether it be "piercing" or "gnawing" of hands and feet, *both* indicate the most gruesome of deaths. And it is reasonable to view lions gnawing at one's hands and feet as a metaphor for crucifixion.

Chapter 5

College Years

AFTER COMPLETING HIGH SCHOOL IN 1964, I BEGAN attending nearby Queens College of the City University of New York. My years there witnessed a number of significant events, some of which affected my maturing Christian faith.

During the mid-sixties, upheavals took place at three levels. On the political level, the Vietnam War was ramped up; on the social level, the Civil Rights Movement escalated into high gear; and on the cultural level, we experienced the birth of the "counterculture." In 1963 President John F. Kennedy had been assassinated. Under our new president, Lyndon B. Johnson, the Vietnam War was intensified. President Johnson also initiated another war, the "War on Poverty," and pushed through Congress the Civil Rights Act of 1964.

The counterculture became an ever more potent force. Its influence was strongest among the younger generation. The movement included radical political activity, new standards of dress and sexual behavior, illegal drug use involving psychedelic mind-altering experimentation, the rise of hard rock music, rock and roll with many musical variations, greater environmental awareness, the formation of communes in rural areas, and the rise of underground newspapers and poster art. Its members were first called "beatniks"; later, "hippies"; then "radicals."

For most of these years I was a college student, and I somehow managed to remain "straight" as opposed to becoming a hippie.

I never found the drug culture and sexual revolution that surrounded me at college appealing. My dramatic Christian conversion experience at sixteen somehow stuck.

The World's Fair ∾

THE WORLD'S FAIR HOSTED BY NEW YORK CITY WAS LOCATED IN Flushing Meadow in Queens, near Queens College. It ran for two years, 1964 and 1965, ending in October. The theme of the fair was "Peace Through Understanding." This proved an ironic theme, given that the years 1964–67 saw a substantial escalation of the Vietnam War.

World Fairs were typically held once every decade, featuring pavilions built by private companies, states, and foreign countries. The fairs were educational, entertaining, and spectacular. This one had 140 pavilions on 646 acres. More than a billion dollars were invested, and the fair drew fifty-one million people.

The Billy Graham Pavilion featured a film called *Man in the Fifth Dimension*. It is a wonder that forty years later in 2005, Billy Graham would conduct the final evangelistic crusade of his career at Flushing Meadows Park.

As a new Christian, I was particularly interested in visiting the Protestant and Orthodox Christian Pavilion, which hosted many varied booths representing innumerable denominations. The Vatican Pavilion displayed Michelangelo's *Pietá* sculpture, depicting the crucified Christ cradled in his Mother Mary's arms. This was the first time the *Pietá* had been exhibited outside its chapel in St. Peter's Basilica in Rome. It was displayed in a darkened room while Gregorian chants played softly in the background. The *Pietá* was the most popular attraction at the fair.

The month the World's Fair closed, October 1965, brought another visitor from Rome, Pope Paul VI. He was the first pope to visit the United States. While in New York, he addressed the United Nations, said Mass at St. Patrick's Cathedral, and visited the Vatican Pavilion at the World's Fair. A few months earlier, Catholic churches across the country had switched from using Latin during the Mass to saying it in English. My Catholic friends were really excited about this change, as they could now understand the prayers. I could relate to this, as the synagogues I used to attend used Hebrew in prayer; but at times they also used English, which I preferred.

The years of the World's Fair drew visitors from all over the world, including a new rock band that made its first appearance on December 27, 1964, on the Ed Sullivan television show. They were unknown in the States before that and had a bizarre name that was fiercely disliked and mocked by conservative folks: "The Beatles."

The Civil Rights Movement ❧

THE CIVIL RIGHTS MOVEMENT AFFECTED ME DEEPLY. IN 1964, only seven percent of voting-age African-Americans in Mississippi were registered to vote. The Mississippi Freedom Summer Project was formed to increase voter registration. A number of college students from our area volunteered to spend their summer assisting in this effort. Many student envoys from the New York City colleges were Jewish, as New York Jews were overwhelmingly liberal Democrats and extremely supportive of and active in the Civil Rights Movement. These young idealists were labeled "outside agitators" by many Southern whites and were not welcomed. The Ku Klux Klan and its offshoots were still active in many areas of the South.

Three young men helping in Mississippi were kidnapped and murdered while returning from investigating the burning of a rural Black church. The search for and discovery of their bodies brought in the federal government and for weeks made national news. (Years later, a movie was made about the event called *Mississippi Burning*.) One of the three young men killed, Andrew Goodman, was a fellow Queens College student. Another, Michael Schwerner, had a brother at Queens. Their becoming civil rights martyrs drew our campus deeper still into the movement. We all closely followed the events unfolding in the South.

Also in 1964, Martin Luther King, Jr. won the Nobel Peace Prize. At thirty-five years of age, he was the youngest ever to do so.

The following spring, on March 7, 1965, a group composed mostly of Blacks marched from Selma, Alabama, to the state capital of Montgomery to protest the growing violence against civil rights activists. They were attacked by Alabama state troopers. The national outrage was so great that a couple of weeks later another march was held, this time with the protection of a beefed-up Alabama National Guard federalized by President Lyndon Johnson.

Two months after this, on May 13, 1965, Martin Luther King, Jr. came to speak at Queens College in appreciation for our support and involvement in the Civil Rights Movement. Though the auditorium was overflowing with thousands present, I managed to sit only a few feet in front of Dr. King. Knowing his audience was predominantly Jewish, he began by speaking briefly about being a "man of the cloth"—a Christian minister. The speech was passionate, and we were moved not only by what he said but by his very presence. His address became known as the "we've come a long, long way, but still have a long, long way to go" speech. It was a moment I will always cherish.

Three short years later, on April 4, 1968, Martin Luther King, Jr. was assassinated in Memphis, Tennessee. He gave his life for a cause he believed in. I couldn't help but wonder—if called on, would I be willing to do the same?

The Great Blackout of 1965 ᕈᕈ

CITIES ARE MORE SUSCEPTIBLE TO APOCALYPTIC TYPES OF DISASTERS than rural areas. This was particularly true of New York City. One such disaster took place on Tuesday, November 9, 1965, at 5:27 P.M. I know the time because the living room clock stopped and remained stuck there for hours.

I had returned home from school and was alone in our apartment. This was no longer behind Dad's candy store; we had moved upstairs after the store was sold. Suddenly we lost power and it was pitch black. I felt my way down the long flight of stairs to the street. As I emerged, I noticed that the street lights were out, as were all of the neighbors' lights.

A number of people were gathered at what used to be Ike's candy store. Some huddled around a portable radio, hoping to hear news about what had happened. I don't recall our having lost power before, as our power lines were underground. I doubted the news program would say anything; I figured the outage was local. Then someone noticed the elevated trains in front of the store were not running. This was very unusual. It took something exceptional to stop the trains, such as someone falling or jumping onto the track before an oncoming train.

Then news of the power loss came through on the radio. The newscaster reported that electricity had been lost in various parts of the city. Details were sketchy. Following some confusion, he came back on and announced that electricity was out throughout the entire New York metropolitan area. This was unbelievable—it had never happened before. About thirteen million people lived in the region. We still had the most people of any metropolitan area, even if the Brooklyn Dodgers and New York Giants had deserted us for sunny, beachy, creepy California. Who cared if hundreds of thousands followed them—we were still the greatest city on earth! That is, when the lights were on.

More people drifted to the store as neighbors emptied into the streets carrying flashlights and candles. For kids, it was really exciting. My friends who were with me said it felt like Halloween night. One asked, "Hey guys, whaddaya say we go trick or treatin'?" Being young people, we wanted to have fun, and did not consider the darker side of this disaster. In contrast, the adults were serious. They discussed what might have happened to people stuck in subways and elevators. It was rush hour and literally millions of people were on the move. The blackout couldn't have happened at a worse time.

Someone commented that he thought the hospitals would be okay as they had backup generators. Another person asked, "What about the guys driving cars in the tunnels under the Hudson and East rivers? Do they have back-up generators?" "They must," someone replied, "'cause the tunnels need to keep the air flowing, otherwise they'd get asphyxiated." New York had not just one, but four tunnels—the Lincoln, Holland, Queens Midtown, and Brooklyn-Battery tunnels—and they were all long.

The evening progressed and neighbors began to cook meals outside on the grills set up on front stoops, lawns, and sidewalks. Then the other shoe fell. Reports came in confirming that electricity was out in upstate New York, New Jersey, and possibly in other states, including Connecticut, Rhode Island, and parts of Pennsylvania. As the evening progressed, confirmation of these reports arrived. What next? Then we heard that Boston was out. And the whole of Massachusetts. Everyone was shocked. What in the world could cause this? We heard nothing about the cause. Later we were told that the whole of the Northeast, including Vermont and New Hampshire, was out, as well as Ontario in Canada!

Heated discussions ensued as to the cause. True to the spirit of the Cold War and the middle-class immigrant mentality of those gathered, the consensus was, "We're under attack!" Some took this seriously, especially the World War II vets. When we heard that Chicago was out, the panic level dramatically increased. It soon subsided when we heard Chicago was not out after all, at which point we cheered!

Eventually we were informed via radio that the blackout had affected about thirty million people. It took days to figure out what actually caused it. Evidently a breakdown had occurred in the electrical power grid. A single faulty relay in Ontario went out, which resulted in escalating power line overloads as power had to be rerouted. This in turn caused overloaded power plants to automatically shut down so as not to be damaged. The cascading shutdowns resulted in the spread of blackouts throughout the entire Northeast.

Neither Dad nor Sol got home that night. Dad had been working at his concession stand in the Times Square subway station when we lost power. He immediately closed the store by pulling down the metal storefront partition and locking it. Dad later told us that he was fearful of being robbed in the dark.

My brother Sol was caught on a packed subway train. The passengers had to exit the train and very carefully walk the stinking, rat-infested underground subway tracks to get to the nearest station.

That night was one we will always remember, made memorable also by the fact that virtually no looting or acts of crime were committed! People really pitched in to help one another, unlike subsequent power failures. One lasting impact was said to be the great increase in births nine months later.

By the following morning, the electricity was back on and the Great Blackout of '65 was only a memory. But it taught me not to take electricity for granted. In fact, one always appreciates light more when one has been stuck in the dark. This is true spiritually as well as physically. My effort as a new believer in Christ was to move from darkness into greater light.

Chapter 6

In the Holy Land

MEANWHILE, AT HOME WITH DAD, THINGS WENT FROM bad to worse. His anger towards me increased as he saw that he and others could not persuade me to return to the Jewish fold. He wanted me out of the house, but also wanted me to be in a situation that would change my mind. So he took drastic action and did what many New York Jewish families did in those days. After I completed my second year at Queens College, he paid my way to take a one-year leave of absence and sent me to Israel.

No doubt about it, I was excited about going. It was the land of the Bible, the land where Jesus lived, where the ancient Church was born and grew. It was also where many of my relatives still lived. So off I went in February 1967 on a jet to Jerusalem. Upon arriving, I spent a couple of months at Kibbutz Gat, near where the Philistines and Goliath lived. Then I settled in Jerusalem.

A Traitor among My People ∾

MANY OF MY RELATIVES ON BOTH SIDES OF THE FAMILY LIVED IN Jerusalem, including my only living grandparent—Dad's mom. My mother's brothers Abe, Morris, and Max and their families lived there as well. All were Orthodox Jews.

As a Christian, I was reluctant to live with religious family members; instead I rented a room on Bethlehem Road, which connected the new city of Jerusalem in Israel with Bethlehem in

Jordan. The house was only a few hundred yards from the border's no-man's-land, and my window presented an unobstructed view of the Jordanian hills.

Here I was, at twenty years of age, in the Holy Land, living within a nation of people who shared a common Jewish heritage and sacred destiny. A sense of awe and anticipation pervaded the Israeli ethos. As a Jew who believed in Christ, I too shared in the celebration of nationhood. Yet I was very guarded, knowing that the Jewish people were my people and yet were not, because of my newfound faith in Christ. I would no longer be viewed as being Jewish; in fact, to many I would be what they called a *mahshoomid*—a traitor.

Meeting Grandmother ❧

MEETING MY FATHER'S MOTHER FOR THE FIRST TIME EVER WAS one of my most memorable experiences in Israel. She looked ancient to me and spoke no English, only Yiddish (a dialect of German) and Hebrew. She was a Hasidic Orthodox Jew living in the ultra-Orthodox Jewish section of Jerusalem, Mea Shearim. In this area signs caution, "No Picture Taking Allowed." The vehicle of anyone foolish enough to drive through there during the Sabbath would be stoned.

So there I was, surrounded by relatives and cousins, none of whom I knew. They looked as if they had just arrived from a ghetto in Eastern Europe—dressed all in black, heads covered, the men wearing ultra-long sideburns called *payous,* and everyone talking at once in Yiddish. They beamed with joy that the long-awaited son of Isaac had arrived; yet they also were embarrassed for me, as I looked more like a goy (Gentile) than a Jew. They had heard rumors that I was interested in Christianity, and that worked against me. But being a chess champion worked in my favor.

❧ SURPRISED BY CHRIST

The cousins acted as interpreters as Grandmother spoke to me in Yiddish. I understood very little of what she said. My parents, with great determination, had raised me knowing only English so that I would be a true American. The only Yiddish words I remembered with clarity were curse words. And Grandmother was not cursing at me. I caught a word here and there: *chutzpah* (gall, guts), *cockamamie* (ridiculous), *goyshka cup* (Gentile head), and a few others.

It was both a wonderful and scary encounter—to be center stage surrounded by Old World Jewish culture. During the subsequent months, I had the opportunity to eat some Sabbath meals at my Uncle Abe's and to meet cousins on my mother's side. These were Orthodox Jews and seemed less intimidating to me than the ultra-Orthodox Jews on my father's side.

The Six-Day War ❧

FOUR MONTHS INTO MY ONE-YEAR STAY, FOREBODING WAR CLOUDS arose. The political climate rapidly deteriorated as Israel's Arab neighbors became increasingly belligerent. Egypt made the first decisive move by transporting large numbers of forces across the Sinai Peninsula towards Israel's border.

During this time the radio was my primary means of keeping up with the news. Virtually all I could get was Jordanian military music, bagpipes and all, accompanied by diatribes in English warning all foreigners—especially Americans—to leave immediately or risk death. In my youthful naiveté, I didn't really think anything would come of it. I was gravely mistaken.

On the morning of June 5, 1967, I was visiting a pastor friend of mine when in the distance, just before noon, I heard some isolated gunfire. At first there were few shots, so I ignored them. Within an hour, however, the chatter of machine-gun fire along the nearby Israeli/Jordanian border increased at an alarming rate.

My apartment was located in the Baka/Talpiot area near the Israeli military base called Allenby Camp. I rushed toward the supposed safety of my apartment, but as I ran it dawned on me that my apartment was closer to the shooting, not farther away. With each step I took, the shots increased in number, rapidity, and volume. I thought, "Why am I here? Why did I not return to America?" My apartment was literally on the border between two armies at war—the Israeli army in Jerusalem, and within eyesight the Jordanian army stretching towards Bethlehem to the south and the Jordanian hills to the east.

All hell was breaking loose—my apartment afforded me as much protection as a cardboard crate in a tornado. Rockets whizzed overhead; the noise of exploding shells sounded like the thunder of nearby lightning strikes. Quickly I gathered some belongings, praying that no bullet would come through the window or bomb through the ceiling. Descending the staircase of the small apartment complex, I heard screams and saw people fleeing—mostly to the basement, where the elderly, mothers with children, and those not able to serve in the military were gathered. I was the lone American. As we settled in, I was not comforted by their words, "Your American passport won't save you."

As the sun set, we watched flares ever so slowly descend from great heights, lighting up no-man's-land to the south. The flares conveyed a most eerie impression—the beauty of light as soft as a full moon. Under that gentle glow many died in battle near my apartment. The incoming mortar shells increased in intensity, some falling nearby.

The first night was the most difficult. We heard rumors that advancing Jordanian troops had captured Government House, also called the United Nations Headquarters Compound, located on the Mount of Evil Counsel directly east of us. This was a strategic hill overlooking Jerusalem, only about half a mile away. We had also heard that Israel was at war with Egypt to the south, Syria to the north, and Jordan to the east, and that a number of other large Arabic countries were providing troops and equipment. This meant that Israel was surrounded and fighting on all fronts against substantially larger forces.

Suicide! ～

THOSE AROUND ME BECAME AGITATED, AND I SENSED THAT something was up. There was great fear that the Jordanian advance could continue and that at any time now we could be captured. The Israelis were terrified that the men's throats would be slit and the women raped and killed, if not by the soldiers, then by the armed civilians following them. They took these threats seriously, as they had heard that Arabs were sharpening their knives in various nearby towns with this in mind.

Then they asked me, "Do you want to join us in this effort?"

I asked, "In what effort?"

I was told they had decided that if the Arabs took our area, those gathered, rather than be captured, would commit suicide! They planned to use pistols. I immediately told them, "No, I'm not going to participate."

During that night and those following, we heard many jets flying overhead and bombs exploding in the distance. We didn't know whose jets they were or who was being bombed. Arabic radio broadcasts bombarded us with a continual stream of reports of Israeli defeats. Not knowing what was happening was a most agonizing part of this experience, as the news reports were sketchy and we had no idea how the war was progressing. Neither side wanted to reveal where their troops were or what they were doing.

Following the local battle, I wandered outside and was

surprised to see how close to us the mortar shells had fallen. Their shrapnel sliced through steel as if through butter. The treads of immense tanks had completely torn up the roadways. While roaming about, I suddenly heard whizzing by me something that made the sound of *shooup, shooup, shooup.* It drew nearer. With horror, I realized it was the sound of bullets—I was right in someone's crosshairs! I ran back to my basement sanctuary, where I patiently remained until the all-clear was given.

The war was short as wars go, lasting only six days. As our lives began to return to normal, we realized that the map of Israel had completely changed. Most significantly, the Old City of Jerusalem, which I could previously only see from afar, was now under Israeli control.

Old Jerusalem ❧

THOUGH SADDENED BY THE LOSS OF LIFE, ALL OF ISRAEL WAS AT the same time ecstatic over the change in circumstances. I immediately visited the Old City, and having made contact with Baptist Christian leaders in both the Old and New Cities of Jerusalem, became one of the first two students at the newly established Jerusalem Bible Institute. Soon afterward, I moved into what was called the Jewish sector of the old walled city of Jerusalem, renting a room from a Christian Arab family. It was awesome to live in the exact area where my father had been born (and who knows—perhaps in the same house).

From the roof I could clearly see the Temple Mount, the Church of the Holy Sepulcher, the Mount of Olives, and in fact all of Jerusalem. My relatives thought that I was *meshuggener* (crazy) for moving into newly occupied territory. They warned, "You'll get your throat slit." It seems the preserving of one's throat is a major Middle Eastern concern. Only a handful of extremely zealous ultra-Orthodox Jews had dared to move into the Old City, reclaiming pre-1948 Jewish synagogue sites. I, being young, naïve, and of an innocent disposition, trusted that God would protect me. Now, looking back many years later at what I did, I agree with my relatives. I was *meshuggener*.

Some viewed me as brave because I lived alone among a sea of Arabs. Others thought perhaps I was not to be trusted because I was friendly with the Arabs. On the other side, an Arab Christian accused me of spying for the Jews. In actuality, I was a free spirit, oblivious to the dangers around me. The fact that I survived intact is a miracle.

What of Old Israel? ❧

ONE DAY, AS I WALKED THE SITE OF THE TEMPLE MOUNT, I STOOD at what is called the pinnacle of the Temple, the highest point on the corner where the south and east walls meet. A man approached me, saying he was a Protestant minister. He said with an air of contempt that the Jews praying at the Wailing Wall were not really Jews. True Jews, he exclaimed, are Christians, and true Israel is the Church.

With mixed feelings I engaged him in conversation. Though I agreed with what Paul says—"For he is not a Jew who *is one* outwardly, nor *is* circumcision that which *is* outward in the flesh, but *he is* a Jew who *is one* inwardly; and circumcision *is that* of the heart" (Romans 2:28–29)—I also believed that there was a destiny for the Jewish people. Thus began for me the struggle to clarify the relationship between Jews and Christians—between what many Christians call Old Israel and New Israel—between the synagogue and the Church.

Are the Jews Still Chosen of God? ☙

THE SECTION OF SCRIPTURE I DISCOVERED THAT DEALS MOST clearly with the relationship of the Jewish people and the Church is Romans 9—11. In this section, St. Paul speaks adamantly of his love and continued attachment to his kinsmen. He says, "For I could wish that I myself were accursed from Christ for my brethren, my countrymen according to the flesh . . . from whom, according to the flesh, Christ *came* . . . Brethren, my heart's desire and prayer to God for Israel is that they may be saved" (Romans 9:3, 5; 10:1).

Paul addresses the issue of Israel's blindness in chapters 9 and 10. In all that is said, it is explicit that he is speaking of the Jewish people and not of the Church. Then beginning in chapter 11, he asks the question, "I say then, has God cast away His people? Certainly not! For I also am an Israelite, of the seed of Abraham, *of* the tribe of Benjamin. God has not cast away His people whom He foreknew" (Romans 11:1, 2).

What immediately struck me was that Paul referred to the Jewish people as "His [God's] people." I had encountered Christians who said that the Jewish people are no longer chosen of God and that the Christian people—the Church alone—are now "His people." I had also been told that I should no longer consider myself a Jew, as the Jews don't believe in Christ and I was now a Christian. Yet how could I reconcile this view with that of Paul, who continued to speak of the Jewish people as his own "countrymen" and "His [God's] people"?

The Mystery of Israel's Blindness ☙

HOW TWO PEOPLES CAN BE REFERRED TO AS "GOD'S PEOPLE" becomes clearer in Romans 11. Paul says of the Jewish people:

I say then, have they stumbled that they should fall? Certainly not! But through their fall, to provoke them to jealousy, salvation *has come* to the Gentiles. . . . For if their being cast away *is* the reconciling of the world, what *will* their acceptance *be* but life from the dead? . . . For I do not desire, brethren, that you should be ignorant of this mystery, lest you should be wise in your own opinion, that blindness in part has happened to Israel until the fullness of the Gentiles has come in. (Romans 11:11, 15, 25)

As I understood it, Paul was saying Christians should not be proud in their belief, because in some mysterious way God has permitted, even perhaps caused, Israel's blindness as a nation in order to accomplish a greater blessing for the Gentiles (see Romans 9:17–23; 11:7, 8).

Then, speaking of the future, Paul says this condition of Israel's blindness will continue "until the fullness of the Gentiles has come in" (Romans 11:25). In saying this, Paul assumes the continued existence of Jews as a distinct people, and divine destiny and providential guidance for them even until Christ's return. He speaks of a future time in which, after the "fullness" of Gentiles become Christian, an awesome event will take place. The event is described in the next verse, "and so all Israel will be saved" (Romans 11:26).

It is evident from the context that the Israel spoken of is the Jewish people and not the Church. This passage has been interpreted to mean, not that literally every individual Jew will become a Christian, but that the people as a whole will come to faith in Christ. Just as the Jewish nation previously rejected Christ (though individual Jews accepted Him), so in the future the Jewish nation will accept Christ (though there will be some individuals who won't).

If there is any doubt as to whom Paul is speaking of—that is, the Jewish people and not the Church—it is made clear in verse 28: "Concerning the gospel *they are* enemies for your sake, but concerning the election *they are* beloved for the sake of the fathers." Immediately following this, we are told more clearly still of the unconditional chosenness of the Jewish people:

> For the gifts and the calling of God *are* irrevocable. For as you were once disobedient to God, yet have now obtained mercy through their disobedience, even so these also have now been disobedient, that through the mercy shown you they also may obtain mercy. For God has committed them all to disobedience, that He might have mercy on all. (Romans 11:29–32)

Years later, I read a sermon by a prominent spokesman for Orthodox Christianity, Bishop Kallistos Ware, entitled, "Has God Rejected His People, the Jews?" In the sermon, Bishop Kallistos focuses on Romans 9—11 and concludes by saying:

> Let us all inscribe these words of St. Paul upon our hearts indelibly in letters of fire. Never for one moment let us forget the incalculable loss which Christianity has suffered through the early separation between the Church and the Synagogue. Let us long, as Paul does, for the ending of that separation, and let us keep steadfastly in view his confident expectation that, willingly and by their own free choice, the Jewish people as a whole will eventually accept Christ as God and Savior. And, until that happens, let us never by deed or word show the slightest disrespect or hatred for the people of Israel. They are still God's Chosen People.

Anti-Semitism, in all its expressions, is the work of Satan.

I beg you, then, to make your own St. Paul's 'great sorrow and unceasing anguish,' and I ask you also to hold fast to his ultimate hope that 'all Israel will be saved'.[3]

Returning to America ∿

MY FAMILY IN NEW YORK FELT THAT A YEAR IN ISRAEL WAS MORE than enough time in which to return to Judaism. The fact that I did not, but remained a Christian, was a source of great frustration to them, and they called me home. In February, 1968, one year after my arrival, I departed from Israel on a ship that traveled through the Mediterranean and North Atlantic.

On the way home, we were buffeted by a treacherous storm. The swells were much higher than the ship. Rope lines were put up so that we could walk without falling, holding onto them for dear life as the ship was tossed to and fro. The dining hall was vacant during mealtimes because so many suffered from seasickness, but I remained well and got much more than my fair share of food.

Eventually we made it safely home, and I must say that I felt a great deal of joy as Lady Liberty greeted us in the New York Harbor. I had seen her many times before, as I often took the ferry ride from lower Manhattan to Staten Island. This time it was different. Having survived a war as well as a perilous journey by sea made my thankfulness for being an American all the more heartfelt. Thank God I was home!

Part II

Discovering the Church

Chapter 7

Evangelical Protestant Ministries

Upon returning to the U.S. from Israel, I resumed my studies at Queens College while living at home. Feeling a need to be more practical, I changed my major from philosophy/history to economics. For about a year, I wore suits and visited Wall Street and the New York Stock Exchange.

The elevated train ride through Brooklyn and over the Williamsburg Bridge took only half an hour and was a straight shot to the financial center of the world. I enjoyed watching huge ticker tape screen displays in the brokerage houses and the seasoned traders sitting comfortably in leather chairs, commenting to one another as multimillion-dollar transactions took place. Billows of smoke rose from cigars and pipes, creating an atmosphere similar to that of the chess clubs I frequented. Both were smoky, male domains that used complex technical language and felt intimidating. I was surrounded by the wealthy and enterprising making and losing fortunes.

It was a delight to sometimes see older tabletop, glass-domed ticker tape printers in use, printing an actual paper tape of trade transactions. When trading volume exploded in the 1960s, ticker tape printers were replaced by computer networks and became obsolete. What I most liked about them was that they made it possible to have authentic ticker tape parades.

Ticker tape parades were spectacular. Lower Manhattan provided the historic route for parades, called the Canyon of Heroes. While the motorcade of those being honored passed through the narrow street below, massive amounts of ticker tape were thrown out of the upper windows of adjacent skyscrapers. Some tapes were many feet long. Others were cut into shorter strips, creating differing lengths of confetti. The strong updrafts typical within the manmade canyon of skyscrapers prevented the streamers of confetti from plummeting to the ground. Instead, they flew in all directions, floating and flipping about. Some seemed to remain suspended indefinitely as they were blown up again and again, caught in powerful gusts. It was an awesome sight to behold.

Two years that I especially recall are 1962 and 1969. Both celebrated history-making accomplishments in space. On March 1, 1962, a ticker tape parade was held in honor of John Glenn, the first American astronaut to orbit the earth. He had accomplished this on the Friendship VII spacecraft as part of the Mercury VI mission. On August 13, 1969, a similar parade was held following the Apollo XI mission to honor the first humans to land on the moon—Neil Armstrong, Edwin Aldrin, and Michael Collins. For a New York kid like me, the ticker tape parades honoring the astronauts were what made celebrating the space conquests so exciting.

In addition to honoring celestial accomplishments, we also proclaimed terrestrial milestones, including baseball victories. On April 9, 1962, a ticker tape parade was held for the New York Yankees, winners of the 1962 World Series; on October 20, 1969, another was held for the New York Mets, winners of the 1969 World Series.

For New Yorkers, 1962 and 1969 were baseball years that would always be remembered. In 1962 the New York Yankees played the San Francisco Giants, who had deserted New York after the 1957 season. The Yankees boasted legends such as Mickey Mantle, Roger Maris, Yogi Berra, and Whitey Ford. The Giants, playing at Candlestick Park, had Willie Mays and Willie McCovey. In the 1969 series the Mets, who played at Shea Stadium in Queens, were in their first post-season appearance with legends such as Tom Seaver, Jerry Koosman, and a new young pitcher in the third year of his twenty-seven–year, record-breaking pitching career named Nolan Ryan. Those were the days when bats were made of wood, a hot dog cost twenty-five cents, steroid use was unknown, and authentic ticker tape was used for parades instead of sheets of shredded paper and toilet tissue.

When I was in Lower Manhattan, I sometimes walked the short distance from the Stock Exchange and brokerage houses to the end of Wall Street, where stood Trinity Episcopal Church. Founded in 1697, it was rebuilt twice, the last time in 1846 in Gothic style. When the first church was built, it was the highest structure in Lower Manhattan. Its spire, surmounted by a gilded cross, could be seen by nearby ships. I found this hard to believe, because the church now seemed totally out of place, dwarfed by adjacent towering skyscrapers that grew higher with the passing years, making the church appear to shrink.

Yet the church's doors were always open, unlike those of the Federal Reserve down the street and the nearby banks and brokerage houses. Sometimes I would quietly slip into another world, a world of stillness permeated with a sense of sacredness and antiquity. Trinity Church stood in stark contrast to the chaos of the bustling business world of empire builders outside, where everyone seemed frantic, as if preparing for the Olympic speed-walking contest. Perhaps my brother Sol, having worked a few years on Wall Street, had been prepared by this for the New York City marathons that he ran in later years.

Our dad had a certain attachment and fascination with Wall Street. He would sometimes say to me in his thick Yiddish accent, "I vould vish fur you dat you should be a schtock brooker (stockbroker), den you could be a philantropist." In this I disappointed him, as I would soon decide against pursuing fame and fortune in the vast world of finance and commerce, choosing instead to enter the world of deeper spirituality I had glimpsed within Trinity Church.

The Vietnam War ∾

BY LAW, I WAS REQUIRED TO REGISTER WITH THE SELECTIVE Service System thirty days after my eighteenth birthday. So in May 1964, I registered and submitted a request to be categorized as a conscientious objector. I did this not so much out of fear as because of my authentic belief in pacifism, and my conviction as a Christian that this was how Christ wanted me to live. I based my conviction on Jesus' commands to His disciples not to resist evil, to turn the other cheek, and to love their enemies. His own life of nonresistance, and those of the earliest Christians, convinced me that the highest expression of spirituality was manifested in one's willingness to be martyred, while authentically loving and forgiving those perpetrating evil.

Graduating from high school and entering college meant that I would automatically receive a student deferment labeled "2-S." So although there was no need to claim conscientious objector status, as I would not be at risk to be drafted, I did so anyway. My request resulted in my having to explain and defend my position before an official Selective Service System board of inquiry.

The cross-examination took place in a dark, intimidating closed room. I stood alone a considerable distance from a long table, behind which sat a number of angry-looking people. The air was thick with smoke—intense and foreboding. This was going to be a battle.

Then came the first question: "Do you swear to tell the truth, the whole truth, and nothing but the truth, so help you God?"

This was followed by an unusually long period of silence. Finally I responded, "As a Christian, I cannot in good conscience take an oath, because Jesus said, 'Do not swear at all, neither by heaven nor by earth, but let your yes be yes and your no, no—for whatever is more than these is from the evil one.'"

One of the examiners gruffly replied, "That swearing is referring to cussing, not to making oaths."

Immediately I shot back, "The context shows clearly that Jesus is speaking about oaths, not about cussing."

This first round set the tone for the cross-examination, during which it became evident to them that I held deep convictions and was beyond hope. Nevertheless, I did not receive conscientious objector status. I suppose because I was entering college and would automatically receive a college student deferment, they put my request on hold.

As a Queens College student I participated in a few anti-war demonstrations, boycotted some classes, and distributed anti-war literature in centrally located areas. At heart I was not politically motivated, so I would often distribute literature about God and the Christian faith rather than about the war.

By 1969, the Vietnam War had become so controversial and the need for more troops so great that the first draft lottery since World War II was held on December 1 of that year. This is how the lottery was done: Each day of the year was printed on a piece of paper. Each piece of paper was placed in a separate plastic capsule, and all 366 capsules were deposited in a deep glass jar. Then the capsules were randomly drawn one at a time. This determined the order of call numbers of all men within the eighteen to twenty-six age range (those born between 1944 and 1951). The first capsule drawn held September 14; this meant that those born on that date would all be drafted first. My birth date of May 6 was number 139 on the list of 366. As it worked out, everyone who received a number lower than 196 was eventually called to report.

Upon graduating from college in 1970, I no longer had student status, and I expected to be inducted. Literally, my number was up. I renewed my conscientious objector appeal, requesting alternative service. Then something totally unexpected happened. A class action lawsuit initiated by a group of anti-war lawyers claimed that I, along with many others, was illegally being drafted during a period in which an official draft moratorium was in place. Surprisingly, they won. I was then assigned a Class I-Y status, in which the "registrant is qualified for military service only in time of war or national emergency." As the war was winding down, this meant that I was being placed on hold and would not be drafted.

In 1973 the Vietnam War officially ended, as did the draft. The United States then adopted an all-volunteer military. I felt great sorrow for the innumerable innocent lives destroyed and broken in the war—a war that has come to be known as a bad war. Most of all I was relieved that I had escaped being sucked into the horrendous vortex of destruction.

This era provided me the opportunity to confront the issue of violence and war within a Christian worldview. At that time I was a staunch pacifist, but through the years I have modified my views. The issues are not uniformly the same and clear-cut. It seems to me that varying degrees of merit exist in the specific circumstances and motivation of those involved. In my younger years everything seemed black or white, right or wrong. There was little room for gray. With the passing years the area of gray has grown substantially. Although I still consider pacifism to have a legitimate basis, I now think that at times the selective and wise use of violence can also be commendable.

InterVarsity Christian Fellowship ❧

In the sixties I was told that about eighty percent of the student body at Queens College was Jewish. But I did not feel at home there. These years were tumultuous, as the Vietnam War was in full swing, the Civil Rights Movement was in its prime, and the social upheaval of the counterculture pervaded everything. Increasing numbers of students were experimenting with drugs and "turning on," especially with marijuana. Sexual promiscuity, renamed "free sex," was becoming the norm rather than the exception. What little religious interest existed was Eastern in nature—Hindu and Buddhist mingled with Native American beliefs.

Christians were a tiny minority on the campus, with the theologically conservative group smaller still. Conservative Christian converts from Judaism, like me, constituted a minority of one. I felt like a stranger in a strange land swimming upstream against a ferocious current. Culturally I was a misfit—I didn't smoke, drink, use drugs, or know many hippies. I was "straight" and felt as if I was becoming straighter.

I recall that the campus had three Christian student organizations, two of which met in adjacent rooms in the Student Union Building. The Lutheran Club was virtually all male and had pictures of motorcycles posted throughout their clubroom. Next to it was InterVarsity Christian Fellowship (IVCF), an evangelical Christian organization whose membership consisted of about twenty women and a sprinkling of men. Its meeting room held pictures of Jesus, the Holy Land, and flowers.

Though I admired the motorcycle pictures on the Lutheran

club walls and was fascinated by their interest in guns, the members were of mostly German descent; motorcycles, guns, and Germans did not seem like a good mix to me. So I gravitated to the conservative evangelical Protestant and predominantly women's IVCF. This placed me in an awkward situation, as I was socially inept and had minimal life experience with women.

IVCF had college and university chapters nationwide. Its primary purpose was to encourage Christian witness and discipleship. At Queens College I manned an IVCF display table of Christian books and literature at the Student Union Plaza. I enjoyed doing this and also distributing Christian literature on campus. Some instructors and classmates were surprised to see me engaged visibly in Christian outreach, because they knew my name, Arnold Bernstein, was very Jewish.

Following a few months of active involvement, I was asked and agreed to become president of the Queens College chapter. It was an exciting and inspiring position, as I soon met dedicated Christian staff workers and chapter presidents from a number of New York City colleges who had a significant and positive impact on my life. The New York City chapter presidents comprised a steering committee engaged in sponsoring varied activities, including inviting various Christian speakers. We once met privately with Billy Graham in order to plan how to encourage campus participation in his upcoming New York City crusade.

Being president of an evangelical Protestant Christian campus ministry presented a personal dilemma, because I had not yet been baptized a Christian. But no one made an issue of it, so neither did I.

The Sicilian-born parents of my neighbor, friend, and fellow Queens College student Tom Carrubba were extremely supportive of me. One day Tom's dad Jim took me to Manhattan to hear a speaker at Beth Sar Shalom Hebrew Christian Fellowship on West

72nd Street. While there I met the group's leader, Daniel Fuchs, and its missionary director, a man who would have a major impact on my life, Martin (Moishe) Rosen.

After that I visited the center often, and finally, on November 30, 1969, was baptized there by Martin, who was a Baptist minister. This baptism was for me a remarkable and life-changing experience, providing me great comfort and a sense of authenticity.

Jews for Jesus ∾

UPON GRADUATING FROM QUEENS COLLEGE WITH A B.A. IN Economics, I discussed with Pastor Martin (Moishe) Rosen what path to take. I was surprised to learn that he was leaving his position with Beth Sar Shalom Ministry in order to establish a brand new evangelical Protestant ministry in the San Francisco Bay Area, to be called Jews for Jesus. A new evangelistic Christian movement called the Jesus Movement beckoned him to the West Coast. This vibrant movement was drawing thousands of young people to Christ.

Moishe was excited about having a Hebrew Christian outreach to Jews that would go beyond the somewhat staid Hebrew Christian Ministries. His vision was to be more creative, energetic, and visible, making use of media to widely communicate the Jews for Jesus message. Implementation included public distribution of leaflets, display of posters, public preaching, and demonstrations. Moishe was extremely dedicated, with a surprisingly subdued personality that concealed his intense fervor. He drew around him a tight group of individuals who loved Jewish culture and were multitalented and enthusiastic about assisting in this new ministry.

Moishe encouraged me to move with him and his family to the Bay Area in order to be part of this effort. Because I had a great respect for Moishe and appreciated his zeal and vision, I agreed to go. In the fall of 1970, I flew with the future founder of the musical ensemble the Liberated Wailing Wall, Stu Dauermann, on a new and exciting adventure to the West Coast. Little did we know that his future compositions with Christian themes and a Jewish klezmer flavor would become well known among evangelical Christians.

As we flew west, I felt sad leaving my family behind. I also was saddened by the realization that in moving to California I was following in the path of the Dodgers and Giants, teams I had ridiculed for years.

During my first year in the Bay Area, I lived in Christian communes—first in Marin County, then in Oakland, and finally in Berkeley. Berkeley was at times called Berzerkley because of its bizarre nature. As this began to rub off on me, I procured a blue denim jacket, painted on the back of it a large Star of David with a bright cross in the middle, and then printed in large letters, "Jews for Jesus." The jacket provoked many comments and interesting conversations. Moishe really liked it. At the time I didn't think much of it.

Thirty-six years later, Moishe wrote me, "You were the first one who ever thought about wearing something that said 'Jews for Jesus' on it. You set the pattern that I followed. After you, I had an embroidered denim jacket that said 'Jews for Jesus,' then all that constituted the original group had very artfully-made 'Jews for Jesus' denim jackets, about thirty in all. Then in the summer we switched to T-shirts that said 'Jews for Jesus'."

Our small but very dedicated cadre immediately set to work. Large numbers of specialized leaflets called broadsides were printed and distributed. Broadsides were printed on 8½" x 11" sheets of paper folded into thirds, making six sides when read. The text was large, often with hand-drawn diagrams and sketches. The leaflets were short, easy to understand, witty, entertaining, and focused on single themes that could be read while on the run. Thought-provoking subjects included "Jesus Made Me Kosher" and "Jesus Gives Peace Now." I remember the first one printed in New York, "A Message from a Square." Two thousand other Jews for Jesus leaflets have since been written, with millions distributed throughout the world.

Love Not Lust ∾

NORTH BEACH IN SAN FRANCISCO FEATURED TOPLESS DANCE nightclubs. It was a gaudy area with lots of libertines and hawkers enticing people passing by to enter their sleazy establishments. Our earliest Jews for Jesus outreach efforts involved prime-time distribution of literature and picketing demonstrations in front of the larger establishments. At times we coordinated our efforts with other evangelical Christians who were part of the Jesus Movement.

We constructed large double-sided posterboard signs and held them up as we walked single file in a large circle, chanting, "Love not lust," "Jesus is the answer," and similar slogans. When not picketing, we distributed broadside leaflets especially crafted for the occasion, which gave us the opportunity to talk (we called it witnessing) to those interested.

Though only a small group of about fifteen participated, we drew large crowds. As the Jesus Movement enthusiasts pitched in, the numbers of demonstrators grew to a couple of hundred and the gawking crowds grew larger still. A great commotion ensued as vehicular traffic backed up and thousands of people sought to find out what was happening. The media arrived, providing Moishe and others an opportunity to further publicize our mission. The television and radio media ate it up.

During one of our larger demonstrations, a woman stabbed Moishe in the hand. It was a superficial wound but nevertheless bled freely. True to character, Moishe refused to stop demonstrating, and instead held his wounded hand up high. We all thought he did this to gain attention, but he later told us he did it to slow the bleeding. I still think it was the former.

The demonstrations continued for a number of successive weekends, causing the nightclubs to lose a significant amount of business. Finally a key proprietor negotiated a deal with us. We offered to cease demonstrating if a few of us were permitted to share the Gospel from the stage of a nightclub during weekend prime time. They agreed. Following the presentation we discontinued our demonstrations, at least for a while.

What lasting impact our effort had upon North Beach only God knows. There was one superficial change: the nightclub we picketed and in which we spoke changed its name to the Garden of Eden. Its exterior neon flashing lights now display Eve standing next to a tree, upon which is a serpent. As was true of the forbidden fruit in the original garden, the exterior of the topless nightclub looks appealing, but the interior is rotten to the core.

Because we were young and impressionable, exposure to the wantonness really did reinforce in us that "Love not lust" was more than a slogan. I knew Bay Area street kids whose lives had been broken through seeking momentary sexual pleasure at the expense of the permanence of authentic love, responsibility, and commitment.

As the Jews for Jesus ministry in the San Francisco Bay Area grew, new outreaches developed, including one called Christ in the Passover. This consisted of presentations given to various groups and churches in which the symbols within the Passover service and meal were explained and shown to have their fulfillment in Jesus Christ. In subsequent years, I organized demonstration meals for groups of interested Christians. These were always a big hit, as most Christians have no exposure whatsoever to Passover, though the feast is often mentioned in the New Testament.

The Jesus Movement ⌘

LIVING IN BERKELEY DISTANCED ME FROM THE ONGOING ACTIVITIES of Jews for Jesus, as they were located in Marin County north of San Francisco and I had moved to the East Bay. I became increasingly involved with efforts to present the Christian faith to those in the counterculture, Gentiles as well as Jews.

Berkeley was a hotbed of political, social, and cultural upheaval, receiving frequent national news coverage for its massive and violent demonstrations and sit-ins against the Vietnam War. The University of California Berkeley campus and extended community drew disenchanted kids from across America who wanted to encounter the San Francisco Bay Area hippie experience. Thousands poured in searching for spiritual and cultural utopia. The atmosphere was energized with anticipation that as the cutting edge of the hippie and anti-war movement in Berkeley deepened, some new and wonderful age was dawning. While some prepared for what was called the utopian Age of Aquarius, others with a more apocalyptic bent expected at worst World War III, and at best another great San Francisco earthquake that would totally destroy the local military industrial establishment. The local hippie-looking Christians known as Jesus freaks were likewise energized and eager to creatively present the Christian faith.

While in Berkeley, I became a member of the Christian World Liberation Front (CWLF), an evangelical Protestant ministry that was an offshoot of Campus Crusade for Christ. Liberation fronts were radical movements that often were Marxist/communist. CWLF adopted this extreme-sounding name in the belief that authentic Christianity is in a sense the *most* radical of all movements. Also, the designation was more acceptable in the counterculture.

Under the leadership of Jack Sparks, CWLF engaged in a number of creative ministries, presenting the Christian gospel in forms and language more understandable to the counterculture. Jack paraphrased portions of the New Testament into the language of the counterculture, which Zondervan published as *Letters to Street Christians.* An example taken from 1 Corinthians: "When we told you about Jesus, we didn't use intellectual jive or rhetoric, but only rapped the straight 'Good News.' Let's face it, people, that's all there is—the person of Jesus the Messiah and the fact of His death on the cross. . . . Dig it! Your faith has to stand on the power of Jesus in your life, not on any philosophical jive."

Some of the more prominent ministries included the *Right On* underground newspaper, distributed widely in the Bay Area and throughout the West Coast to similarly minded Jesus Movement centers; and Crash Pad house ministries, about five in number, in which individuals living on the streets or passing through Berkeley could stay for a few nights (during which they would be witnessed to by young Christian staff workers and hear the gospel). The Spiritual Counterfeits Project (SCP) provided evangelical Protestant Christian apologetics critiquing non-Christian religious movements, especially Eastern-based Buddhism and Hinduism.

At a time when prayer was being legally excluded from public schools, a competing system of prayer called transcendental meditation (TM) was increasingly accepted as religiously neutral. Hindu-based TM rapidly found public funding and inclusion within a broad range of public institutions as a substitute for Judeo-Christian prayer. This system of meditation had been popularized by the Beatles, whose spiritual guru was TM's founder Maharishi Mahesh Yogi from India. A significant effort of the

SCP was to raise public awareness that TM was religiously based, and to lobby against its public funding and use in schools and other public institutions as a non-religious substitute for prayer. In this effort the SCP was largely successful.

Christian Street Theater ~

THE MINISTRY OUTREACH I WAS MOST INVOLVED WITH WAS STREET theater. Christian street theater is a form of guerrilla theater presenting the Christian message in short, creative skits using minimal props.

Among our troupe of seven or so was my Queens College buddy Charlie Lehman, who as a child had been adopted by a loving German Lutheran family in Queens. He decided to join me out on the West Coast after graduating with a degree in drama. His presence on the team encouraged me and reminded me of home.

Under the able direction of Frank Couch and Eugene Burkett, we created from scratch a series of six or so skits, each lasting about ten minutes and presenting a subtle, thought-provoking message. We often used parables from the Scriptures or elsewhere. One of my favorite skits was taken from *The Giving Tree*, in which the tree was presented as a metaphor for God. We linked the individual skits together in order to convey a common Christian theme, presenting aspects of Christ's life and teachings as the answer to life's greatest issues.

Our street theater troupe used no stage, amplification, sophisticated costumes, or expensive props. We performed outside wherever people congregated, with plazas and public parks our sites of preference. The troupe sought mobility, flexibility, and minimal expense, so we didn't advertise or reserve sites. Guerrilla theater was simply about appearing and performing.

At Berkeley we usually gave skits at the free speech plaza next to Ludwig Fountain, where Jack Sparks at other times would conduct public baptisms.

The crowds at our presentations numbered in the hundreds. Those gathered were decisively anti-Christian, making our effort especially challenging. This awareness made our presentations all the more rewarding, as in spite of our conservative theological Christian message we were warmly received, often with enthusiastic applause. They loved us in spite of our message because the skits were presented creatively with artistic excellence and respect for our audience.

Jews for Jesus' Jan Moskowitz, also a New Yorker, was a participant in one of our annual summer workshops in which we trained others to do street theater. Jan became co-founder in 1972 of the New Jerusalem Players street theater troupe. Jews for Jesus had a very utilitarian approach to evangelism, whereas our directors tended to view artistic excellence as having a value beyond its use in bringing people to Christ. At times we would discuss the role of art and how, as performers, we should view it. Is the Christian use of the arts primarily utilitarian—to spread the Gospel—or does good art have its own intrinsic value even without an overt message? Both sides were opinionated in their views.

Years later I read a book called *The Philokalia*, which in Greek means "love of beauty." It is a collection of texts written by ascetic saints of the Eastern Orthodox Christian Church between the fourth and fifteenth centuries. These texts present the love of and desire for moral and spiritual beauty as an intrinsic created aspect of human nature. My extrapolated understanding held that all which is truly beautiful—including good art—has inherent value and power, manifesting the creative love and beauty of God. In a sense I discovered both viewpoints to be true. All beauty comes from God and reflects His creative love, with or without the attachment of a message. On the other hand, all of creation—including beauty—serves to remind us of God. So beauty and art have both intrinsic value and the power to draw us to God.

Chapter 8

Why the Scriptures Are Not Enough

IN MY EARLY YEARS AS A CHRISTIAN, MUCH OF MY RELIGIOUS education came from private Bible reading. By the time I entered college, I had a pocket version of the whole Bible that was my constant companion. I committed favorite passages from the Scriptures to memory, and often quoted them to myself in times of temptation—or to others as I sought to tell them about Christ. I heartily proclaimed with St. Paul the Apostle, "All Scripture *is* given by inspiration of God, and *is* profitable for doctrine, for re-proof, for correction, for instruction in righteousness" (2 Timothy 3:16). Unfortunately, I took this as license to decide for myself what the Scriptures meant. So I marked verses about Jesus with my yellow highlighter, but passed over passages concerning God the Father, the Church, or baptism.

I saw the Bible as a heavenly instruction manual. I didn't think I needed the Church, except as a good place to make friends or to learn more about the Bible so I could be a better do-it-yourself Christian. I sought to build my life by the Book, and took *sola scriptura* ("only the Bible") seriously. Salvation history was clear to me: God sent His Son; together they sent the Holy Spirit; then came the New Testament to explain salvation; and finally, almost as an afterthought, the Church developed.

A Maelstrom of Confused Doctrines ⌥

NOT LONG AFTER MY CONVERSION TO CHRISTIANITY, I FOUND myself swept up in the tide of religious sectarianism, in which Christians would part over one issue after another. I encountered this in the very first church I attended, the Assemblies of God, in which I wrestled with whether speaking in tongues was "of God" or not and whether it was a necessary sign confirming one's salvation. Whether I could be saved without speaking in tongues became a very personal issue. Some in the church said yes, but many declared no. Feeling very self-conscious, I didn't stay long enough to find out.

In subsequent churches and Christian parachurch movements, I developed friendships with enthusiastic Christians whom I respected and who influenced my theological formation. Being relatively new to Christianity, I had to sort through many varied and conflicting doctrines in order to settle on what I personally believed to be true. Unfortunately, my friends often held opposing views that left me conflicted, confused, and frustrated. They all claimed one thing in common—"It's clearly taught in the Bible."

I attended services at a few Baptist churches, in part because the pastor who baptized me, Moishe Rosen, was an American Baptist, as were other friends. These churches emphatically taught that salvation is an instantaneous born-again experience in which we are saved by faith alone without the need of good works. This they based upon the scripture, "For by grace you have been saved through faith, and that not of yourselves; *it is* the gift of God, not of works, lest anyone should boast" (Ephesians 2:8, 9).

This position fit in well with my own life experience, as on a very specific day and time I had experienced a life-changing dramatic conversion. On the other hand, I also knew godly

⌁ SURPRISED BY CHRIST

Christians who could not point to a specific day and hour when they were "born again." Though raised in what are called Bible-believing churches, they had grown into the faith slowly, without any dramatic experience. These friends of mine could point to the time when they had been baptized as young adults, when they rededicated their lives to Christ, but not when they had experienced an instantaneous conversion.

In addition to the Baptists, the Lutherans who met next door to our Queens College IVCF chapter also believed in salvation by grace alone. Their founder, the sixteenth-century reformer Martin Luther, called the doctrine *sola fide* ("faith alone"). In contrast, other friends of mine in college held that salvation is a lifelong process, because faith alone is insufficient without good works. This view was held by my Pentecostal, Methodist, and Holiness Movement friends, some of whom traced their spiritual lineage to the great reformer John Wesley.

This group of friends also referred to Scripture to support their position. For example, they pointed out that the passage the Baptists and Lutherans loved to quote—that salvation is by faith and grace, and not of works—continues, "For we are His workmanship, created in Christ Jesus for good works, which God prepared beforehand that we should walk in them" (Ephesians 2:10).

These friends directed me to the Epistle of James, which seems to state the exact opposite of what Paul says in Ephesians: "What *does it* profit, my brethren, if someone says he has faith but does not have works? Can faith save him? . . . Thus also faith by itself, if it does not have works, is dead. . . . You see then that a man is justified by works, and not by faith only" (James 2:14, 17, 24). The opposing camps each lined up innumerable proof texts in support of their position and passionately presented them to me. Both sides seemed convincing.

As president of IVCF, I got to know some Christian Reformed Church members who taught what is called reformed theology. These included two of my closest college buddies, George and Harry, who led IVCF chapters in other NYC colleges. They later attended seminaries, including Westminster Theological Seminary, and became missionaries and staff workers. They presented still a third view about salvation, called five-point Calvinism. One of its most prominent expositors was the contemporary theologian Francis Schaeffer, highly regarded among college students and author of widely read books.

These strict Reformed Calvinists based their understanding of salvation on the 1618 Synod of Dort, which held that in the original Fall mankind became "totally depraved," a slave to sin and no longer possessing free choice or free will to turn to God. In this system of understanding, an individual can only be saved if God gives him saving grace. The ones to whom God gives saving grace cannot resist receiving it, nor can the ones to whom God does not give it ever receive it. An individual's salvation is determined by God's choice, not his own.

My Christian Reformed friends also claimed to base their views solidly on scripture. They pointed to verses such as, "There is none who seeks after God" (Romans 3:11b), and, "Therefore He has mercy on whom He wills, and whom He wills He hardens. You will say to me then, 'Why does He still find fault? For who has resisted His will?' But indeed, O man, who are you to reply against God? Will the thing formed say to him who formed it, 'Why have you made me like this?' Does not the potter have power over the clay, from the same lump to make one vessel for honor and another for dishonor?" (Romans 9:18–21).

I found horrific this view that I had no ability to choose salvation because I was totally depraved, and could only be saved if God chose to save me. What if God chose not to save me? Though two of my best college buddies believed this, I would not. I had a much greater attraction to the position of those in the other two opposing camps, both of which pointed to the scripture that says God "desires all men to be saved and to come to the knowledge of the truth" (1 Timothy 2:4).

Thus, the very first step in understanding salvation was in much dispute among my closest Christian friends. They all claimed to believe "only the Bible," but they interpreted its teachings on salvation in diametrically opposite ways. To complicate this question, the issue of the future state of non-Christians arose. Was there any hope for them in the life to come? Some said the Scripture says yes, and some no. If Christians had such widely differing views on something as basic as salvation, then how diverse must their views be on less basic issues?

Within my circle of Bible-believing friends, I witnessed a mini-explosion of sects and schismatic movements, each claiming to be "true to the Bible," each in bitter conflict with the others. Serious conflict arose over every topic imaginable: charismatic gifts, interpretation of prophecy, the proper way to worship, communion, church government, discipleship, discipline in the Church, morality, accountability, evangelism, social action, the relationship of faith and works, the role of women, and ecumenism. It seemed there were as many opinions on the Second Coming as there were people in a given discussion.

These were just a few of the subjects I wrestled with. Any issue could—and often did—cause Christians to part ways. We all appealed to the Scripture, saying, "If it's not in the Bible I don't believe it." Each claimed the same biblical authority, yet it seemed to me that it was not the Bible, but each person's private interpretation of it that became the ultimate authority. In an age that highly exalts independent thought and self-reliance, each of us was becoming his or her own pope.

The fruit of this sectarian spirit was division in my small circle of friends, which became a microcosm of Christendom, reflecting the theological chaos that has given birth to literally thousands of independent churches and denominations since the Protestant Reformation.

A Struggle for Understanding ⌇

THE GUIDELINE I USED IN INTERPRETING SCRIPTURE SEEMED simple enough. It was expressed in this little saying: When the plain sense of Scripture makes common sense, seek no other sense. I believed that those who were faithful and honest in following this principle would achieve Christian unity.

To my surprise, however, this common-sense approach led not to increased Christian clarity and unity, but to a spiritual free-for-all. Those who most strongly adhered to believing "only the Bible" tended to become the most factious, divisive, and combative of Christians—although perhaps unintentionally. In fact, it seemed to me that the more someone held to the Bible as the only source of spiritual authority, the more factious and sectarian that person became. We even argued heatedly over verses on love!

As I became increasingly sectarian, my radicalism intensified, and during the late 1960s and early 1970s I came to believe that *all* churches were unbiblical: to become a member of any church was to compromise the Faith. For me, "church" meant "the Bible, God, and me." This hostility towards the churches fit in well with my Jewish background. I naturally distrusted all churches because I felt they had betrayed the teachings of Christ by having participated in or passively ignored the persecution of the Jews throughout history. But the more sectarian I became—to the point of being at times obnoxious and antisocial—the more I began to realize that something was seriously wrong with my approach to Christianity. My spiritual life wasn't working.

Clearly, my privately held beliefs in the Bible and what it taught were leading me *away* from love and community with my fellow Christians, and therefore away from Christ. As St. John the Evangelist wrote, "He who does not love his brother whom he has seen, how can he love God whom he has not seen?" (1 John 4:20). This division and hostility were not what had drawn me to Christ.

I knew the answer was not to deny the Faith or reject the Scriptures. Something had to change. Maybe it was I. I began a study of the history of the Church and the New Testament, hoping to shed some light on what my attitude toward the Church and the Bible should be. The results were not at all what I expected.

The Bible of the Apostles ❧

MY INITIAL ATTITUDE WAS THAT WHATEVER WAS GOOD ENOUGH for the apostles was good enough for me. This is where I got my first surprise. Though I knew that the apostle Paul regarded Scripture as being inspired by God (2 Timothy 3:16), I had always assumed that the Scripture spoken of in this passage was the whole Bible—both the Old and the New Testaments. In reality, there *was* no New Testament when this statement was made. Even the Old Testament was still in the process of formulation, for the Jews did not decide on a definitive list or canon of Old Testament books until after the rise of Christianity.

As I studied further, I discovered that the early Christians used a Greek translation of the Old Testament called the Septuagint. This translation, which was begun in Alexandria, Egypt, in the third century BC, contained an expanded canon that included a number of the so-called "deuterocanonical" (or "apocryphal") books. Although there was some initial debate over these books, they were eventually received by Christians into the Old Testament canon.

In reaction to the rise of Christianity, the Jews narrowed their canons and eventually excluded the deuterocanonical books—although they still regarded them as sacred. The modern Jewish canon was not rigidly fixed until the third century after Christ. Interestingly, it is this later version of the Jewish canon of the Old Testament, rather than the canon of early Christianity, that is followed by most Protestants today.

When the apostles lived and wrote, there was no New Testament and no finalized Old Testament. The concept of "Scripture" was much less well defined than I had envisioned.

Early Christian Writings ❧

THE SECOND BIG SURPRISE CAME WHEN I REALIZED THAT THE first complete listing of the New Testament books as we have them today did not appear until over 300 years after the death and Resurrection of Christ. (The first complete listing was given by St. Athanasius in his Paschal Letter in AD 367.) Imagine it: If the writing of the New Testament had been begun at the same time as the US Constitution, we wouldn't see a final product until the year 2076.

The four Gospels were written from thirty to sixty years after Jesus' death and Resurrection. In the interim, the Church relied on oral tradition—the accounts of eyewitnesses—as well as scattered pre-gospel documents, such as those quoted in 1 Timothy 3:16 and 2 Timothy 2:11–13, and also on written tradition. Most churches only had parts of what was to become the New Testament.

As eyewitnesses of Christ's life and teachings began to die, the apostles wrote as they were guided by the Holy Spirit in order to preserve and solidify the scattered written and oral tradition. Because the apostles expected Christ to return soon, it seems they did not have in mind that these gospel accounts and apostolic letters would in time be collected into a new Bible.

I discovered that during the first four centuries after Christ, there was substantial disagreement over which books should be included in the canon of Scripture. The first person on record who tried to establish a New Testament canon was Marcion, in the second century. The main body of Christians excluded him from fellowship because of his heretical views. He wanted the Church to reject its Jewish heritage, and therefore he dispensed with the Old Testament entirely. Marcion's canon included only one gospel, which he himself edited, and ten of Paul's epistles. I was shocked to learn that the first attempted New Testament was heretical.

Many scholars believe that it was partly in reaction to this distorted canon of Marcion that the early Church determined to create a clearly defined canon of its own. The destruction of Jerusalem in AD 70, the breakup of the Jewish-Christian community there, and the threatened loss of continuity in the oral tradition probably contributed to the sense of the urgent need for the Church to standardize the list of books Christians could rely on.

During this period of the canon's evolution, most churches had only a few, if any, of the apostolic writings available to them. The books of the Bible had to be painstakingly copied by hand, at great expense of time and effort. Also, because most people were illiterate, these books could only be read by the privileged few. Most Christians' exposure to the Scriptures was confined to what they heard in the churches—the Law and Prophets, the Psalms, and some of the apostles' memoirs. The persecution of Christians by the Roman Empire and the existence of many documents of nonapostolic origin further complicated the matter.

This was my third surprise. Somehow I had naively envisioned every home and church as having a complete Old and New Testament from the very inception of the Church. It was difficult for me to imagine a congregation surviving and prospering without a complete New Testament. Yet unquestionably they did. This may have been my first clue that there was more to the total life of the Church than just the written Word.

Who Decided? ∿

THE ECUMENICAL COUNCILS OF THE FIRST FEW CENTURIES OF THE Church met to discern and confirm what was already generally accepted within the Church at large. The councils did not legislate the canon so much as set forth what had become self-evident truth and practice within the churches of God. The councils sought to proclaim the common mind of the Church and to reflect the unanimity of faith, practice, and tradition as it already existed in the local churches represented. Nevertheless, the New Testament books did not choose themselves. Christian leaders chose them.

The councils provide us with specific records in which the Church spoke clearly and in unison as to what constitutes Scripture. Among the many councils that met during the first four centuries, two are particularly important in this context:

(1) **The Council of Laodicea** met in Asia Minor about AD 363. This is the first council that clearly listed the canonical books of the present Old and New Testaments, with the exception of the Apocalypse (Revelation) of St. John. The Laodicean council stated that only the canonical books it listed should be read in the church. Its decisions were widely accepted in the Eastern Church.

(2) **The third Council of Carthage** met in North Africa about AD 397. This council, attended by Augustine, provided a full list of the canonical books of both the Old and New Testaments. The twenty-seven books of the present-day New Testament were accepted as canonical. The council also held that these books should be read in the church as Divine Scripture to the exclusion of all others. This council was widely accepted as authoritative in the West.*

Human and Divine ⌒∾

As I delved deeper into my study of the history of the New Testament, I saw my previous misconceptions being demolished one by one. I understood now what should have been obvious all along: that the New Testament consisted of twenty-seven separate documents, which, while certainly inspired by God, had been written and compiled by human beings. It was also clear that this work had not been accomplished by individuals working in isolation, but by the collective effort of all Christians everywhere—the Body of Christ, the Church.

Committed to belief in the inspiration of Scripture, I had understood the New Testament to be God's Word only, not man's. I supposed the apostles were told by God exactly what to write, much as a secretary takes down what is dictated, without providing any personal contribution.

Ultimately, my understanding of the inspiration of Scripture was clarified by the teaching of the Church regarding the Person of Christ. The Incarnate Word of God, our Lord Jesus Christ, is not only God but also Man. Christ is a single Person with two

---

* For a fuller explanation of the evolution of the New Testament canon, see my booklet "Which Came First: the Church or the New Testament?" published by Conciliar Press.

natures—divine and human. To deemphasize Christ's humanity leads to heresy. The ancient Church taught that the Incarnate Word was fully human—as human as it is possible to be—yet without sin. In His humanity, the Incarnate Word was born, grew, and matured into manhood.

I came to realize that this view of the Incarnate Word of God, the Logos, Jesus Christ, paralleled the early Christian view of the written Word of God, the Bible. The Holy Scriptures reflect not only the divine thought, but a human contribution as well. The Old and New Testaments convey truth to us as *written by men*, imparting the thoughts, personalities, and even limitations and weaknesses of the writers—yet inspired by God, to be sure. This means that the human element in the Bible is not overwhelmed and lost in the ocean of the divine.

It became clearer to me that as Christ Himself was born, grew, and matured, so did the written Word of God, the Bible. It did not come down whole—plop—from heaven, but was of human origin as well as divine. The apostles did not merely inscribe the Scriptures as would a secretary, but freely cooperated with the will of God through the inspiration of the Holy Spirit.

In contrast, I discovered Moslems believe their sacred scripture, the Koran, was communicated to Mohammed word-for-word by an angel, and because the Arabic language alone is sacred, should only be read in Arabic.

A Question of Authority ◞

THE SECOND ISSUE I HAD TO GRAPPLE WITH WAS EVEN MORE difficult for me—the issue of church authority. It was clear from my study that *the Church* had, in fact, determined which books composed the Scriptures; but still I wrestled mightily with the thought that the Church had been given this authority.

Ultimately, it came down to a single issue. I already believed that God spoke authoritatively through His written Word. The written Word of God is concrete and tangible. I can touch the Bible and read it. But for some strange reason, I was reluctant to believe the same things about the Body of Christ, the Church— that she was visible and tangible, located physically on earth in history. The Church to me was essentially mystical and intangible, not identifiable with any specific earthly assembly.

This view permitted me to see each Christian as being a church unto himself. How convenient this was, especially when doctrinal or personal problems arose! Yet this view did not agree with the reality of what the apostolic era understood the Church to be. The New Testament is about real churches, not ethereal ones. Could I now accept the fact that God spoke authoritatively not only through the Bible, but through His Church as well—the very Church which had produced, protected, and actively preserved the Scriptures I held so dear?

The Church of the New Testament ᘰ

IN THE VIEW OF THE EARLIEST CHRISTIANS, GOD SPOKE HIS WORD not only *to* but *through* His Body, the Church. It was *within* His Body, the Church, that the Word was confirmed and established. Without question, the Scriptures were looked upon by early Christians as God's active revelation of Himself to the world. At the same time, the Church was understood as the household of God, "having been built on the foundation of the apostles and prophets, Jesus Christ Himself being the chief corner *stone*, in whom the whole building, being joined together, grows into a holy temple in the Lord" (Ephesians 2:20, 21).

God has His Word, but He also has His Body. The New Testament says:

(1) "Now you are the body of Christ, and members individually" (1 Corinthians 12:27; compare Romans 12:5).

(2) "He [Christ] is the head of the body, the church" (Colossians 1:18).

(3) "And He [the Father] put all *things* under His [the Son's] feet, and gave Him *to be* head over all *things* to the church, which is His body, the fullness of Him who fills all in all" (Ephesians 1:22, 23).

My discovery that in early times there was no organic separation between Bible and Church, as we so often find today, was for me shocking. The Body without the Word is without message, but the Word without the Body is without foundation. As Paul writes, the Body is "the church of the living God, the pillar and ground of the truth" (1 Timothy 3:15).

The Church is the living Body of the Incarnate Lord. The apostle does not say that the *New Testament* is the pillar and ground of the truth. The *Church* is the pillar and foundation of the truth, because the New Testament was built on her life in God. In short, she wrote it. She is an integral part of the gospel message, and it is within the Church that the New Testament was written and preserved.

The Word of God in Oral Tradition ❧

THE APOSTLE PAUL EXHORTS US, "THEREFORE, BRETHREN, STAND fast and hold the traditions which you were taught, whether by word or our epistle" (2 Thessalonians 2:15). This verse was one I had not highlighted because it used two phrases I didn't like: "hold the traditions" and "by word [of mouth]." These two phrases conflicted with my understanding of biblical authority.

But then I began to understand: the same God who speaks to us through His written Word, the Bible, spoke also through the apostles of Christ as they taught and preached in person. The Scriptures themselves teach in this passage (and others) that this oral tradition is what we are to keep. Written and oral tradition are not in conflict, but are parts of one whole. This explains why ancient church fathers teach that he who does not have the Church as his Mother does not have God as his Father.

In coming to this realization, I concluded that I had grossly overreacted in rejecting oral Holy Tradition. In my hostility toward Jewish oral tradition, which rejected Christ, I had rejected Christian oral Holy Tradition, which expresses the life of the Holy Spirit in the Church. And I had rejected the idea that this Tradition enables us properly and fully to understand the Bible.

Let me illustrate this point with an experience I had later on in life. In the 1990s, while living in Washington State, I decided to build a shed behind my house. In preparation, I studied a book on carpentry that had "everything" in it. It was full of pictures and diagrams, enough so that "even a kid could follow its instructions." It explains itself, I read. But simple as the book claimed to be, the more I read it the more questions I had and the more confused I became.

Disgusted at not being able to understand something that seemed so simple, I came to the conclusion that the book needed interpretation. Without help, I just couldn't put it into practice. What I needed was someone with expertise who could explain the manual to me.

Fortunately, I had a friend who was able to show me how the project should be completed. He knows because of oral tradition. An experienced carpenter taught him, and he in turn taught me. Written and oral tradition together got the job done.

Which Came First? ❧

WHAT CONFRONTED ME AT THIS POINT WAS THE BOTTOM-LINE question: Which came first, the Church or the New Testament? I knew that the Incarnate Word of God, Jesus Christ, had called the apostles, who in turn formed the nucleus of the Christian Church. I knew that the Eternal Word of God therefore preceded and gave birth to the Church.

When the Church heard the Incarnate Word of God and committed His Word to writing, she thereby participated with God in giving birth to the written Word, the New Testament. Thus it was the Church that gave birth to and preceded the New Testament. To my question, "Which came first, the Church or the New Testament?" the answer, both biblically and historically, was crystal clear.

I asked myself, "Does it really make any difference which came first? After all, the Bible contains everything we need for salvation." The Bible is adequate for salvation in the sense that it contains the foundational material needed to establish us on the correct path. On the other hand, I had learned that it is wrong to consider the Bible as being self-sufficient and self-interpreting. The Bible is meant to be read and understood by the illumination of God's Holy Spirit within the life of the Church.

I am reminded that the Lord Himself told His disciples, just prior to His Crucifixion, "When He, the Spirit of truth, has come, He will guide you into all truth; for He will not speak on His own *authority*, but whatever He hears He will speak; and He will tell you things to come" (John 16:13). He also said, "I will build My church, and the gates of Hades shall not prevail against it" (Matthew 16:18). Our Lord did not leave us with only a book to guide us. He left us with His Church. The Holy Spirit within the Church teaches us, and His teaching complements the Scripture.

I came to see how foolish it was for me to believe that God's full illumination ceased after the New Testament books were written, not to resume until the Protestant Reformation in the sixteenth century, or—to take this argument to its logical conclusion—until the very moment when I myself started reading the Bible. Either the Holy Spirit was in the Church throughout the centuries following the New Testament period, leading, teaching, and illuminating her in her understanding of the gospel message, or the Church had been left a spiritual orphan, with individual Christians independently interpreting—and often teaching with an assumption of authority—the same Scripture in radically different ways. I became convinced such chaos could not be the will of God, "for God is not *the author* of confusion but of peace" (1 Corinthians 14:33).

Though he may have coined the slogan, the fact is that Luther himself did not practice *sola scriptura*. If he had, he would have tossed out the creeds and spent less time writing commentaries. The phrase came about as a result of the Reformers' struggles against the added human traditions of Romanism. Understandably, they wanted to be sure their faith was accurate according to the New Testament standards. But to isolate the Scriptures from the Church, to deny fifteen hundred years of history, is something the slogan *sola scriptura* and the Protestant Reformers—Luther, Calvin, and later Wesley—never intended to do.

At this point in my spiritual journey, the late 1970s, I felt I had to make a decision. If the Church were not just a tangent or a sidelight to the Scripture, but rather an active participant in its development and preservation, then I felt compelled to identify and reconcile my differences with her and abandon my prejudices. Rather than trying to judge the Church according to my modern preconceptions about what the Bible was saying, I needed to humble myself and come into union with the Church that produced the proper understanding of Holy Scripture. My task now became to identify that Church.

Chapter 9

Worship in the Ancient Church

THE DESIRE TO DISCOVER *WHAT* CHURCH HAD DEFINED the New Testament Canon led me to search the Scripture and the earliest Christian writings for telltale signs. I examined what I considered the most central act of Christians—worship. If I could determine how the ancient Christians worshiped and find a church that worshiped similarly today, perhaps it would help me identify the church that compiled the New Testament.

I was disappointed to find that the New Testament has little to say about worship, other than indicating that the original Jewish Christians continued to worship as Jews in both the Jerusalem temple and the synagogues. They did so for as long as they were able, stopping only after the temple's destruction and their exclusion from the synagogues by non-Christian Jews.

The New Testament epistles were written to provide spiritual encouragement and to address problems and disputes within the Church. The fact that issues concerning worship are largely absent from the epistles indicates that worship was not a problem. Neither did I find worship an issue of controversy in the post-New Testament writings. Though many theological issues were disputed during these first few centuries, the form of worship was not.

This seemed strange, given the great differences of worship styles and resulting conflicts existing among Christians today. Why was this? Was it because diverse forms of worship were practiced and everyone tolerated everyone else's style of worship? I found the opposite to be true. Diversity was limited, as universally there was a single form of Christian worship.

As I delved into the study of worship in the ancient Christian Church, I came to realize how many writings from the first four centuries contain detailed descriptions of its services. These documents, which we will look at in detail later on, reveal a form of worship based on temple and synagogue forms, and remarkably unified throughout all the churches of Christendom, both in the East and in the West.

Of what did this worship consist? My first discovery was that worship services were universally centered on weekly Holy Communion or Eucharist, with the sermon filling a secondary, supportive role. The unanimous and universal practice during the first four hundred years of the Church was to center the worship of God around receiving Holy Communion. This was shocking to me, as the circle of Christians I knew rarely had communion services, and receiving communion was always optional and often deemphasized. The only exceptions to this were my Roman Catholic friends.

A Deep Distrust of Roman Catholicism 〰

HAVING BEEN RAISED IN NEW YORK CITY, I KNEW A LOT OF Catholics. Some went to mass often. In fact, the first person who spoke to me about Jesus was my lifelong friend George Linkus, whose parents were Catholic immigrants from Lithuania. Years before I was given a New Testament by another friend, Frank Sorbi, George had asked me, "Why don't you believe in Jesus?"

At the time I answered, "Because we don't believe that he is God."

With the passage of time my knowledge of the Roman Catholic Church's dark history with Jews increased, resulting in my deep distrust, indeed dislike, of Roman Catholicism. Of all the Christians I knew, Catholics were the ones most likely to call me names like "Christ-killer," "Jew bastard," "Kike," "Yid," or other profanities. On more than a few occasions, Catholic neighbors vehemently spewed streams of profanities about Jews. I had the impression that hatred of Jews was a central Roman Catholic tenet.

As part of my Jewish upbringing, I read many books and saw documentaries chronicling the persecution of Jews by Christians. Roman Catholic history was particularly abhorrent, as it included a long history of blatant anti-Semitism. This history included the Medieval Blood Libels, in which Jews of Europe were accused of stealing, slaughtering, and drinking the blood of Christian children during Passover; the Black Death (bubonic plague), which Jews were accused of causing by poisoning wells; the Crusades, during which great numbers of Jews were slaughtered by the crusading armies as they marched to and from the Holy Land; the Spanish Inquisition, in which many Jews were subjected to forced baptism, and those who did not convert were expelled from Spain; and the seemingly friendly relations between the Vatican and fascist dictators Mussolini and Hitler before and during World War II.

These events so colored my mind that, for example, to me 1492 was not so much the year that Columbus discovered America as it was the year in which the Spanish monarchs Ferdinand and Isabella expelled the Jews from Spain. "In the same month in which their Majesties [Ferdinand and Isabella] issued the edict that all Jews should be driven out of the kingdom and its territories, in the same month they gave me the order to undertake with sufficient men my expedition of discovery to the Indies." So begins

Christopher Columbus's diary. The edict of expulsion was given on March 30, 1492, and the Jews were given exactly four months in which to leave. On July 30 of that year, the entire Jewish community, some 200,000 people, were expelled from Spain.

In contrast, the devout Protestants I knew were often friendly towards Jews and even supportive of the Zionist movement and the establishment of Israel. Some even went so far as to view this as the fulfillment of biblical prophecy.

Though I believed in Christ, I was Romophobic in my theology and understanding of Christianity. This prejudice included rejecting any ritual, ceremony, liturgy, or other expression of Christian worship that appeared too formal, organized, traditional, or Catholic.

Ancient Worship Was Liturgical and Sacramental ◆

THIS PREJUDICE MADE MY DISCOVERY ABOUT HOW EARLY CHRIS-tians worshiped all the more challenging. The agreement among the earliest Christian writings with regard to a highly liturgical, sacramental, and hierarchical form of worship was difficult for me to accept. That was not at all the kind of worship I wanted to find in the ancient Church.

The writings I studied, readily available and easy reading, included:

- The letters of St. Ignatius of Antioch (first century).
- St. Justin Martyr of Rome (second century), whose *First Apology*, written to the Emperor Marcus Aurelius, explains Christianity, describing its worship and in particular the Eucharist.
- St. Clement of Alexandria (second century) describes what the Eucharist is.
- Hippolytus of Rome (third century), in *The Apostolic Tradition*,

provides a detailed description of how the church in Rome worshiped.

- St. Cyril of Jerusalem (fourth century), in his *Catechetical Lectures,* tells how to prepare for Communion and describes the service.
- Egeria (fourth century), in her *Diary of a Pilgrimage,* describes in great detail worship services she personally witnessed in Jerusalem and at Mount Sinai.
- St. Ambrose of Milan (fourth century), in *On the Sacraments,* speaks about the Eucharist.

In addition, I studied the extensive writings and sermons of St. John Chrysostom (fourth century), St. Augustine (fifth century), as well as many others. I found that all the accounts of worship from that era without exception agree as to how the early Church worshiped.

The first account I read was Justin Martyr's *First Apology,* written in the middle of the second century to the emperor Marcus Aurelius as a defense of the Christian Faith. Having read Justin's other writing, *Dialogue with Trypho the Jew,* in which he displays an understanding and sensitivity to Jews, I was particularly eager to hear what he had to say about early worship. Justin Martyr's writings are among the earliest known.

The second account was *The Apostolic Constitutions,* a late-fourth-century document. This is a guideline and manual of church teaching and practice based on still earlier works. It claims to be the teaching of the apostles transmitted to the Church by Clement of Rome (AD 30–100). He is believed to be the same Clement mentioned in Philippians 4:3: "And I urge you also, true companion, help these women who labored with me in the gospel, with Clement also, and the rest of my fellow workers, whose names *are* in the Book of Life."

The form of worship or liturgy is contained in the eighth book of *The Apostolic Constitutions* and is often called the Clementine Liturgy. Regardless of its origin, it is commonly understood to present how the church at Antioch worshiped, and is the earliest complete eucharistic text to have survived. This thrilled me, as Antioch was the site of the first mission to the Gentiles and was greatly influenced by the Jewish Christian church of Jerusalem. Because of this, much of its worship form was of Jewish origin. In time, the worship rite of Antioch was inherited by Constantinople. Book eight of the *Apostolic Constitutions* has among its sources a still earlier writing called *The Apostolic Traditions,* compiled by Hippolytus of Rome about AD 215. *The Apostolic Traditions* contains what is believed to be the eucharistic service served at Antioch and later adopted in Rome.

The third ancient document I found to be most impressive presents the account of a wealthy woman named Egeria, perhaps from Rome, who went on pilgrimage to the Holy Land in the fourth or fifth century. She describes at length the worship that she participated in at Jerusalem and on Mount Sinai. This journal, *The Diary of a Pilgrimage,* excited me as it presents perhaps the earliest detailed account of worship in Jerusalem and the Holy Land.

It became evident from the accounts contained in these three ancient documents, as well as others, that a very uniform pattern or shape to worship existed throughout the Roman Empire. The Christians in Jerusalem, in Antioch-Syria, in Rome, in Alexandria, Egypt, in Constantinople, in Spain, in Gaul, and in the British Isles all worshiped in essentially the same way.

How the Earliest Christians Worshiped ∾

A COMPOSITE LIST OF ELEMENTS FOUND IN EARLY CHRISTIAN worship follows. Its details collectively provide a clear picture of what the ancients considered to be worship.

- The church pointed east, was rectangular in shape, and was built with sacristy rooms on either side at the east end.
- The people stood while worshiping, with men on one side and women on the other.
- The service began with Old Testament, epistle, and Gospel readings.
- The Psalms of David were sung between the readings.
- The sermon, typically delivered by the bishop, followed the Gospel reading.
- The bishop greeted the people by making the sign of the cross, and preached sitting while the people stood.
- The sermon was followed by a dismissal of those who were not entitled to take part in Holy Communion/Eucharist. The text refers to various groups who were dismissed, including *catechumens* (those being prepared for baptism), *illuminati* (those in the final stages of preparation for baptism), *energums* (those believed to be possessed by unclean spirits), and *penitents* (those excluded from Communion while they did penance for grave sins). Each group was dismissed in a similar way, with a litany.
- When only the faithful remained, the deacon led them in praying a comprehensive litany for the whole Church. The litanies comprised a list of petitions or intercessions set in written form. The petitions began with, "Let us pray for . . ." and continued, "that the Lord may . . ." Following each petition, the people responded with *"Kyrie eleison,"* which means "Lord, have mercy."
- The kiss of peace was exchanged. The clergy greeted the clergy, the laymen the laymen, and the women the women.
- The deacons brought the gifts of bread and wine to the bishop at the altar.
- The celebrant consecrated the bread and wine.

- The celebrant called the people to Communion with the words, "Holy things are for the holy [people]." The people responded with, "There is one holy, one Lord Jesus Christ, to the glory of God the Father."

- Communion was given with the words, "The Body of Christ" and "The Blood of Christ," to which the communicant responded, "Amen."

- Following Communion, the celebrant gave thanks in the name of all. The deacon instructed the people to bow their heads while the celebrant prayed for them. The deacon then dismissed the people.

Dom Gregory Dix (1901–1952), the Anglican priest/monk/historian, writes in his classic study on the history of the development of worship in the ancient Church:

> The main lines of all the Eastern traditions had been reached before the end of the fourth century, and after this the process in all of them is no more than one of adjustment and development of detail. . . . The basis chosen is the rite of the "holy city" Jerusalem in the East, and Rome in the West . . . the general tendency [in the East] was to adopt the Syrian liturgy of the Jerusalem-Antioch type. The Byzantine rite itself, clearly of Antiochian-Syrian derivation, continued to develop along its own lines down to the seventh century and did not become absolutely rigid until the ninth century.[4]

My discovery astounded me. I discovered in these ancient documents that services were typically led by one person, either a bishop or priest, who alone had authority to say the prayers consecrating the bread and wine. The service included a recounting of the Last Supper, the words of Institution, and an *epiclesis*, or calling down the Holy Spirit upon the faithful and upon the bread and wine. Worship was understood to have a sacrificial aspect, as it re-presented the once-for-all sacrifice of Christ. Following the consecration, the bread and wine were called the Body and Blood of Christ.

Statements in the various documents clearly indicate that the ancient Church *universally* understood the Eucharist to be literally the glorified Body and Blood of Christ. Communicants were required to be baptized, living a moral life, and reconciled with those within the Church. Only the faithful, those properly received into the Church and in good standing within it, were permitted to receive Communion. The clergy were responsible for the implementation of the rules of discipline and for deciding who would and would not be permitted to commune.

Does Ancient Worship Matter? ᥐ

DISCOVERY OF THE ANCIENT CHURCH'S FORM OF WORSHIP WAS A major breakthrough in my search to identify which Church wrote and compiled the New Testament. But knowing this intellectually and being willing to accept and believe it were two different things. My prejudice ran deep against "high church" liturgical worship, which I considered spiritually dead.

As I discussed my findings about the worship of the ancient Church with friends, something very revealing surfaced. Most of them didn't care! What they really cared about was finding worship they enjoyed and felt comfortable with. All that mattered was having a vibrant community of friends who shared similar values. Their concerns were practical in nature, whereas I was driven by ideology and the desire to know what was true. I longed to acquire the biblical and post-biblical model, even if it proved personally uncomfortable and meant sacrificing the familiar.

This journey was a continuation of my journey to Christ. For me, as a Jew, believing in Christ meant creating a breach with the Jewish people, my relatives, and my parents. Now, in pursuing a church unlike any I had experienced, I would likely experience a breach with my Christian family—my Protestant, IVCF, Jews for Jesus, and Jesus Movement friends. Starting with a totally different type of church and brand new friends was not something I desired. And at present all I knew was how the early Christians worshiped—I did not know whether that ancient form of worship was still practiced.

The Centrality of the Eucharist ◡

I HAD COME TO REALIZE THAT THE CENTRAL ACT OF ANCIENT church worship was what is called the Eucharist, or Communion. The circle of Christians I knew did not use the word Eucharist. Eucharist was a "high church" word that usually implied the bread and wine were regarded as more than symbolic. The Communion services I participated in used grape juice, not wine, on the assumption that Jesus drank grape juice at the Last Supper. Almost all the Christians I knew believed that at Communion the bread and grape juice remained bread and grape juice, and that no transformation took place when they were consecrated or prayed over.

In my studies I made another major discovery. The ancients universally used wine, not grape juice, and adamantly held that after the prayers of consecration the bread and wine became the glorified Body and Blood of Christ, at the same time retaining the appearance of bread and wine. For them, Communion was more than symbolic—it was actual.

Many statements from the earliest era of the Church clearly demonstrate the universal belief in the centrality of the Eucharist in worship, and belief that after being consecrated the bread and wine become the glorified Body and Blood of Christ.

St. Ignatius of Antioch, first century:

> Do ye all come together in common . . . in obedience to the bishop and the presbytery with an undivided mind, breaking one and the same bread, which is the medicine of immortality, and the antidote to prevent us from dying, but [which causes] that we should live for ever in Jesus Christ.[5]

St. Justin Martyr, second century:

> Having ended the prayers, we salute one another with a kiss. There is then brought to the president of the brethren bread and a cup of wine mixed with water; and he taking them, gives praise and glory to the Father of the universe, through the name of the Son and of the Holy Spirit, and offers thanks at considerable length for our being counted worthy to receive these things at His hands. And when he has concluded the prayers and thanksgivings, all the people present express their assent by saying Amen. This word Amen answers in the Hebrew language *to genoito* [so be it]. And when the president has given thanks, and all the people have expressed their assent, those who are called by us deacons give to each of those present to partake of the bread and wine mixed with water over which the thanksgiving was pronounced, and to those who are absent they carry away a portion.[6]

> And this food is called among us *Eukaristia* [the Eucharist], of which no one is allowed to partake but the man

who believes that the things which we teach are true, and who has been washed with the washing that is for the remission of sins, and unto regeneration, and who is so living as Christ has enjoined. For not as common bread and common drink do we receive these; but in like manner as Jesus Christ our Saviour, having been made flesh by the Word of God, had both flesh and blood for our salvation, so likewise have we been taught that the food which is blessed by the prayer of His word, and from which our blood and flesh by assimilation are nourished, is the flesh and blood of that Jesus who was made flesh. For the apostles, in the memoirs composed by them, which are called Gospels, have thus delivered unto us what was enjoined upon them; that Jesus took bread, and when He had given thanks, said, "This do ye in remembrance of Me, this is My body;" and that, after the same manner, having taken the cup and given thanks, He said, "This is My blood;" and gave it to them alone.[7]

St. Cyril of Jerusalem, fourth century:

Even of itself the teaching of the Blessed Paul is sufficient to give you a full assurance concerning those Divine Mysteries, of which having been deemed worthy, ye are become of the same body and blood with Christ. For you have just heard him say distinctly, That our Lord Jesus Christ in the night in which He was betrayed, took bread, and when He had given thanks He brake it, and gave to His disciples, saying, Take, eat, this is My Body: and having taken the cup and given thanks, He said, Take, drink, this is My Blood. Since then He Himself declared and said of the Bread, This is My Body, who shall dare to doubt any longer? And since He has Himself affirmed and said, This is My Blood, who shall ever hesitate, saying, that it is not His blood?

He once in Cana of Galilee, turned the water into wine, akin to blood, and is it incredible that He should have turned wine into blood? When called to a bodily marriage, He miraculously wrought that wonderful work; and on the children of the bride-chamber, shall He not much rather be acknowledged to have bestowed the fruition of His Body and Blood?

Wherefore with full assurance let us partake as of the Body and Blood of Christ: for in the figure of Bread is given to thee His Body, and in the figure of Wine His Blood; that thou by partaking of the Body and Blood of Christ, may be made of the same body and the same blood with Him. For thus we come to bear Christ in us, because His Body and Blood are distributed through our members; thus it is that, according to the blessed Peter, we became partakers of the divine nature. . . .

Consider therefore the Bread and the Wine not as bare elements, for they are, according to the Lord's declaration, the Body and Blood of Christ; for even though sense suggests this to thee, yet let faith establish thee. Judge not the matter from the taste, but from faith be fully assured without misgiving, that the Body and Blood of Christ have been vouchsafed to thee. . . . Having learnt these things, and been fully assured that the seeming bread is not bread, though sensible to taste, but the Body of Christ; and that the seeming wine is not wine, though the taste will have it so, but the Blood of Christ.[8]

St. Ambrose, Bishop of Milan, fourth century:

The Lord Jesus Himself proclaims: "This is My Body." Before the blessing of the heavenly words another nature is spoken of, after the consecration the Body is signified. He Himself speaks of His Blood. Before the consecration it has another name, after it is called Blood. And you say, Amen, that is, It is true. Let the heart within confess what the mouth utters, let the soul feel what the voice speaks. Christ, then, feeds His Church with these sacraments, by means of which the substance of the soul is strengthened.[9]

St. Leo I the Great of Rome, fifth century:

For when the Lord says, "unless ye have eaten the flesh of the Son of Man, and drunk His blood, ye will not have life in you," you ought so to be partakers at the Holy Table, as to have no doubt whatever concerning the reality of Christ's Body and Blood.[10]

If Communion is, as the early Church held, literally the glorified Body and Blood of Christ, it made sense to me that it should be approached with a certain fear and trembling, and not shared with someone who believes the sacrament to be only symbolic. I knew that the Scriptures indicated in a number of passages that Communion was a vital aspect of the Christian life and worship.

Jesus Himself instituted the practice at the Last Supper when He said, "'Take, eat; this is My body.' Then He took the cup, and gave thanks, and gave *it* to them, saying, 'Drink from it, all of you. For this is My blood of the new covenant, which is

❧ SURPRISED BY CHRIST

shed for many for the remission of sins'" (Matthew 26:26–28).

In 1 Corinthians 10:16, the apostle Paul asks, "The cup of blessing which we bless, is it not the communion of the blood of Christ? The bread which we break, is it not the communion of the body of Christ?" St. Paul indicates that the bread and wine were to be viewed as being more than symbolic:

> For I received from the Lord that which I also delivered to you: that the Lord Jesus on the *same* night in which He was betrayed took bread; and when He had given thanks, He broke *it* and said, "Take, eat; this is My body which is broken for you; do this in remembrance of Me." In the same manner *He* also *took* the cup after supper, saying, "This cup is the new covenant in My blood. This do, as often as you drink *it*, in remembrance of Me." For as often as you eat this bread and drink this cup, you proclaim the Lord's death till He comes. Therefore whoever eats this bread or drinks *this* cup of the Lord in an unworthy manner will be guilty of the body and blood of the Lord. But let a man examine himself, and so let him eat of the bread and drink of the cup. For he who eats and drinks in an unworthy manner eats and drinks judgment to himself, not discerning the Lord's body. For this reason many *are* weak and sick among you, and many sleep. (1 Corinthians 11:23–30)

The fact that those who received Communion unworthily became sick and even died was a strong indication to me that the consecrated bread and wine were more than merely symbolic.

Chapter 10

A New Commitment

LITTLE DID I KNOW WHILE IN BERKELEY ENGAGED IN street ministry that my involvement would soon lead to a much more enduring engagement. Our CWLF community had planned a Christian retreat for New Year's weekend at Meteor Ranch in Upper Lake. It was a majestic site near Clear Lake—California's largest freshwater lake. The conference would have a guest speaker as well as lots of fellowship and singing.

I went with my friend Tom Carrubba, who was visiting from New York. Having been raised as city boys, we regarded spending a few days in the Northern California forests as an adventure akin to going to the Amazon jungle. At twenty-four, I had been in true wilderness forests only a couple of times. I did not know how to drive and had gone on only very short excursions, so our trip of a few hours seemed to take forever.

In 1970, New Year's Eve fell on Thursday. That evening as the magic hour of midnight drew near, Tom and I talked to a few others in the main conference room. We were seated around a blazing woodstove in the center of the hall. At a most enchanting moment as the new year was to begin, two young women approached the fire from the other side. One was a tall, Nordic-looking blonde with high cheekbones and a quiet, gentle manner. Her name was Bonnie Lynn Halstrom. In seven months she would be my bride.

It is strange how the most monumental, life-changing events

often begin with the most subtle and unheralded encounters. Bonnie and I spent a couple of hours together around the blazing fire as the first moments of the new year arrived. The winter's cold could not diminish the fire's warmth nor the blossoming of love's flower at our first encounter. As I write, thirty-six years and four children later, I remember those first moments together as if they took place yesterday.

Following the retreat, Bonnie and I met once or twice a week. She lived with her parents an hour's drive to the south in San Jose, and studied nursing at San Jose State. Her parents came from cultures quite different from mine. Her father Walter was raised on a vineyard near Fresno, California. His parents, Alban and Mary, were immigrants from Sweden. They were of religious evangelical Protestant stock and refused to sell their grapes to wineries. Walt served in the Army in World War II, with a specialty in communications that took him to Morocco, Algeria, Tunisia, Sicily, Italy, France, and Germany.

Bonnie's mother Bobbie and her twelve siblings were raised in a dirt-poor family in the San Fernando Valley of California. Her grandparents had migrated from Oklahoma/Kansas to southern California during the Dust Bowl years of the Great Depression. They were some of the people of whom John Steinbeck wrote in *The Grapes of Wrath*. Family folklore has it that some family members were too poor to travel to California and devised a scheme to get there. Using an old clunker of a car that had no engine, but claiming engine problems, they asked others driving by to help by pushing the car, overflowing with their belongings, to the nearest town. They were pushed from one town to the next and then to the next and so on, always moving westward towards California, until they finally arrived in the promised land.

Life was terribly hard, even in the land of their dreams. Bobbie moved away from home to work as a domestic worker at thirteen years of age and matured under difficult conditions. She married twice, had a daughter by each husband, and was left a widow as a relatively young woman. After the war, she met and married Walter, who was for her a deliverer.

Bonnie was born in a dusty little oil town in central California in 1951, the year the United Nations headquarters opened, the Korean War was being fought, and Mickey Mantle and Willie Mays began their major league baseball careers. The family lived in Bakersfield, California, and attended a Southern Baptist church. Work was hard to come by. Being by profession a glazier, Walt was drawn to work in booming San Jose, about four hours to the north. Eventually the family moved there and attended a Baptist General Conference church.

Needless to say, Bonnie and I were of contrasting backgrounds. She told me that though she had read about Jews in the Bible, she had never knowingly met one. I was the first, and a New Yorker besides. I told her that I had never knowingly met someone of Okie and Swedish descent as beautiful and mellow as she. I shared with her my love of classical music, opera, art, museums, chess, earth sciences, news, newspapers, lox and bagels, Chinese food, Italian Chianti wine, and cannolli pastries. She shared with me her love of gardening, camping, hiking, swimming, horseback riding, walking barefoot, and eating natural, unprocessed, back-to-nature foods and granola. Her parents introduced me to eating meat three times a day, and to mashed potatoes, cornbread, and black-eyed peas.

Sometimes opposites attract. In terms of ethnic/cultural upbringing and physical appearance, this was true of us. There were also contrasts in terms of our personalities. I was talkative, blunt, confident, theoretical, idealistic, and abstract; Bonnie was soft-spoken, reserved, logical, ordered, methodical, and extremely bright. Bonnie typically grasped practical concepts more easily than I, whereas I more readily understood abstract and theological concepts. She also had a fantastic memory. Bonnie read books like a hare and I like a tortoise.

These contrasts of personality and culture made for interesting, exciting, but also difficult times relating to one another. Often marriages flounder unless there is much love, patience, compromise, and humility with which to ask for and to grant forgiveness. There is no doubt that our common faith in God and our commitment to one another and to pursuing purity of life enabled us to overcome the trying times of conflict. We allowed our differences and conflicts to spur us to grow spiritually as we prayed more and sought to be more humble and loving.

Our Wedding ⌒

JULY 4, 1971, WAS OUR PERSONAL LAST DAY OF INDEPENDENCE, AS we were wed on July 5. It was a hippie, Jesus Movement type of wedding. Jews for Jesus founder Moishe Rosen presided wearing a black robe. CWLF founder Jack Sparks gave the sermon in his best bib overalls. Bonnie wore a modest vintage wedding dress. The ceremony was held outdoors in front of the Brazilian Room at Tilden Park in the Berkeley Hills. The temperature was in the nineties and flowers were in bloom everywhere. The guests sat before us on the spacious lawn, except for a few special guests, including Bonnie's parents, who were given chairs.

My parents refused to attend because I was marrying a Gentile and it was a Christian wedding. The only relative of mine who came was my beloved brother, Sol. Most in attendance wore their finest hippie clothes with lots of emblems on their shirts, beads, Birkenstock sandals, long hair and beards. They listened appreciatively as guitars played songs like "Turn Turn Turn, for Everything There Is a Season" from the Book of Ecclesiastes. We included the Jewish rite of crushing the common wine glass underfoot.

The reception was held in the Brazilian Room, where bagels and cream cheese were served. It was there that Bonnie's sister Jeanie met her future husband Ken Winkle, called Koala Bear by all of us because of his round face. All my Berkeley friends were there, even the nationally famous street preacher Holy Hubert. It was a most typical early seventies hippie wedding with all the cultural additions, including patchouli oil and hippie jargon: "Far out, now get this, brothers and sisters, we are all God's Forever Family, and Jesus is King."

The back-to-nature movement was strong then, so Bonnie and I decided to spend our honeymoon in the mountains. We drove our Mercury Comet to majestic Yosemite National Park, which held a special place in our hearts.

Upon returning to Berkeley, we first lived in an apartment near Grove and University Avenue, then bought our first house together with another married couple, Gene and Peggy Burkett. In the fall of 1975 our first child, Heather Noel, was born. Heather grew to be very friendly and artistic. Over the next seven years we had three more children. Holly was born in July, 1979. She would grow to be gregarious and adventurous, with an intense love for the poor and needy. Peter was born in February, 1981. He looked very Scandinavian, like his grandfather Walt. He would grow to be contemplative, a gentle spirit, soft-spoken, artistic, poetic, and musical. Our fourth and last child, Mary, was born in November, 1982. She has grown to be a friendly, happy lover of children.

By 1975 I no longer worked for CWLF. For a short time I was a bookkeeper, then a silkscreen painter—a job that I was laid off from only two months after Heather's birth. Bonnie worked as a part-time nurse. Yet we were able to sell our half interest in our home and buy full interest in another house. Our new home was of redwood construction, located on Ashby Avenue directly across the street from Alta Bates Hospital, where Bonnie worked.

As newlyweds, our shared Christian faith was central to our lives. We viewed ourselves as having begun a lifelong spiritual journey together in which we were in transition and not certain where it would lead. Little did we know that we were walking a path that would culminate in substantial changes in our understanding of Christianity.

Left to right:
Fr. James's
paternal
great uncle,
great grandfather
Samuel,
and grandfather
Solomon;
circa 1900.

Below:
Fr. James's
mother, Belle
(the girl in the
white dress), with
her parents and
brothers;
circa 1918.

Arnold
(Fr. James)
as a young
boy; Bronx,
New York; 1950.

Ike's Candy Store, 74-38 Jamaica Avenue, Queens, New York.

Arnold Bernstein Wins Title of Jr. National Chess Champion

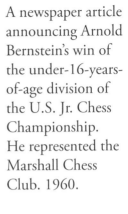

Arnold Bernstein, a fourteen-year old freshman at Lane, was named the Junior National Chess Champion after competing in an annual national tournament in West Orange, New Jersey.

Becoming interested in the game under the influence of a friend, Arnold has been a chess enthusiast for a year and a half. He entered the national tournament with sixty-three other competitors whose ages varied but did not exceed twenty-one. The ten-round tournament extended through an entire week. Arnold was declared winner by a one-half point lead over his opponent.

Prior to his entrance into the tournament which would determine the Junior National Chess Champion, Arnold had competed in several local tournaments. The majority of the competitors in these events were professional chess players. "This accounts for the fact that I was rarely a winner in these events," said Arnold. "This competition, however, gave me invaluable experience and taught me many skills in the art of chess; it gave me the self-confidence necessary to enter and win a major tournament."

Arnold is currently a member of the Marshall Chess Club. This is an organization composed of chess enthusiasts from every borough of New York City. Its purpose is to provide for those interested in the game of chess a place to meet and play the game for personal enjoyment. The Marshall Chess Club meets in Manhattan.

Not planning at present to enter professional chess, Arnold intends to study science and maintain his amateur chess standing.

A newspaper article announcing Arnold Bernstein's win of the under-16-years-of-age division of the U.S. Jr. Chess Championship. He represented the Marshall Chess Club. 1960.

Below:
Chess trophies; circa 1961.

Franklin K. Lane High School in Brooklyn, New York.

Arnold Bernstein in Nazareth, Israel; 1967.

Fr. James's parents, Isaac and Belle Bernstein; Queens, New York; circa 1970.

Arnold with Moishe Rosen, the founder of Jews for Jesus; Manhattan, New York; 1969. This photo was taken prior to their moving to California to establish Jews for Jesus.

Staff photo for CWLF's *Right On* free newspaper; Berkeley, California; early 1970s. Arnold is standing at far left. Jack Sparks is standing second from the right.

A street theater scene in Berkeley, California; early 1970s.

Berkeley Christian Street Theater performing in front of Sproul Hall; University of California, Berkeley; early 1970s.

Jack (Fr. Jack) Sparks and Arnold Bernstein baptizing someone in Ludwig's Fountain; UC Berkeley; early 1970s.

Arnold and Bonnie Bernstein, at their wedding on July 5, 1971; Tilden Park, Berkeley.

Arnold and Bonnie; Queens, New York; 1973.

The Bernstein family; Queens, New York; 1977.
Top row: Arnold and Bonnie Bernstein, Isaac (Fr. James's father), Heather (Fr. James's oldest daughter), and Solomon (Fr. James's brother). Bottom: Belle (Fr. James's mother).

Bishop Antoun and Archdeacon Hans at Fr. James's ordination to the diaconate; St. Anthony Antiochian Orthodox Church, Bergenfield, New Jersey; 1988.

Archbishop Michael Shaheen and Fr. Joseph Allen at Fr. James's
ordination to the priesthood; East Coast Parish Life Conference
in Parsippany, New York; 1988.

Fr. James at his seminary graduation; St. Vladimir's Seminary,
Crestwood, New York; 1989.

Fr. James and
Kh. Martha;
1995.

Fr. Thomas Davis, Bishop Joseph, Fr. James, and Fr. Joseph
Copeland, at Fr. James's elevation to archpriest; St. Paul
Antiochian Orthodox Church, Brier, Washington; 1999.

Deacon James Bryant, Peter Jenson, Fr. James, and Deacon Philip Jenson; Holy Saturday, 2005; St. Paul Church, Brier, Washington.

Fr. James and Kh. Martha; 2007.

Fr. James with his whole family.
Top row, left to right: Baby Noah, Mary, and J.D. Curry;
Holly Bernstein; Fr. James Bernstein; Peter Bernstein;
Kh. Martha Bernstein; Kh. Heather and Fr. David Sommer.
Children in front row: Nicholas, Ephraimia, and John Sommer.

The four Bernstein children: Peter. Holly, Heather, and Mary; 2008.

"Surprised by Christ"

Chapter 11

Finding the Original Church

I CONTINUED MY SEARCH FOR THE CHURCH THAT WROTE and compiled the New Testament. I had already discovered that two earmarks of that original church were its form of worship and its stress on the centrality of Communion in worship. By now it was evident to me that both had been uniquely retained in the present-day Orthodox Christian Church.

I had come into contact with the Orthodox Church as a result of my association with Jack Sparks and the CWLF. Jack had friends who were former Campus Crusade for Christ leaders with whom he increasingly discussed theological issues. These "apostolic workers" formed the core leadership of a movement away from informal, low-church Jesus Movement Protestantism into a more traditional, structured, liturgical, sacramental, and hierarchical view of the Church. These men included Peter Gillquist, Jon Braun, Dick Ballew, Ken Berven, Gordon Walker, and Jack Sparks. The church communities under the leadership of this apostolic band were on the same journey. Bonnie's and my transition from Protestantism to Orthodoxy paralleled theirs but was greatly accelerated, taking only about four years.

In 1973 the apostolic workers met in Berkeley and agreed to divide up the study of the ancient Church into sections. Their hope was that by systematically studying the early Church without preconceived prejudices, they would come to an understanding of what the original post-biblical Church was like and be able to identify her. Jack's area of research was worship.

In February of 1975 they met again, this time in Seattle, to share their findings. With shock, they discovered that the ancient Church was liturgical, sacramental, and hierarchical. This understanding led to a decision to form a closer association, thus establishing the New Covenant Apostolic Order (NCAO). On April 5, 1975, I was ordained a pastor of a house church in Berkeley as Jack Sparks' assistant.

In early 1977 Jack moved to Goleta, California, in order to be in the same church community as Peter Gillquist, Jon Braun, and Dick Ballew. The NCAO's first encounter with an Orthodox priest took place when some of the leaders in Goleta met with Fr. Ted Wojcik in Santa Barbara. At the same time, my friend and new co-pastor Gerald Crawford and I made our first contact with Fr. Michael Procurat in the Bay Area.

In February of 1978, we sold our house in Berkeley and moved to San Ramon, California, where the small house church was relocating under the oversight of Bob Guio, one of the expanded band of apostolic workers. In early 1978 the NCAO had its first exposure to Orthodox worship in Tarzana, California; in late 1978 the dean of St. Vladimir's Seminary, Fr. Alexander Schmemann, visited the church community in Goleta for the first time.

In February of 1979, the NCAO and its associated churches became the Evangelical Orthodox Church (EOC), thus incorporating "Orthodox" into its official name. At that time the former "apostolic workers" ordained one another as bishops.

While the NCAO was evolving into the EOC, I continued my own study of the nature and history of the Church that created the New Testament.

Fencing the Table 〜

I NOW SOUGHT TO IDENTIFY OTHER CHARACTERISTICS OF THE ancient Church that would help me determine whether it still exists today. In this effort I came to understand how the biblical and apostolic Church related *doctrine, morality, and obedience* to the receiving of Communion. In addition to the form of ancient worship, these three issues were so incredibly important that the early Church actually excluded from Communion those baptized Christians who had forsaken them. (A non-baptized person partaking was completely unheard of.) This practice is called closed Communion.

In further research I learned that the practice of closed Communion was not only adhered to by all Eastern and Western churches since the earliest days—in other words, all of ancient Christendom—but it continues to be the standard, not only of the Orthodox Church, but of the Roman Catholic Church and, until recently, most Protestant denominations as well. For example, until the beginning of the twentieth century, Anglicans and Episcopalians practiced closed Communion. The various Lutheran synods did as well, and some of the more conservative still do. Most Baptist groups had closed Communion, as do many Southern Baptist congregations to this day. Methodists were required to renew a "note of admission" to Communion from the bishop every quarter. Reformed Presbyterians issued certificates or "sacramental tokens" to those who, after examination, were considered to be in good standing—a practice called "fencing the table."

Why was this careful guarding of Holy Communion, which numerous contemporary believers have ignored so widely, practiced by such a broad spectrum of churches? Let us examine its biblical and historical basis.

Orthodox Christian Doctrine ❧

I IDENTIFY WITH AND ADMIRE THE ORIGINAL JEWISH CHRISTIAN Church because of my heritage. Nevertheless, it had serious problems. The apostle Paul fought major battles with Jewish believers who demanded that Gentiles be circumcised and keep all the provisions of the Mosaic Law. Finally, the Council of Jerusalem, presided over by the apostle James, decided that Gentiles could become Christians without circumcision or adherence to the Mosaic Law (Acts 15:1–31).

In his Epistle to the Galatians, St. Paul specifically addresses those desiring to impose Judaic legalism on Gentile believers. "But even if we," he writes, "or an angel from heaven, preach any other gospel to you than what we have preached to you, let him be accursed. As we have said before, so now I say again, if anyone preaches any other gospel to you than what you have received, let him be accursed" (Galatians 1:8, 9).

St. Paul's conflict with the "Judaizers" (subsequently called Ebionites) was not minor, but was in fact so significant that he excluded them from fellowship. In dealing with the issue of Gentiles mingling covenants, the apostle was clearly restrictive.

It's a paradox: the apostle Paul, who probably brought more people into the Church than any other apostle, also *excluded* from the Church—and thus from Communion—those believers who did not hold orthodox Christian doctrine. So adamant was St. Paul that he twice states his position toward the doctrinally aberrant using a most severe Greek term: *anathema* (which means "accursed").

Throughout the New Testament, doctrine was always

considered to be a matter of great importance. St. Luke tells us concerning the new believers on the Day of Pentecost, "And they continued steadfastly in the apostles' doctrine" (Acts 2:42).

The apostle John, known as the apostle of love, wrote with regard to the gnostic heretics, "For many deceivers have gone out into the world who do not confess Jesus Christ *as* coming in the flesh. This is a deceiver and an antichrist. . . . If anyone comes to you and does not bring this doctrine, do not receive him" (2 John 7, 10).

And the apostle Paul wrote, "But we command you, brethren, in the name of our Lord Jesus Christ, that you withdraw from every brother who walks disorderly and not according to the tradition which he received from us . . . note that person and do not keep company with him, that he may be ashamed. Yet do not count *him* as an enemy, but admonish *him* as a brother" (2 Thessalonians 3:6, 14, 15).

To "keep company" is to "break bread" together; both terms are understood biblically as referring to Holy Communion. This passage and others contain a directive to exclude offenders from eucharistic fellowship, while also fulfilling St. Paul's exhortations to "repay no one evil for evil . . . live peaceably with all men . . . do not avenge yourselves. . . . Do not be overcome by evil, but overcome evil with good" (Romans 12:17–21).

As I continued my examination of this ancient practice of closed Communion, I came to realize that soon after the New Testament books were written, other heretical groups arose which, by their error, excluded themselves from the Eucharist. In the third century, the Modalists rejected the Orthodox Christian doctrine of the Trinity. They denied that God the Father is the Fountainhead of the Trinity, teaching instead that God is somewhat distinct from the Trinity and has multiple modes of existence. The Sabellians, also in the third century, rejected the apostolic doctrine that the three Persons of the Trinity are distinct. They sought to fuse Father and Son.

In the fourth century Arianism arose, and for approximately two centuries engaged in mortal combat with the Church. The Arians attacked the divinity of Christ, holding that in Jesus' preincarnate existence as Logos—Word of God—He had been *created* by God and was therefore neither divine nor God incarnate. That century also witnessed the rise of other heretical groups called Macedonians. They rejected the Holy Spirit as the third Person of the Trinity, teaching instead that the Holy Spirit is not divine but merely a creation of God. The Apollinarians were another fourth-century group not in communion with the Church. They taught that Jesus did not have a human mind.

The fifth century witnessed the rise of the Nestorians. They taught that the Virgin Mary did not conceive within her womb the preexistent Son of God in the flesh. These false teachers recognized only the humanity of Christ in her womb, not His divinity. Add to these sects the Antinomians, Docetists, Novatians, Donatists, Monarchianists, Monophysites, Monothelites, Montanists, and Theopaschites, and we still have only a partial list of those who departed from the original Faith.

All these groups held one thing in common: *they claimed to be Christian and to believe in Jesus Christ.* But they were universally excluded from Holy Communion by the Church because they rejected the fullness of the apostolic Faith, "once for all delivered to the saints" (Jude 3).

I came to appreciate that, in excommunicating these people as heretics and schismatics, the early Church was not making a statement as to their eternal destiny. This realization was a great relief to me, as I was convinced that many who did not share Orthodox understanding or theology were closer to God than I, and their eternal destiny was for God alone, not for me or the Church, to decide. In excluding the non-Orthodox from Communion, the Church was simply following the biblical injunction of Christ Himself to be sure the worship of the Father was conducted "in spirit and truth" (John 4:23).

In the historic Church, orthodox doctrine was a prerequisite for eucharistic unity. It became clear to me that orthodox doctrine was one of the telltale signs identifying the Church I was searching for—the Church that determined the New Testament canon.

Orthodox Christian Morality ◠◡

I REMEMBER AS A YOUNG JEW READING IN THE OLD TESTAMENT, "My son, do not despise the chastening of the LORD, / Nor detest His correction; / For whom the LORD loves He corrects, / Just as a father the son *in whom* he delights" (Proverbs 3:11, 12).

The apostle Paul quotes this passage in the Book of Hebrews, adding, "If you endure chastening, God deals with you as with sons; for what son is there whom a father does not chasten? But if you are without chastening, of which all have become partakers, then you are illegitimate and not sons. . . . Now no chastening seems to be joyful" (Hebrews 12:7–8, 11). The discipline of which the Scripture speaks is not punitive or abusive, but corrective, loving, and applied with wisdom and restraint.

The biblical exercise of discipline in the Church was based on the teaching of Jesus. How does the Church relate to an unrepentant brother? If a personal word does no good, Jesus says, "And if he refuses to hear them, tell *it* to the church. But if he refuses even to hear the church, let him be to you like a heathen and a tax collector. Assuredly, I say to you, whatever you bind on earth will be bound in heaven, and whatever you loose on earth will be loosed in heaven" (Matthew 18:17, 18).

Remarkable! These words come from the same Lord who

forgave the woman caught in adultery, saying to those who would have stoned her, "He who is without sin among you, let him throw a stone at her first" (John 8:7). This is the same Lord who said we should forgive our brother, not "up to seven times, but up to seventy times seven" (Matthew 18:22)—the Hebrew idiom for infinity. And this is the same Lord who cried out upon the Cross, "Father, forgive them, for they do not know what they do" (Luke 23:34). How difficult it was for me to balance the love of God with His discipline and not place them in opposition.

I discovered that this tell-it-to-the-church passage in Matthew 18 has universally been understood as referring to the Church's responsibility to maintain internal discipline. What it was saying to me was that though we are called to be a loving and forgiving people, our kindness is not to prevent us from providing reasonable moral boundaries, guarding the integrity of our communion with God and with one another.

The apostle Paul's castigation of the church in Corinth for ignoring the serious moral sin of an unrepentant Christian brother reinforces the Church's responsibility to maintain a moral standard for communicants. In 1 Corinthians 5, St. Paul says:

> It is actually reported *that there is* sexual immorality among you, and such sexual immorality as is not even named among the Gentiles—that a man has his father's wife! And you are puffed up, and have not rather mourned, that he who has done this deed might be taken away from among you. For I indeed, as absent in body but present in spirit, have already judged (as though I were present) him who has so done this deed. . . .
>
> I wrote to you in my epistle not to keep company with sexually immoral people. Yet *I* certainly *did* not *mean* with the sexually immoral people of this world, or

with the covetous, or extortioners, or idolaters, since then you would need to go out of the world. But now I have written to you not to keep company with anyone named a brother, who is sexually immoral, or covetous, or an idolater, or a reviler, or a drunkard, or an extortioner—not even to eat with such a person. . . . Therefore "put away from yourselves the evil person." . . .

Do not be deceived. Neither fornicators, nor idolaters, nor adulterers, nor homosexuals, nor sodomites, nor thieves, nor covetous, nor drunkards, nor revilers, nor extortioners will inherit the kingdom of God. (1 Corinthians 5:1—6:10)

According to St. Paul, Christian love within the Church was not wishy-washy warmth that ignored or winked at serious sin. For the apostle to the Gentiles, love within the Church is tough love that calls the sinning brother to repentance *for his own good.* It is a love that excludes an immoral brother or sister from the eucharistic meal so as to stress the seriousness of sin. For our Savior and for St. Paul, love was more demanding and discipline more severe toward those within the Church than toward those outside it. It became clear to me that the Church has a responsibility for the moral conduct of her own that she doesn't have for others.

In addition to our individual responsibility for ourselves, our Mother Church also gives us a collective responsibility. Within the Church, we call one another brothers and sisters. We bear the same last name: *Christian.* As with our nuclear family, the Church is morally accountable for her people and sets conditions for receiving Holy Communion. I came to realize that right doctrine and right morality are biblical prerequisites for eucharistic unity and would help me identify the Church that compiled the New Testament canon.

Orthodox Christian Obedience ❧

In addition to unity of worship being encompassed by unity of faith (doctrine) and unity of practice (morality), communion also expresses unity of obedience. I discovered that in the early Church, a person could be excommunicated not only for blatant heresy or immorality, but also for severe and persistent factionalism or divisiveness.

This area of offense would be perhaps the toughest for me as a modern Westerner to accept. After all, everyone is entitled to his or her own opinion, right? This is a democracy, is it not? Besides, it's good to seek unity in diversity. We know these lines well—we've all used them. And certainly there are places for appropriate diversity, such as in the use of gifts, ministries, and activities (see 1 Corinthians 12:4–6).

But as we have seen, there is no room for diversity in doctrine or morals. Nor is there a diversity in obedience. While our civil government aims for democracy, I knew that the Kingdom of God is a theocracy: it is ruled by God. The Church is the presence of the Kingdom in the world. Thus in the Church, as was true in the Old Covenant, God's people refrain from "doing whatever *is* right in [their] own eyes" (Deuteronomy 12:8). Uncomfortable as it was for me as an independent Protestant, I was repeatedly confronted with the fact that for the early Christians, Christianity was not a "do your own thing" affair.

In Israel of old, God governed His nation through prophets, patriarchs, kings, elders, and judges. He raised up leaders who would bring unity and order to His people. In the Church, there should be leadership and order as well. St. Paul speaks of apostles, prophets, evangelists, pastors, and teachers. In fact, as far as polity is concerned, it became increasingly clear that the New Testament reveals the Church as composed of her bishops surrounded by the presbyters, deacons, and "the people of God," the laity. Thus we have such exhortations as, "Obey those who rule over you, and be submissive, for they watch out for your souls, as those who must give account. Let them do so with joy and not with grief, for that would be unprofitable for you" (Hebrews 13:17; see also 1 Peter 5:1–3).

In this statement I made note that our obedience is voluntary—as is our adherence to true doctrine and morality. In the first New Testament book written, St. Paul instructs his flock, "And we urge you, brethren, to recognize those who labor among you, and are over you in the Lord and admonish you, and to esteem them very highly in love for their work's sake. Be at peace among yourselves" (1 Thessalonians 5:12, 13). Then in the very next verse, he says, "Warn those who are unruly," a word which means insubordinate or ungovernable—people who are out of control.

In the New Testament, refusal to obey the apostles and their coworkers was a serious offense. Thus the Scriptures teach, "Reject a divisive man after the first and second admonition" (Titus 3:10). The willfully divisive were ultimately excluded from communion.

A Broken Unity ∾

FOR THE APOSTLES AND THE EARLY CHURCH, ISSUES OF HOW TO worship and the way that worship expressed true doctrine, morality, and obedience were never considered irrelevant or extraneous to a person's relationship with Christ. In regard to Holy Communion, the Sacrament of sacraments, it became evident to me that no right-believing priest of the early period of the Church's history would have thought to offer Communion to a person he knew had separated himself or herself from the Church in any of those areas.

Though I had taken in college a class on medieval world history, taught by a most demanding professor who was an elderly Jewish immigrant from Germany, for some reason I was oblivious to the fact that for the first thousand years of her history, the Church in East (Orthodox) and West (Roman Catholic) was one. This meant that if a Christian was in good standing in any local church, he was in good standing and could receive Communion in all churches. All the churches had unity of worship, as well as of doctrine, morality, and obedience to the bishops. By the same token, if a Christian had fallen out of fellowship with the One Church in any of those areas, he could not simply walk out in a huff, expecting to receive Communion at the next Christian church down the street.

The Church's unity was most clearly manifest in her protection of the purity of the sacraments. For centuries, when at the Divine Liturgy the deacon proclaimed, "The doors, the doors," it was a sign that all but baptized believers in good standing were to depart. It was time to begin the eucharistic portion of the Liturgy.

Obviously, this state of unity no longer exists today. How did the Church become so fragmented and divided? What happened to tear apart the unity that was so apparent in those early days of the Church's development?

The answer was in part to be found in the eleventh century—a time of grave significance for the Church. In that century an event occurred which, more than any other single episode, came to symbolize the sharp division that had grown up between the Christian East and the Christian West—a division that was to have a direct impact on the Church of our own day. The Orthodox theologian, Bishop Kallistos Ware, vividly describes this episode in his book, *The Orthodox Church:*

One summer afternoon in the year 1054, as a service was about to begin in the Church of the Holy Wisdom at Constantinople, Cardinal Humbert and two other legates of the Pope entered the building and made their way up to the sanctuary. They had not come to pray. They placed a Bull of Excommunication upon the altar and marched out once more. As he passed through the western door, the Cardinal shook the dust from his feet with the words: "Let God look and judge." A deacon ran out after him in great distress and begged him to take back the Bull. Humbert refused; and it was dropped in the street.

Bishop Ware goes on to state:

It is this incident which has conventionally been taken to mark the beginning of the great schism between the Orthodox east and the Latin west. But the schism, as historians now generally recognize, is not really an event whose beginning can be exactly dated. It was something that came about gradually, as the result of a long and complicated process, starting well before the eleventh century and not completed until some time after.[11]

Whatever else can be said about this disastrous course of events, one thing is certain. Whereas a united Christian Church once existed in both the East and the West, a terrible and undeniable schism had now taken place—a "great divorce" of epic proportions. For the first time since the Church's foundation, Orthodox Christians of the East were unable to receive Communion in a Western, Roman church, or vice versa. How could this have come about?

Some historians lay the entire blame for this tragedy at the feet of the Western Church. Others point the finger eastward. Still others see failure on both sides, perhaps factoring in the difficult geographical and political considerations that served to complicate the situation further. No matter which perspective you accept—or even if you are totally unaware of these events, believing that no other period of the Church's history matters except that described in the Book of Acts—the reality is unchanged. What took place centuries ago, exemplified by that disastrous occurrence in Constantinople in 1054, has had a direct and all-encompassing impact on the Christianity of our own era. The Church has never been the same since that day.

As I delved further into what became of the original one, united Church, I saw that following the initial separation between Rome and the Orthodox East, which came to be known as the Great Schism, both sides drifted further and further apart, following separate and often very distinct paths. The Roman West added a phrase, *filioque* (Latin for "and [from] the son"), to the basic statement of the Church's Faith, the Nicene Creed, thus altering its definition of the Trinity—changing "the Holy Spirit . . . who proceeds from the Father" to "the Holy Spirit . . . who proceeds from the Father and the Son."

Rome also turned increasingly to the papal office for its understanding of the Faith. Collegiality, agreement between bishops from different areas, became less a means of decision-making. A high-water mark occurred in the nineteenth century, when the First Vatican Council declared that the Pope was infallible when he defined that a doctrine concerning faith or morals was part of the deposit of divine revelation.

Orthodoxy, although severely hampered by various regional and national persecutions that arose throughout the ensuing centuries, staunchly refused to follow the Roman West in what it considered to be a departure from the Church's historic understanding of the Faith. The Eastern Church remained collegial in its understanding of church government (no one bishop exercised a position of ultimate, unilateral authority), steadfast in its adherence to the unaltered creeds and council decisions, and committed to the united teachings of the early Church, both East and West. Some say that this fact alone explains why no "Reformation" took place in Orthodoxy, as it did in the West. Many of the concerns raised by early reformers were reactions against Western innovations which the East had refused to embrace from the beginning.

Once the Protestant Reformation took place in the West in the sixteenth century, the results were immediate and irrevocable. The German monk Martin Luther was one of the original leaders of the Reformation and the father of Lutheranism. In France, John Calvin broke from Rome and from Lutheranism, thereby widening the schism and becoming the father of the Presbyterian and Reformed churches.

Additional groups subsequently broke from both the Lutherans and the Calvinists. The radical wing of Protestantism known as the Anabaptists gave birth to the Amish, Mennonites, and Quakers. In England, the Anglicans broke away from Rome when, among other things, the pope refused to grant King Henry VIII's request for annulment of his marriage to Catherine of Aragon.

Each of these groups departed, whether directly or indirectly, from Rome, but they never reconnected with the Orthodox Church. Because Rome had already severed communion with the Orthodox Church, the Protestants were, *de facto,* also out of communion with the Orthodox Church. Thus today, a sincere, faithful Catholic or Protestant Christian still finds himself out of communion with Eastern Christendom, and vice versa.

An ever-increasing number of modern offshoots have developed from the major branches of Protestantism. From the Church of England came the Puritans, Baptists, and Methodists. From the Methodists came the Nazarenes and the Salvation Army. Still later there developed the Disciples of Christ, Assemblies of God, and various Pentecostal groups. All of these Protestant denominations themselves became further fragmented, breaking up into still more factions.

At present there are thousands of Protestant denominations, many of which are out of communion with one another. In addition, there exist thousands of independent churches. All of these groups are, knowingly or unknowingly, out of communion with both the Roman Catholic Church and the Orthodox Church as they have existed throughout the centuries.

Communion in the Orthodox Church ∾

WHAT DID THIS MEAN FOR MY FAMILY AND ME AS NON-ORTHODOX Christians wanting to come to worship in an Orthodox Church?

Applying these three criteria of unity rooted in the worship of the ancient Church—doctrine, morality, and obedience—the Orthodox Church, which claims to maintain the ancient Faith in its fullness, refuses to admit to Holy Communion anyone who is not a baptized, chrismated Orthodox Christian. (Furthermore, I later learned that even Orthodox Christians must be in good standing with the Church and must properly prepare themselves through regular confession and spiritual discipline.)

The more I researched the history of doctrine, the more I realized that there is no non-Orthodox denomination that holds to the fullness of the Orthodox Faith as expressed in the original, unaltered Nicene Creed. All but the Orthodox have either added to the Faith or subtracted from it. With regard to morality, of course there are many believers in other churches who lead upright, moral lives; but if they are not part of an Orthodox parish, regularly confessing their sins and receiving absolution, the priest has no way to be certain that they are not partaking unworthily. With regard to worship, no other church to my knowledge observes the ancient liturgy unaltered and believes the Eucharist to be in a mystery—not by any physical means of transubstantiation—truly the Body and Blood of Christ.

I came to realize that even if I decided to experience correct worship by attempting to recreate Orthodox worship with others (a Protestant sort of thing to do), and adhered to the correct belief and practice, if I were not a baptized, chrismated Orthodox Christian, the third criterion of obedience to the authority of the Church would still be lacking. The Orthodox Church teaches that one must be born into the Church of God through these sacraments of baptism and chrismation (anointing for the reception of the Holy Spirit), established by Christ Himself, to be fully in communion with her. If one is not in communion, one may not partake of Communion.

But what of other Christians? This policy of closed Communion does *not* imply that those outside the Orthodox Church are considered not to be Christians, or not to be saved. The Church explicitly refuses to pass judgment concerning the salvation of any individual, within or outside her walls. But having received the deposit of Faith from the Lord and His apostles, and having faithfully kept it intact down to this day, the Church holds that she must protect that deposit by extending Communion only to those who have united themselves to her.

At one level I was saddened to learn that non-Orthodox cannot take Communion at an Orthodox Church. But at a deeper level it seemed reasonable. I realized that it was not because of callous indifference or pride that the Orthodox Church refuses Communion to non-Orthodox Christians. It is rather an expression of the profound importance the Orthodox Church throughout time has placed on the Holy Eucharist—the partaking of the Body and Blood of Christ. I agreed that the current state of division and schism—a schism devout Orthodox Christians pray often that God will bring to an end—should not obscure the transcendent reality of this great sacrament. To lose sight of this, even for the sake of compassion, would be to lose sight of the Orthodox Faith.

Yet I also understood that no Christian living today is responsible for what happened almost one thousand years ago, or for the chaotic state of Christendom that has resulted. We are, all of us, survivors of a cataclysmic disaster—a disaster that took place long before we were born and over which we had no control whatsoever. I did have control, however, over the way I would respond to this tragic situation. I knew that it is open to each and every Christian to embrace the fullness of the apostolic Faith once more, and to choose to unite himself or herself to the Church that holds this Faith intact.

Discovering the Church's ancient form of worship had been a major breakthrough in my search to identify which Church wrote and compiled the New Testament. The subsequent discoveries of ancient doctrine (belief), morality (practice), and obedience, and of the practice of closed Communion further reaffirmed to me the authenticity of the Orthodox Christian Church as the Church that wrote and compiled the New Testament.

Chapter 12

Orthodoxy: Jewish and Christian

IN THE FALL OF 1977, MY COPASTOR GERALD CRAWFORD and I read *The Orthodox Church* by Timothy Ware and some other Orthodox books, and were so impressed that we decided to make our first visit to an Orthodox church. I went somewhat warily, as my high church experiences were for the most part negative. To my pleasant surprise, I immediately felt a distinct sense of being in the presence of God the moment I walked inside the church. It was like stepping back in time with Christ and entering the ancient Jewish Temple in Jerusalem. Everything about the service was centered in the worship of the Most High God.

The music was very different from what I was accustomed to hearing in Protestant churches. It was more subdued and had a mystical quality about it. Visually, the interior of the church reminded me of the ancient Temple—it was stunning. In front stood an altar with a Jewish-looking candelabrum on it. Following the service I went home and found the sweet aroma of the incense had pervaded my clothes. It was as if I had brought some of the heavenly presence home with me.

Worship in Scripture ❦

EVEN BEFORE ATTENDING AN ORTHODOX WORSHIP SERVICE, I HAD concluded that the early Christians of the first four centuries were universally liturgical, sacramental, and hierarchical in their worship. As I continued my research I discovered that the Bible itself presents the same elements of worship. Whenever God revealed Himself to man in Scripture, it was in a setting of worship that included beauty, order, and majesty. Both Old Testament and New Testament worship sought to reflect on earth the majesty of God as revealed from heaven.

The prophet Ezekiel (sixth century BC) had such an intense vision of God being worshiped in heaven that he had difficulty describing it in conventional terms. He speaks of a whirlwind, a great cloud with raging fire engulfing itself, lightning, a breathtaking crystal, the voice of an army, and a throne. He saw on the throne a Being with the appearance of a man, and fell on his face in awe.

I also discovered in the New Testament a reaffirmation of the heavenly majesty of God. The writer of the Book of Hebrews says, in contrasting the New Covenant with the Old Covenant:

> But you have come to Mount Zion and to the city of the living God, the heavenly Jerusalem, to an innumerable company of angels, to the general assembly and church of the firstborn *who are* registered in heaven, to God the Judge of all, to the spirits of just men made perfect, to Jesus the Mediator of the new covenant, and to the blood of sprinkling that speaks better things than *that of* Abel. See that you do not refuse Him who speaks. (Hebrews 12:22–25)

He concludes by saying, "For our God *is* a consuming fire" (Hebrews 12:29).

In the last book of the Bible, St. John describes a vision of Our Lord Jesus Christ enthroned and worshiped in heaven in which "His countenance *was* like the sun shining in its strength" (Revelation 1:16). When John saw Him, he fell at His feet as dead. John speaks further of the throne as surrounded by twenty-four other thrones on which twenty-four elders sit. There are four living creatures which "do not rest day or night, saying: 'Holy, holy, holy, Lord God Almighty, / Who was and is and is to come!'" (Revelation 4:8).

The Scriptures were clearly saying to me that God is worshiped in great glory in heaven, with great solemnity and grandeur. His worship is awe-inspiring. Unfortunately, many modern Christians tend to think of God as a cosmic "buddy." This familiar view of God, I felt, greatly undermines worship. God loves us and is in the deepest sense our friend. But He is also the everlasting God, our Creator, King, and Judge. Even the apostle John, who is described in the Gospels as "the beloved" of the Lord because of his closeness to Christ, "fell at His feet as though dead" on seeing Christ enthroned in heaven. If this beloved apostle and friend of Christ fell at His feet in worship, how much more readily, it seemed to me, should we worship Him in the dignity of humility?

As a Jew, I knew that God had established the ancient Temple in Jerusalem, with all its elaborate ritual, to give us a glimpse of that worship which continually goes on in heaven. Moses had been instructed by God to make the tabernacle after the pattern of the heavenly prototype as seen in Exodus 25:9–40 (and later described in Hebrews 8:5; 9:23, 24). This is the background against which the early Jewish-Christian Church understood worship—seeking to reflect the glory of heavenly worship in their worship on earth.

Jewish worship was always physical. The Old Testament people of God worshiped with music, with color, with light and candles, with sweet aroma and incense, with art, with rhythmic chant, with feasts and fasts, with cycles of holy days, and with godly order and liturgy. I came to realize these things were neither pagan in origin nor temporal in character. They were fulfilled in Christ and retained.

As I attended subsequent Orthodox services, it became clear that the Orthodox Church had inherited, kept, and practiced biblical worship in a way that no other church I knew had—with icons and incense, with multicolored vestments and ringing bells, with flickering candlelight, melodious chant, and processions, with cycles of feast days and fasts. In these services, those on earth mystically understand themselves as joining with those in heaven, together lifting up holy hands towards Him who sits on the celestial throne, singing, "Holy, Holy, Holy, Lord God Almighty, heaven and earth are filled with Your glory!"

Discovering Christian Roots ❧

DEEPLY IMPRESSED WITH ORTHODOX CHRISTIAN WORSHIP, I began to seriously consider the continuity of the historical Orthodox Church. As a Jew, having roots had always been important to me. I now contemplated the importance of having Christian roots as well.

The evangelical Gentile Christians who told me, "I am Jewish too," thought of themselves as spiritual Jews, but somehow in their confusion also thought of themselves as physical Jews. Many had a similar view of the Church. They tended to spiritualize everything, often at the cost of the physical. They would not identify themselves with any specific historic church, yet considered themselves to be somehow in the Church. It was not important to them to have historical continuity with the ancient Church. In contrast, I now believed that the Church is every bit as physical and historical as the Jewish people. As an authentic Jew, I desired to be a Christian in an authentic

Christian Church, one that was physically locatable throughout the ages.

I believed that my evangelical Protestant brethren were authentic Christians who "knew" Jesus, lived holy lives, and seemed heaven-bound. In fact, in my estimation, many lived far holier lives than I. Did this mean they manifested the Church in authentic worship and doctrine? I was not sure. But I was sure of one thing: I didn't want to be in a make-believe church. I wanted to be in that Church which is historically connected with the ancient Jewish-Christian body of believers.

Certainly, the Orthodox Church has clearly identifiable roots. She has a historical continuity of doctrine that can be traced back to the apostles. This deposit of truth, called Holy Tradition, is held to have been passed down faithfully from person to person and from generation to generation. Orthodox lineage is undeniably visible, discernible, and historical. The Church claims to be, as the apostle Paul said, "the pillar and ground of the truth" (1 Timothy 3:15).

In addition to this lineage of truth, the Orthodox Church honors another succession: that of bishops, the apostolic continuity rooted in the ancient Jewish-Christian Church. From the New Testament I learned that from the very beginning, the apostles established individuals within local churches who functioned as apostolic representatives and were called bishops (*episcopoi* in Greek).

Numerous, readily available early accounts reveal that the office of bishop existed universally in the early Church. During the summer of 1975, I had the opportunity to spend many hours reading the church fathers at the Graduate Theological Union Library in Berkeley. There I discovered that by all accounts, bishops were present everywhere, even while the Church was illegal and being persecuted by the Roman Empire. Bishops were not a later "corruption," but were present in the Church from the beginning. The great martyr and bishop of Antioch, Ignatius, who lived in the first century, wrote:

> In like manner, let all reverence the deacons as an appointment of Jesus Christ, and the bishop as Jesus Christ, who is the Son of the Father, and the presbyters as the sanhedrin of God, and assembly of the apostles. Apart from these, there is no Church.[12]

Irenaeus of Lyons, at the end of the second century, likewise wrote:

> It is within the power of all, therefore, in every Church, who may wish to see the truth, to contemplate clearly the tradition of the apostles manifested throughout the whole world; and we are in a position to reckon up those who were by the apostles instituted bishops in the Churches, and [to demonstrate] the succession of these men to our own times; those who neither taught nor knew of anything like what these [heretics] rave about. For if the apostles had known hidden mysteries, which they were in the habit of imparting to "the perfect" apart and privily from the rest, they would have delivered them especially to those to whom they were also committing the Churches themselves. For they were desirous that these men should be very perfect and blameless in all things, whom also they were leaving behind as their successors, delivering up their own place of government to these men; which men, if they discharged their functions honestly, would be a great boon [to the Church], but if they should fall away, the direst calamity.[13]

Though I realized that the succession of bishops does not automatically ensure a succession of truth, apostolic continuity did seem to be God's intent for His Church. It made good sense to me, for it helped provide a physical and tangible link as well as a spiritual link with the ancient Jewish-Christian Church.

The Church of the Holy Land ❧

FOLLOWING THE SIX-DAY WAR IN JUNE OF 1967, I WAS AMONG the first to move from the New City of Jerusalem into the Old City. I lived with Arab Christians close to where my father was born. As I don't know exactly where his birth occurred, I may have been living in that very house. During my few months' stay there, I had many opportunities to visit the holy sites and churches in Jerusalem. The Protestant side of me had difficulty appreciating the more ornate and traditional churches. But as I met Jerusalem Christians, I realized that the indigenous Arab Christians in the Holy Land are neither Protestant nor Roman Catholic. They are Orthodox.

Acts 1:8 says that prior to His Ascension, the Lord Jesus told the apostles, "You shall receive power when the Holy Spirit has come upon you; and you shall be witnesses to Me in Jerusalem, and in all Judea and Samaria, and to the end of the earth." The fact that the Orthodox Church is the indigenous Church in the Middle East and in the Holy Land, the land of the Bible and of our ancient Jewish forefathers, did not seem accidental to me.

The Orthodox Church existed for a millennium and a half before Protestantism was born. From this Jerusalem birthplace, Orthodox Christianity spread westward to Rome and Greece, northward to Europe and Russia, southward to Egypt, and eastward to Persia and India. As I recall my Holy Land experience, I cannot help but think there is a providential purpose in the continuous presence of Orthodox Christianity in the Holy Land—just as there is in the continued existence of the Jewish people.

The Orthodox Church is more than a mystical body of believers. She is also an institutional, concrete, and historical reality with clearly recognizable expansion. As the indigenous Church in the Holy Land, the Orthodox Church can be traced back to the beginning—to Christ Himself and to the apostles. This physical, historical continuity rooted in the Holy Land is very meaningful to me as a Jewish Christian.

Rediscovering the God of the Jews ◦

I WAS IMPRESSED THAT THE ORTHODOX CHURCH'S WORSHIP WAS awesome, heavenly, indeed divine, her roots deep, and her origin in the Holy Land. As a Jewish Christian, I was drawn to Orthodoxy, but what about Orthodox theology? How did the Orthodox view of God compare with the Protestant view? How did it relate to the Jewish view?

As a child, I had often prayed, "Hear, O Israel: The LORD our God, the LORD *is* one" (Deuteronomy 6:4). Later, as a Protestant Christian, I longed for the Judaic emphasis of worshiping God as Creator and King. When I was a child, during the Jewish High Holy Day morning services, we would recite a prayer with over forty petitions, each beginning with, "Our Father, our King [in Hebrew, *Avehnu Malchanu*]." Though I believed in the Trinity and in the divinity of Christ and of the Holy Spirit, I was often confused over questions such as how the Son and the Holy Spirit related to the Father, and to whom I should direct my prayers. I discovered that Orthodox Christians primarily direct their worship to God the Father. The Orthodox believe there is One God because there is One Father.

When the word "God" is used in the New Testament, it almost always refers to God the Father. The Son and the Holy Spirit are often spoken of as being *of* God—as in "Son of God" or "the Spirit of God." The Bible never says "Father of God," for the Father is not *of* God but *is* God. This emphasis on God the Father as the source of unity within the Trinity was lacking in my Protestant experience. Yet it seemed to me to be very Jewish, for it explained more clearly the relationship of the Son and the Holy Spirit to God the Father.

Orthodoxy teaches clearly that both the Son and the Holy Spirit have their eternal origin in the Father, fully sharing the complete Divine Nature with Him. The Father is called the fountainhead of the Trinity; He is the eternal source of the Godhead, and His headship is the unity of the three Persons. So we speak of the Father first. This is why the apostle Paul greets the church to whom he is writing by saying, "I thank my God through Jesus Christ for you all" (Romans 1:8), or, "Grace to you and peace from God our Father and the Lord Jesus Christ" (Ephesians 1:2). This terminology of greeting is typical throughout Paul's writings.

This is also why the Nicene Creed says, "I believe in one God, the Father Almighty, Creator of heaven and earth, and of all things visible and invisible; and in one Lord Jesus Christ, the Son of God. . . . And I believe in the Holy Spirit, the Lord, the Giver of Life, who proceeds from the Father."

It was with sadness that I discovered why both the Protestants and Roman Catholics, in contrast to the Orthodox, deemphasized the One God and Father of the Lord Jesus Christ and the Holy Spirit. The original Nicene Creed of the undivided fourth-century Church said that the Holy Spirit "proceeds from the Father" alone. But in the West, beginning in fifth-century Spain, the Latin word *filioque* ("and the Son") was added, changing the Creed to say that the Holy Spirit proceeds "from the Father *and the Son*."

This change was initially resisted by the pope of Rome, who actually had the original Nicene text engraved on two silver tablets and publicly displayed at the Tomb of St. Peter. Only in the eleventh century did a greatly weakened papacy under political pressure accept the *filioque* clause into the Creed (when the Creed was added to the mass). All Protestants inherited this altered Creed when they broke from the Roman Catholic Church in the sixteenth century.

The addition of the *filioque* clause results in an emphasis on the common Divine Nature of the Trinity as the source of unity rather than on the Person of the Father, who, the Creed says, is the "One God" and source of unity. In worshiping God the Father as the Creator of the universe, as the King of Israel, and as God and Father of our Lord Jesus Christ as the Orthodox do, I was beginning to learn how to worship God the way my New Testament Jewish Christian brethren had done.

Rediscovering Our True Sacrifice ∾

IN 1967 I VISITED THE WAILING WALL AND WALKED ABOUT THE temple mount where the ancient Jewish Temple once stood. I was struck with the centrality of temple worship and sacrifice for the ancient Jews. The Old Testament clearly shows that the sacrificial system was an integral part of the Jewish religion and of temple worship.

I knew from reading Jewish history that with the destruction of the Jewish Temple and the sacrificial system in the first century, devout Jews were thrown into great confusion. Many of the Jewish people were sympathetic to the misguided Pharisees, who decided sacrifice was not necessary. They held that prayers and good deeds could replace sacrifice. So they emphasized local synagogue worship (focusing on scripture reading and homilies) rather than the form of worship that took place in the ancient Jewish Temple in Jerusalem (focusing on sacrifice and ornate liturgical worship), which ceased with the destruction of the Temple in AD 70. Such is the inheritance of present-day Judaism.

On the other hand, many devout Jews became Christians and held that Christ, the Lamb of God, has been provided by God the Father as the fulfillment of the Temple's sacrificial system. The early Jewish Christians saw Christ as a new and superior Sacrifice, of which the earthly temple sacrifices were only types. At Communion, the Orthodox re-present Christ's once-for-all Sacrifice to God the Father. The priest during the Divine Liturgy exclaims, "Thine own of Thine own we *offer* unto Thee, in behalf of all and for all."

Rediscovering Jewish Mysticism ☙

IN THE ORTHODOX CHURCH I ALSO BEGAN TO REDISCOVER HOLY mystery. I love mystery, I suppose because God Himself is not only awesome, He is mysterious. Jews are considered to be a mysterious people, in part because of our continued existence against all odds and our involvement in the establishment of the Judeo-Christian religions. Modern rationalists disdain mystery, but I found that Orthodox Christians thrive on it. In fact, St. Paul calls our very life in Christ a "mystery."

The English word "mystery" comes from the Greek term *mysterion*, which means anything hidden or secret. The biblical Greek concept, though, does not mean a secret for which no answer can be found. Rather, it is a temporary secret, which is being revealed by God to men through His Spirit. The concept of mystery is close to the Greek word *apokalypsis*, which is translated into English as "revelation."

As a Jew, I desired worship that contained a sense of mystery, was rooted in ancient Jewish practice, and centered on God and our Communion meal with Him. But the worship I experienced as an evangelical Protestant tended to view mystical worship as dangerous because it went beyond "reason." This was particularly true of the Communion service.

I had been taught as a new Christian that the bread and wine of Communion were symbols and nothing more, and that to go beyond this was to risk falling into a view of Communion as magic. Though I had read in the Bible that our Lord Jesus said of the Communion bread, "This is My body," and of the cup of wine, "This is My blood," I was told that the bread and wine merely *signified* His body and blood.

This rationalistic view of Communion appealed to my mind, but not to my heart. It was significant that the ancient Christians simply referred to Communion as "O Great Mystery." The gutting of mystery from the Eucharist greatly impoverished Protestant worship, making it seem bare-bones. It was empty not because God and faith were absent—many Protestant Christians were very vibrant and alive. But in pursuing a rationalistic approach to spiritual truth, Protestant worship had unwittingly lost God's mystery.

For the most part, the early Protestant reformers had reacted against what they saw as a magical understanding of the Eucharist implicit in medieval Roman practice. Furthermore—and here most Orthodox would agree—the reformers were impatient with the scholastic form of Rome's teaching of the Eucharist, which tended to formalize mystery.

The Orthodox Church presented me with a New Testament balance. On the one hand, the Orthodox Church does not seek to explain mystery as does the Roman Church; and on the other hand, it does not deny mystery as many Protestant churches do. Mystery in the Eucharist is simply presented, permeating the Faith and providing at every Communion service the reality of God's presence in our midst.

Orthodoxy revealed in me a sense of the awe of God and life, a sense of wonder and mystery. I was reminded of the great acts of God in history: the creation of the world, the Flood, the delivery of the Hebrews from Egyptian bondage, the birth and life of Christ, our Lord's Resurrection, the healing ministry of the apostles. As a Jew, I longed to experience God as supernatural mystery. In light of all that God has done, it was not difficult for me to believe that, if He so chose, He could make bread and wine to be also, in a mystery, the Body and Blood of Christ.

Rediscovering the Joy of the Lord ∾

JEWS LOVE TO CELEBRATE! MAYBE IT'S BECAUSE WE HAVE SUFFERED so much. We take every opportunity we can to give thanks, even if the event seems small.

As a new Christian, I missed the intensity of Jewish asceticism (praying and fasting), and also the intensity of Jewish mirth. I missed the happy music, the folk dancing, the magnificent combination of feasting and asceticism that is uniquely Jewish. It is a paradox that in order to truly and fully celebrate, one must also know how to truly and fully sacrifice, pray, and fast. It is therefore no coincidence that an Orthodox Jew would know how to do both, because these two streams of spirituality—the ascetic (the emptying) and the festal (the filling)—encourage and enhance one another.

Without celebration I found myself drowning in a sea of darkness. There was no tradition of dance in Protestantism. Many Protestants forbade wine and discouraged any type of celebrating that might demonstrate too much festivity. Joyous celebration often was seen as being "of the world." Mystical celebrating was foreign. It was a major challenge to figure out how we Christians should celebrate, so to be on the safe side we often did little or nothing.

I found the Orthodox Church to be sensitive to the centrality of celebration as a fundamental and obvious human need. As an Orthodox Christian, one knows how and what to celebrate. Celebrating festal holidays is part of the Orthodox Christian tradition rooted in the Bible.

When Orthodox Christians celebrate Easter (Pascha), for example, they don't just celebrate one day; they celebrate forty days! And when they celebrate Christmas, they don't just celebrate one day; they celebrate for almost two weeks! Christmas and Pascha are preceded by days of forefeast in which to prepare for the celebration through intense prayer and fasting. The more seriously the preparations are taken, the greater the festal joy that follows.

The proper joining of the sacrificial and festal streams of spirituality is a work of God. I came to believe that Orthodox Christians know how to celebrate because the Church has lived two millennia under the guidance of the Holy Spirit. As a struggling Christian who had difficulty developing any degree of spirituality, I found it a wonderful relief that my life of struggles could be punctuated at many glorious times along the way with feasting.

As the Church's human face is revealed to us, her heavenly face is not forgotten. Our Lord Jesus said, "Therefore you shall be perfect, just as your Father in heaven is perfect" (Matthew 5:48). The Orthodox Faith presents the highest possible goal for us to pursue, the ideal of perfection: to become by grace what God is by nature. Ideal standards and saintly lives are set forward in Scripture and in the Church to inspire us in our struggle. These ideals include the concepts of poverty, chastity, and obedience—fleshed out in practice by those who give all to the poor (Matthew 19:21), love their enemies (Matthew 5:43–48), submit to spiritual authority

(Matthew 8:5–13; John 5:19), pray constantly (Ephesians 6:18; 1 Thessalonians 5:17), and live holy and blameless lives.

On the other hand, I found that the Orthodox Church recognizes that we are far from what we should be. With this in mind, she accepts us as sinners, while continuing to condemn our sins. She does not lower the standard to which we are called, but offers forgiveness and healing of our human weaknesses and sins. Recognizing our human frailty, the Church is concerned not to overwhelm us spiritually, but to accept us where we are and lead us step by step towards God. I found this sensitivity to human frailty, this human face of Orthodoxy, to be very Jewish.

Coming Home ∿

BY THE TIME THE NCAO BECAME THE EOC, BONNIE AND I HAD become convinced of the authenticity of Orthodoxy's claims. As a Jewish Christian, I knew I would be at home in the Orthodox Church. But we became increasingly frustrated with the EOC. On one hand, the EOC leadership seemed very serious in their pursuit of Orthodoxy, but on the other hand some felt they were already Orthodox and displayed what we considered to be elitist, triumphalist, and controlling tendencies. Additionally, a number of the second-rank leaders were far behind the founding fathers in their appreciation of Orthodoxy.

In part because Bonnie and I were uncertain about the EOC's future and in part because of the weirdness of our own church experience in San Ramon, in 1980 we began actively to seek to become Orthodox through the Orthodox Church in America (OCA) jurisdiction. Because the EOC was in active dialogue seeking what they described as "union" with the OCA, it was difficult to make the transfer—though I wanted to do so as a layman and not as a priest.

In April of 1981 Bonnie, the kids, and I attended our first Orthodox Pascha/Easter service, the most magnificent service we had ever experienced. In August of 1981 I resigned as an EOC pastor and officially requested to be received as a layman in the Orthodox Church, along with Bonnie and the children. On November 8, 1981, Bonnie and our three children became Orthodox Christians at St. Michael the Archangel Orthodox Church (OCA) in Danville, California, pastored by Fr. Michael Procurat. Because of ecclesiastical politics, I had to wait to be received. It seemed very strange to see my family enter the Orthodox Church without me.

I was received into the Orthodox Church the next month in a two-stage process. The first stage took place on Saturday, December 12, 1981, following the evening Vespers service. This was called the Rite for the Reception of Converts. It consisted of prayers of exorcism, renunciation of Satan, my spitting (literally) towards the west on him, and the profession of faith, which included the Creed. Fathers Basil Rhodes and Jonathan Mayo were present, as well as my family.

The church was dark, the air thick with incense. I wrote in my journal that it felt very eerie, even spooky. Parts of the service felt like a dream to me, as if prayers were being said over someone who had died. At the conclusion of this rite, our infant son let out a piercing wail. Peter seemed to be expressing in a mysterious way the heartfelt sorrow of my confession.

The second part of the Rite of Conversion took place on Christmas Eve, 1981. I was received by Holy Chrismation, and it was a bright service in contrast to the one two weeks before. After years of struggle, I was finally Orthodox.

What a consolation it was to "come home," comforted in the knowledge that the Orthodox Church provides what I had sought for so long: worship of the One God and Father of Our

Lord Jesus Christ, biblically based and true to the Nicene Creed, at the same time recognizing the divinity of the Son and of the Holy Spirit. The Church offers a sacrifice on earth reflecting that which is forever offered in heaven. She has a clear continuity of history and of apostolic succession going back to Christ and the apostles, and is the original Church of the Holy Land. Orthodox Christianity respects divine mystery and does not press for false clarity. And she provides both an ascetic and festive ideal, being at the same time sensitive to our human frailty. Most of all, I found the Orthodox Church was in continuity with the ancient Jewish-Christian Church and was the fulfillment of Orthodox Judaism.

Chapter 13

What Became of the Apostolic Jewish Christian Church?

ONE FURTHER DISCOVERY CONFIRMED MY BELIEF THAT Orthodox Christianity was the fulfillment of Orthodox Judaism. As a convert from Judaism to Christianity, I had always been troubled by the fact that every race and ethnic group had its niche within Christianity except the Jews. There are Greek, Russian, Arabic, Oriental, African, and Indian churches. There are Italian, Irish, Spanish, German, Swedish, Filipino, Ethiopian, Egyptian, Korean, and Persian churches. All have deep roots with many years of history.

In contrast, my early Jewish Christian exposure was with either experimental, Messianic Jewish fellowships—who called themselves Jewish Christian but for the most part were simply Gentile Christians pretending to be Jews—or with Jews for Jesus parachurch fellowships. These places of fellowship and worship had no history and often were centered around a single charismatic leader. The irony is that God used the Jews to give birth to the Christian Faith. In the beginning, there *was* an authentic and vibrant Jewish Christian Church. What happened to it? Where did it go? Does it exist today?

As I researched the early Church, I discovered that scholars have tended to assume the main body of postapostolic Jewish

Christians branched away from the mainstream Gentile Church into heretical movements, including the Ebionites and gnostics, that denied the divinity of Christ. This assumption seemed to stem in part from the strong anti-Jewish bias that arose within the postapostolic Church.

The Jewish people, estimated to have comprised from one-seventh to one-tenth of the Roman Empire's population, revolted against Rome in at least three major uprisings. These had a profound impact on the Empire, possibly causing the deaths of hundreds of thousands of Gentiles. Nevertheless, in these uprisings many more Jews than Gentiles were killed, providing support for the prevailing view among the church fathers that the Jews were cursed by God for having rejected Christ.

As I studied the early sources, it became clear that the post-apostolic Jewish Christians were more orthodox than we are often led to believe. I also was very surprised to discover that there exists a reasonably good idea of where they went.

The Nazarenes 〰

THE NEW TESTAMENT SAYS THAT JESUS LIVED IN NAZARETH so that "it might be fulfilled which was spoken by the prophets, 'He shall be called a Nazarene'" (Matthew 2:23). The Hebrew term "Nazarene" was perhaps the earliest designation for those who followed Christ. St. Paul was accused of being "a ringleader of the sect of the Nazarenes" (Acts 24:5). The Greek word "Christian" was first used in Antioch, the predominantly Gentile capital city of Syria (see Acts 11:26). There is reason to believe that the word "Christian" came to be used to describe Gentile converts to Christianity, whereas Jewish believers, in the earliest sources, came to be called "Nazarenes."

Two Movements of Jewish Christians ⌒

JUSTIN MARTYR, THE SECOND-CENTURY LEADER OF THE CHURCH whose writing, *Dialogue with Trypho the Jew,* we previously referred to, was born in Samaria of Greek parents. He recognized two kinds of Jewish Christians. The first was a group that became known as the Ebionites (a word probably derived from the Hebrew word meaning "poor"). They sought to keep the Mosaic Law and denied the divinity of Christ, for which Justin Martyr declared them to be heretical. The other group of Jewish Christians, who were considered mainstream Christians, also sought to keep the Mosaic Law, but in sharp contrast, believed in the divinity of Jesus.

In the *Dialogue,* Trypho asks Justin if it is possible to believe in Jesus and still try to keep the Law and be saved. Justin responds, "In my opinion, Trypho, such a one will be saved, if he does not strive in every way to persuade other men—I mean those Gentiles who have been circumcised from error by Christ—to observe the same things as himself, telling them that they will not be saved unless they do" (47,1). Justin Martyr also says of these Jewish Christians, "I hold that we ought to join ourselves to such, and associate with them in all things as kinsmen and brethren" (47).

Origen (AD 184–254), sometimes called the first systematic theologian, indicates in his *Contra Celsum* that both he and the pagan Celsus had personal contact with Jewish Christian communities. He also describes two groups of Jewish Christians. But unlike Justin Martyr, Origen calls *both* Ebionites. Though both groups sought to keep the Mosaic Law, one believed Jesus was born of a virgin and was divine, while the other did not (5,1). The great Church historian Eusebius of Caesarea (c. 262–339), in his *Ecclesiastical History,* also describes two kinds of Ebionites, and calls both heretical.

The Great Escape ❧

EPIPHANIUS (AD 315–403) WAS BORN IN JUDEA OF JEWISH PARENTS. His native language was Syriac, but he also knew Greek, Hebrew, Latin, and Coptic. He studied in Egypt, and upon returning to Judea established a monastery over which he served as abbot for thirty years. In 367 Epiphanius became Bishop-Metropolitan of Cyprus. He spent much of his life fighting heretical teachings and wrote the *Refutation of All Heresies*, also called the *Panarion*, which detailed eighty false beliefs. Epiphanius is the first recorded person to speak of the Jewish Christians as "Nazarenes."

Epiphanius wrote that the Nazarenes "by birth are Jews and dedicate themselves to the Law and submit to circumcision" (*Panarion* 29,5,4) and also read the Old Testament in Hebrew (29,7,4). The Nazarene group, he said, "took its beginning after the exodus from Jerusalem when all the disciples went to live in Pella because Christ had told them to leave Jerusalem and to go away since it would undergo a siege. Because of this advice they lived in Perea after having moved" (29,7,8). Pella was a city south of the Sea of Galilee and east of the Jordan River. Perea was a larger geographical area on the east bank of the Jordan River, between the Sea of Galilee and the Dead Sea, in present-day Jordan.

Regarding this Jewish Christian exodus from Jerusalem prior to the outbreak of the Jewish War with Rome (AD 66–73), Eusebius in his *Ecclesiastical History* wrote:

> Furthermore, the members of the Jerusalem church, by means of an oracle given by revelation to acceptable persons there, were ordered to leave the City before the war began and settle in a town in Perea called Pella. To Pella those who believed in Christ migrated from Jerusalem; and as if holy men had utterly abandoned the royal metropolis

of the Jews and the entire Jewish land, the judgment of
God at last overtook them (3,5).

Following the destruction of Jerusalem in the Jewish War with
Rome, the Sadducees ceased to exist; the Pharisees under Rabbi
Yohanan ben Zakkai settled in Yavne, west of Jerusalem, where
they developed rabbinic Judaism; and the Jewish Christians settled
in Pella, east of Jerusalem.

A Gentilized Christianity ⌒⌣

THOUGH THE NAZARENES UNDERSTOOD THAT SALVATION WAS TO
be built on faith in Christ and not on the Mosaic Law, for the
most part they continued to observe the Law. They sought to
mingle the Law with grace, believing that it would provide the
form and discipline in which holiness would take root. The Apostolic Council of Jerusalem, described in Acts 15 and Galatians 2,
met to decide what Mosaic laws the Gentiles converting to Christianity would have to observe.

The decree of the council, considered the first canon law,
read thus:

> The apostles, the elders, and the brethren, To the brethren
> who are of the Gentiles in Antioch, Syria, and Cilicia:
> Greetings. Since we have heard that some who went
> out from us have troubled you with words, unsettling
> your souls, saying, '*You must* be circumcised and keep
> the law'—to whom we gave no *such* commandment—it
> seemed good to us, being assembled with one accord,
> to send chosen men to you with our beloved Barnabas
> and Paul, men who have risked their lives for the name
> of our Lord Jesus Christ. . . . For it seemed good to the

Holy Spirit, and to us, to lay upon you no greater burden than these necessary things: that you abstain from things offered to idols, from blood, from things strangled, and from sexual immorality. If you keep yourselves from these, you will do well. Farewell. (Acts 15:23–29)

Christians today often forget that this decree was not directed to all Christians—only to Gentile Christians. Jewish believers, it implies, could continue to observe much of the Mosaic Law. It appears from both the New Testament and patristic sources that many Jewish Christians in fact did so. On the other hand, those Jewish Christians called to minister among the Gentiles, such as Paul, evidently did not observe much of the Mosaic Law.

Given the tremendous gulf separating Jewish Mosaic culture from Gentile pagan culture, the Jewish Christian Council of Jerusalem made a truly heroic effort to bridge the gap by greatly lessening the requirements for Gentile Christians. This is all the more astounding when we consider how strict James and his party were in observing the Mosaic Law (see Galatians 2:12). They did not require the Gentile Christians to adhere to the Mosaic Law, to learn Hebrew or Aramaic, to adopt Jewish customs and traditions, or to become Jewish. The Jewish Christians were not only very accepting, but were also highly supportive of the development of a Gentilized Christianity.

Into the Abyss ❧

THE FIRST TWO CENTURIES OF THE CHRISTIAN ERA WERE ABYSMAL for all Jews, whether followers of Christ or not. As stated earlier, during this period three major uprisings against Imperial Rome occurred: the Great War of AD 66–73, the wars under Trajan in 115–117, and the great revolt under Hadrian, led by Bar-Kokhba in 132–135, in which hundreds of thousands of Jews were killed. Though the Jewish Christians for the most part fled Judea prior to the first uprising, they were caught in the searing conflict between Jew and Gentile. Along with the main body of Jews that did not follow Christ, the Jewish Christians were despised by the pagan Gentiles for being Jews; and in addition, they were despised by the Jews for being Christian.

The abyss into which Jewish Christians were thrown was immeasurably deepened by the fact that their spiritual brethren, the Gentile Christians, rejected them as heretics because they sought to keep the Mosaic Law. This was truly astounding to me. They were rejected by Gentile Christians as heretics for upholding the Mosaic piety held by the apostolic church of Jerusalem, which had brought the Gospel to the Gentiles in the first place. The original apostles, especially those who preached to the Jews, doubtless never intended that lessening the Mosaic guidelines for the Gentiles, in order to facilitate their *inclusion* into the Church, would be used against their own Jewish Christian descendants to ensure their *exclusion* from the Church. While St. Justin the Martyr accepted the Jewish Christians as brethren, it appears that those who came after rejected them.

Epiphanius said that the Nazarene Jewish Christians were excluded from the Church because they sought to keep the Mosaic Law: "only in this respect do they differ from the Christians" (29,7,5). Though they professed belief in Jesus, he said, "they are rather Jews and nothing else" (29,9,1). Then immediately he adds, "However, they are very much hated by the Jews . . . who three times a day pronounce curses over them when they say their prayers in the synagogues. Three times a day they say: 'May God curse the Nazarenes . . . because they proclaim as Jews that Jesus is the Christ.'"

It appears that the original Nazarenes split over the issue of the divinity of Christ. Those with Orthodox Christology continued as Nazarenes, and those who denied His divinity became Ebionites. Because the two groups lived near one another and both sought to observe the Mosaic Law, they were disliked by Gentile Christians, who often confused the two groups and called both Ebionites. Yet Filaster, the contemporary of Epiphanius, does not mention the Nazarenes in his book condemning 156 different heresies, thereby implying that they were not heretical but Orthodox.

According to Epiphanius, the Nazarenes used both the Old and New Testaments (29,7,2). This indicates an adherence to Orthodoxy because heresies, especially Jewish Christian ones, typically reject some portion of the Scripture. In excluding the Nazarenes from the Church, it seemed to me that Epiphanius, like subsequent church fathers, exercised a double standard. They declared the Nazarenes heretical because they sought to keep the Law, while at the same time they accepted the Jewish Christian founders of the Church as fully Christian.

The Scriptures state that the bishop of Jerusalem, St. James, along with the elders, told St. Paul, "You see, brother, how many myriads of Jews there are who have believed, and they are all zealous for the law" (Acts 21:20). In making this statement, St. James assumes that being "zealous for the law" is a positive and desirable characteristic. There were some aspects of the Law that St. Paul said even Jews should not strive to keep (see Galatians). But the primary issue of keeping or not keeping the Law applied essentially to Gentiles, not to Jews.

Further North ∾

ACCORDING TO EPIPHANIUS, THE NAZARENES MOVED TO "BEROEA in the neighborhood of Coele Syria and the Decapolis in the region of Pella and in Basanitis in the so-called Kokabe" (29,7,7). Both Epiphanius and Jerome mention the Nazarenes living in Beroea of Coele Syria, which is modern-day Aleppo in northwestern Syria. Epiphanius wrote his *Panarion* for two presbyters who came from Beroea. Their origins in the area of which he speaks provide added credibility to what he says of the region. This is the last site in which the Nazarenes are said to have lived.

St. Jerome (331–419), best known for translating the Bible into Latin, was born in Italy and journeyed to Antioch. While traveling he spent time in the wilderness near Beroea, where he learned Hebrew under "a believing brother from among the Hebrews" (*Patrologia Latina* 22,1079). He also tells us, "The Hebrew itself [of the original Gospel of Matthew] has been preserved until the present day in the library of Caesarea, which Pamphilius the Martyr so diligently collected. From the Nazarenes who use the book in Beroea, a city in Syria, I also received the opportunity to copy it" (PL 23,613). St. Jerome also claimed to have copied the Gospel according to the Hebrews, "which is read by the Nazarenes," and translated it into Greek and Latin. In 390 he began his project of translating the Hebrew Old Testament into Latin.

Evidently St. Jerome, unlike most fathers of the Church, had substantial personal contact with the Nazarenes while in the vicinity of Beroea. About AD 404 he wrote to St. Augustine concerning the Nazarenes, "They believe in Christ, the Son of God, born of Mary the Virgin" (Ep. 112,13). He understood them to have believed in the divinity of Jesus. He also states that they had a Gospel in Hebrew and lived in Beroea "and in all the Synagogues of the East." According to St. Jerome, "The Nazarenes accept Christ in such a way that they do not cease to observe the old Law" (*On Isaiah* 8:14). But their respect for the Law did not win the respect of the Jews, who "three times each day anathematize the Christian name in every synagogue under the name of Nazarenes" (*On Isa.* 5:18, 19).

Whereas the Ebionites and other schismatic Jewish Christians tended to dislike St. Paul, the Nazarenes had a positive view of the apostle and of his ministry to the Gentiles. Instead of resenting their diminished role in the Church, the Nazarenes appear to have been thankful for the success of St. Paul's ministry. In general, Jerome speaks of the Nazarenes in somewhat respectful terms.

The Turning Point ❧

ST. AUGUSTINE OF HIPPO (354–430), OFTEN THOUGHT OF AS THE father of Western theology, accepted Epiphanius's view that the Nazarenes were heretical because they sought to keep the Mosaic Law. Augustine, who never traveled beyond Italy and North Africa, had no direct exposure to them. He wrote, "They persist to the present day who call themselves Nazarene Christians and circumcise the carnal foreskins in the Jewish way" (PL 43,225). Augustine tells us that they profess to be Christians, believe that Christ is the Son of God, and baptize. Their attempt at keeping the Mosaic Law included circumcision, the observance of the Sabbath, and food restrictions.

After Jerome, no writer appears to have had any direct encounter with the Nazarenes. If Jerome is correct, the Nazarenes survived into the early fifth century. A number of earlier church fathers failed to mention them not because they did not exist, but probably because they were considered to be Orthodox Christians. It was Epiphanius who, by confusing the Nazarenes with the Ebionites, created a misunderstanding that remains with us to this day.

Where Are the Descendants of the Nazarenes? ᐊ

THE BABYLONIAN TALMUD SPEAKS OF RABBI ELIEZER, WHO SAYS, "Once I was walking in the upper street of Sepphoris, and found a man of the disciples of Jeshu the Nazarene, and Jacob of Kfar Sechania was his name" (Avodah Zarah 16b–17a). This and many other Talmudic references indicate that following the destruction of Jerusalem in AD 70, the Jewish Christians continued to exist in the region of Galilee.

All records make it clear that the Jewish Christians sought to maintain their identity as they migrated first eastward to Pella, then northward to Aleppo. As the indigenous people of the area in which the Nazarenes lived converted to Christianity, and the number of Gentiles within the Church multiplied, it can be assumed that intermarriage also increased. As the number of Jewish converts to Christianity steadily decreased, it became increasingly difficult for the Nazarenes to maintain their identity. In time they became assimilated into the ever-rising tide of Gentile believers.

The subsequent history of the indigenous Christians of northwest Syria provides some clues indicating that their heritage can in part be traced back to the Nazarenes. During the persecution of Christians under the pagan Roman Empire, many Christians hid in the mountains along the western coast of Syria. A large number lived in caves carved into the limestone cliffs. Some of these caves still exist in Maalula, north of Damascus and close to the modern border of Lebanon. When the Omayyad Moslems overtook Syria in the seventh century, the Christians moved further west into the mountains to escape persecution, and remain there today.

At least two facts indicate that the imprint of the ancient Nazarene Jewish Christians is to be found within the predominantly Arabic Orthodox Christian Church of that region. First, Aramaic, the language of Christ, the apostles, and early Jewish Christians, is still spoken among Christians in and around Maalula and has been used in the worship services of the Syrian Orthodox Christian Church. Western Aramaic is used nowhere else in the world. Second, the region where most of the Syrian Orthodox Christians live today is east of Laodicea (Latakiya) near the river Orontes and below the coastal mountain range known as Jabel al-Nusayriya (Arabic for Nazarene), in what is today known as the Valley of the Nazarenes.

These Christians have historically been under the administration of the Orthodox Christian patriarch of Antioch, who since the fourteenth century has resided in Damascus. Strange as it may seem, the spiritual descendants, and in part physical descendants, of the ancient Nazarene Jewish Christian Church of Jerusalem are the present-day Semitic Antiochian Orthodox Christians living in and around the Valley of the Nazarenes.

This extensive research resulted in my realizing more clearly that Jewish Christians who, like me, desire to rediscover their Jewish Christian heritage should not look in Western post-Reformation Caucasian churches with shallow roots in northern Europe. Rather, we need to look in the place where Christianity began: the Middle East, in the indigenous Semitic Orthodox Christian Church that has deep roots, clear lineage, and continuity with the original apostolic Church. In America, the present expression of that Church is the Antiochian Orthodox Christian Church and her sister Orthodox Christian churches.

What happened to the ancient Jewish Christian Church? Where did it go? Does it exist today? When asked these questions, I now feel comfortable responding that its soul lives within the Orthodox Church, rooted in the spirit of Antioch and the Valley of the Nazarenes.

Part III

Discovering Salvation with Depth

Chapter 14

How Fallen Are We?

OUR CONVERSION TO ORTHODOX CHRISTIANITY WAS initially a bittersweet experience. The Orthodox Church had fantastic worship, true doctrine, apostolic succession, everything we sought except for one thing—committed, welcoming members.

Jesus said of His disciples, "You will know them by their fruits" (Matthew 7:16), and "By this all will know that you are My disciples, if you have love for one another" (John 13:35). But among the Orthodox churches we visited, we discovered many of the people viewed their respective churches as Greek, Russian, or Arabic ethnic clubs rather than as the One Holy Catholic and Apostolic Church. Because of this, they extended little warmth towards outsiders. We dearly missed the zeal and hospitality of our evangelical friends.

Knowing our frustration, our priest told us kindly that "Orthodox Christianity is the right Church with the wrong people." Amusing as the statement was, it helped us realize that the truth of Orthodoxy did not necessarily rub off onto her people.

Bonnie was having more difficulty than I rising above this disconnect. She became increasingly disillusioned and eventually asked that we move out of San Ramon, where we were being shunned by the Protestants we had left, and worse, did not feel at home within the Orthodox communities we frequented. Though a city boy at heart, I finally agreed, and in June 1983 we bought a house in Arnold, a small town at the four-thousand-foot level of the Sierra Nevada Mountains.

Arnold was a magnificent site, bordering a national forest, halfway between Yosemite and Lake Tahoe, about three miles from Big Trees State Park, where the giant sequoia trees grow. During the winter we got plenty of snow. Firewood provided us with our only source of heat.

At this time I was working in Silicon Valley as a production supervisor making integrated circuit chips. I worked three twelve-hour days per week, during which I slept near work—at first in my pickup and later at the in-laws'. Following my workdays, I drove three and a half hours to the mountains and remained at home for four days. It was a good arrangement, and Bonnie didn't need employment as my income was substantial.

During this time we distanced ourselves a bit from the Orthodox Church, and a wonderful thing happened. Whenever we did go to church, which was perhaps once a month, Bonnie grew increasingly appreciative of it. Her original decision to become Orthodox had been based in large part on her trust in me. Now she was gaining ownership of the Orthodox Faith. Eventually we both came to agree that as much as we loved the forest and mountains, we missed and loved the Orthodox Church more. We would enjoy our mountain paradise for only two and a half years.

Back to New York ᐸᐳ

Silicon Valley's high-tech chip industry is either boom or bust. As a supervisor, if I was not in hiring mode I was in firing mode. There was nothing in between. In 1985 the chip industry was hit by a recession. During this time Bonnie and I discussed my making a major occupational move.

Four years had passed since I had ceased serving as a part-time

EOC pastor to become Orthodox, and I was now thirty-nine years old. I had completed the three-year Late Vocations Program, which prepares individuals to become Orthodox deacons. I was restless and desired to serve as a pastor again. Priests and good friends confirmed that they thought I had a call to the priesthood and should go to seminary. We began to seriously consider attending St. Vladimir's Seminary in Crestwood, New York.

Just when we had decided that I would quit my job and go, I got laid off. We had four young children, and agreed that it was unreasonable to have the entire family move from coast to coast to discover whether I liked the seminary and wanted to pursue the priesthood. We decided I would spend one semester back East alone, assessing whether it was worth taking the giant leap of moving the entire family there. I entered the seminary in the fall of 1985, living in the student dorm for singles. The experience was intense, including daily morning and evening services and concentrated studies.

During Thanksgiving break, Bonnie visited and fell in love with the seminary services. We decided to purchase a house while she was there, and also to put our home on the West Coast up for sale. We weren't able to find a suitable house until the very last one we looked at, on the final day of Bonnie's visit. With glee we learned that our offer had been accepted. The huge house, located in the Italian neighborhood of Tuckahoe, was within walking distance of both the seminary and a major train line that could transport us to Grand Central Station in downtown Manhattan in only thirty minutes. The house was situated next to a marble quarry, from which we were told marble had been extracted to build the Capitol Building in Washington, D.C. When people asked us where we lived, I would sometimes answer, "Next to where the Capitol Building used to be."

With great effort we moved everyone and everything across

this wide nation of ours. We left our mountain paradise with a certain sorrow, knowing that our life on the outskirts of New York City would be very different. I felt sad for Bonnie, knowing she preferred living in the country; also, our move would mean that she would have to work at the local hospital. We invited my brother Sol, who had been living alone in Queens, to live with us. His acceptance of our offer became a great blessing for us, as he provided both moral and material support.

Is Death from God? ◠

BOTH OF MY PARENTS HAD PASSED ON BY THIS TIME, DAD in February of 1978 and Mom in the same month in 1983. Being back on the East Coast meant that I had returned to my hometown minus my parents, whose graves I visited at Cedar Park Jewish Cemetery in Westwood, New Jersey. Their absence, and the fact that our children would never know them in this life, challenged me to meditate on the reality of death and its origin. It was appropriate that I more seriously examine this subject, as I was now a seminarian.

I had always had a special appreciation for the first book of the Bible, Genesis. This was in part due to the fact that among some Jews, one way of teaching children how to read Hebrew is to begin at the beginning, meaning with the very first verses of Genesis. Genesis relates how human sin and death originated when Adam and Eve disobeyed God and ate of the forbidden fruit in the Garden of Eden.

The Scripture says, "And the LORD God commanded the man, saying, 'Of every tree of the garden you may freely eat; but of the tree of the knowledge of good and evil you shall not eat, for in the day that you eat of it you shall surely die'" (Genesis

2:16, 17). Regardless of how the passage is interpreted—whether literally or figuratively—all interpretations assume that man turned away from God, and as a result fell from a position of intimacy with God to a state of confusion and death. Sin, mortality, and death, both spiritual and physical, were the direct result of man's disobedience.

In this scenario of what is called "the Fall," the next major assumption often made by non-Orthodox churches is that death was the direct result of a punitive sentence pronounced by God. That is, God made a law—"you shall not eat of the fruit, for if you do you will surely die"—and when Adam and Eve broke that law, death resulted from God's punitive proclamation. The action and resultant punishment are understood as being of a juridical nature. In this non-Orthodox understanding of the Fall, God had no choice but to declare that Adam and Eve would die. The punitive action was demanded by a necessity to which God Himself was bound. What was this necessity? The necessity of being just.

To tell the truth, I had never really thought about this in depth. Now, I realized that I did believe that because God is just He could not simply forgive Adam and Eve's sins. Therefore, their spiritual and physical death was directly related to God's justice. It was quite a shock to discover that what I had always assumed to be obvious and true about this most basic doctrine of Christianity was in fact false and not Orthodox.

In contrast to this juridical view of the Fall, the Orthodox hold that when God told Adam he would die if he ate the forbidden fruit, it was a simple statement of fact. The Lord was essentially saying, "If you turn from Me, the only source of life, then death will be the outcome." The Orthodox understood the statement to be a warning, not a threat of retributive justice. St. Gregory Palamas (fourteenth century) describes the scenario as follows:

For those who hear such sayings with wisdom, it is possible to know that God created neither the death of the soul nor the death of the body. For in the beginning, neither did He command saying, 'Die on the day when thou shalt eat,' but 'On the day when thou shalt eat, thou shalt die.' And neither did He say, 'Return thou to the earth' but '. . . thou shalt return,' announcing beforehand and allowing freedom, and not even justifiably staving off the outcome.[14]

The Scripture says God told Adam and Eve that if they ate from the fruit of the tree of the knowledge of good and evil, they would die. For the first time I realized that God did not say, "I will kill you," but, "you will die." Because God alone has life in Himself and is the source of all life, only life can come from Him. In turning away from God, the fountain of life, man turned towards death.

In eating of the fruit, Adam and Eve ceased desiring God. They ceased looking to Him for their sustenance, for their food, and instead ate a fruit that represents the world. In eating the world, they looked to creation itself for sustenance instead of to God. So in this act, the first parents sought to exclude God from their lives and to live autonomously.

In Orthodox thought, the great sin is not that they disobeyed a law, but rather that they sought to discover knowledge and sustenance apart from God. St. Basil the Great wrote:

[Life] is God, and the deprivation of life is death. Thus, Adam prepared death for himself through his withdrawal from God. . . . Therefore, God did not create death, but we brought it upon ourselves by our wicked purpose.

Neither did He prevent the dissolution . . . so that the illness would not be preserved immortal in us.[15]

In contrast, the Roman Catholic Council of Trent (1546) stated:

> If any one does not confess that the first man, Adam, when he had transgressed the commandment of God in Paradise, immediately lost the holiness and justice wherein he had been constituted; and that he incurred, through the offence of that prevarication, *the wrath and indignation of God, and consequently death, with which God had previously threatened him,* and, together with death, captivity under his power who thenceforth had the empire of death, that is to say, the devil, and that the entire Adam, through that offence of prevarication, was changed, in body and soul, for the worse; let him be anathema [emphasis mine].[16]

The more I thought, the more I understood that the difference between the two views could not be overstated: the non-Orthodox view stressed that death is God's direct retributive judgment on man for having broken His law, while the Orthodox view stressed that death is a self-imposed condition resulting from man's turning away from God, who alone is the source of life.

The differences were crucial, for if I believed that death was somehow from God, I would be tempted to approach God Himself as an obstacle that must be overcome if I were to gain salvation. Clearly, the goal then comes to be appeasement of God. Sadly, some Christians view the Trinity this way: God the Father is seen as a totally unapproachable Old Testament Ancient-of-Days figure with a long, flowing white beard—fierce, harsh, vindictive, and unsympathetic. He is the God of justice and judgment, like the Viking god Odin who sent bolts of lightning upon puny, frail, mortal humans. In contrast, Jesus Christ is viewed as the loving, compassionate, gentle Lamb of God who as Son seeks to appease His angry Father. The Holy Spirit is the odd Person out, so He is usually ignored.

The Virgin Mary is the soft, sensitive, kindly, feminine figure who is very approachable, very human. So among those who have an abiding dread of the Father, there tend to be proportionally more prayers directed to the Blessed Mother for intercession. She appeals to her Son on their behalf as only a mother can, encouraging Him to approach the unapproachable Father. In this scheme of things, the Father is the one people want to evade at all costs. In fact, He becomes the figure one must make an end run around in order to get into heaven. This may sound like an exaggeration, but I have known devout and godly Christians who view the Trinity and the Virgin Mary much as I have described.

In contrast, the Orthodox understanding of the Fall focuses on *our* condition or state, rather than on a broken law or God's judgmental anger. It centers on Adam and Eve's state of being, the essence of who they were and how that was changed in their disobedience. By turning away from God, the source of life, they began to die. The issue is not legal or juridical, but ontological. In a sense it has nothing to do with God and everything to do with man. It is less a relational issue and far more an issue of interior change of heart at the deepest level.

Because death is not viewed as a juridical issue, neither is its cure. Fr. John Romanides wrote a well-researched book on this subject called *The Ancestral Sin,* in which he writes:

As we shall see, the juridically framed problem of guilt inherited from Adam and the consequent punishment of mankind because of an offense against divine justice do not even exist for the Greek Fathers simply because they teach that God is not the cause of death. Man's withdrawal from God unto his own death, like the freedom of human will, is outside God's jurisdiction. And it is outside of His jurisdiction by His own will. The fact that God desires the salvation of all does not mean that all are saved. God saves only through love and freedom. This point is exactly what theologians under the influence of Augustine have never comprehended.[17]

My youthful experience in Judaism taught me that God loves. Though we had many laws to fulfill, God was always presented as merciful and forgiving. Salvation was never taught as our being delivered from God's wrath. In my eighteen years as a Protestant, I came to view salvation as our being saved from the wrath of God and from the hell that He created for the lost. Salvation essentially meant to avoid hell and go to heaven. Now, as an Orthodox, I was being taught that salvation means being saved not from God's wrath, but from the power of the three great enemies: sin, death, and the devil.

How Fallen Are We? ❧

THE ANSWER TO THIS QUESTION DEPENDS ON TWO THINGS: WHAT was the state *from which* we fell, and *to what* state have we fallen? I discovered that in non-Orthodox Christianity, *both* the height from which we fell and the depth to which we have fallen are held to be much greater than in Orthodoxy. The Orthodox Christian approach meshed well with the Orthodox Jewish understanding with which I was raised. Both have a much more favorable view of man than is presented in non-Orthodox Christianity, especially in the Calvinist view that man fell from a state of perfection to a state of total depravity, retaining no ability within himself to return to God.

In his book, *The Orthodox Church,* perhaps the foremost presentation of Orthodoxy in the English language, Timothy (Bishop Kallistos) Ware says the Orthodox "cannot agree with Augustine, when he writes that humans are under 'a harsh necessity' of committing sin, and that 'human nature was overcome by the fault into which it fell, and *so came to lack freedom.*' The image of God is distorted by sin, but never destroyed; in the words of a hymn sung by Orthodox at the Funeral Service: 'I am the image of Your inexpressible glory, even though I bear the wounds of sin.' And because we still retain the image of God, we still retain free will, although sin restricts its scope. Even after the fall, God 'takes not away from man the power to will—to will to obey or not to obey Him.'"[18]

The great nineteenth-century Russian saint John of Kronstadt said, "Never confuse the person, formed in the image of God, with the evil that is in him; because evil is but a chance misfortune, an illness, a devilish reverie. But the very essence of the person is the image of God, and this remains in him despite every disfigurement." Faithful to the idea of synergy, Orthodoxy repudiates any interpretation of the Fall that allows no room for human freedom.

So from what state does Orthodoxy view man as having fallen? St. Irenaeus (second century) wrote, "Man having received existence was to grow and mature, then become strong, and reaching full maturity should be glorified, and being glorified, should be enabled to see God."[19]

According to St. Irenaeus, man's original state was one of spiritual childhood, innocence, and simplicity joined to moral purity. Man was to gain the divine likeness through a slow process.

He does not view man's fall as a full-blown rebellion, but rather as an impulsive desire to grow before his time.

The metaphor of the damaged eye helped me to understand the difference between the two views. The total depravity model views the Fall as having destroyed man's spiritual eye so that he is no longer capable of having any spiritual sight whatsoever. His only hope is to be given a completely new eye from God. God unilaterally decides who is given a new eye and who is not. This is called double predestination, as God alone decides (predestines) who will be given faith and go to heaven, and who will not be given faith and will go to hell.

In contrast, in the Orthodox view, the Fall damages the spiritual eye but does not destroy it. We are not totally blind, because having been created in the image and likeness of God, we still retain free will and some degree of desire for God. Faith remains within us, though it may be the size of a mustard seed. Having faith is not an all-or-nothing issue. Just as differing levels of fallenness exist, so do varying degrees of faith.

What Is Inherited from Original Sin? ⌒

I HAD BEEN A GREAT ADMIRER OF ST. AUGUSTINE (FOURTH/FIFTH century), who is viewed by much of Western Christianity as the father of Western theology. In studying the tremendous impact he has had on Western Christianity, I discovered that his conflict with the monk Pelagius, a Briton who lived in Rome, was critical. Pelagius (fifth century) denied the inheritance of any kind of sin by Adam's descendants. While St. Augustine answered Pelagius well in most ways, he resorted to some extremes that led to later distortion and overemphasis. St. Augustine's writings were the first to use the term "original sin" (*peccato originali*).

The scriptural text central to the issue of original sin is

Romans 5:12, in which St. Paul refers to Adam. The following passage is translated from the Greek as Orthodox would translate it: "As sin came into the world through one man, and through sin death, so death spread to all men and *because* [of death] all men have sinned." The last four words in Greek are *eph ho pantes hemarton*.

Here a major issue of translation emerges. These four words were translated into Latin as *in quo omnes peccaverunt*, "in whom [Adam] all men have sinned." This wording was used in the West from the time of St. Jerome's translation of the Scriptures into Latin (fourth/fifth century), to justify the doctrine of guilt inherited from Adam and spread to his descendants. The Greek does not say this. *Eph ho* is a contraction of *epi* with the relative pronoun *ho*; it can be translated "because." Most modern scholars agree that this is the original meaning.

Thus, St. Paul is not saying that we are all guilty of personal sin merely because we are conjointly included in Adam, but that, like Adam, we have all committed personal sinful acts and have thus experienced death. We are subject to death and corruption because of Adam's sin, but we are guilty only of our own personal sinful acts. Unfortunately, Western Christianity has often accepted variations of the following mistranslated version: "Therefore, just as through one man sin entered the world, and death through sin, and thus death spread to all men, *in whom* all have sinned." This translation misleads readers into believing that the *guilt* of original sin is inherited.[20]

Additionally, confusion arises from two Greek words used for "sin." The Greek word *hamartema* means an *individual sinful action,* while *hamartia* denotes a *generic sinful condition*. It is this latter concept that shaped the Augustinian teaching about original sin, moral disability, and inherited guilt. The distinction between the two words reveals an important assumption: With *hamartia* (generic sinful condition), the idea of the *sin nature*, as distinct from concrete sinful *acts* or sinning *persons*, gained currency in Western theology. Moreover, the Greek Fathers' term *propatorikon amartema* is best translated "ancestral sin" (literally, it means "forefatherly sin"). This term predates St. Augustine's Latin term meaning "original sin."

It was revealing to learn that "ancestral sin" does not convey the idea of the passing on of sin. In contrast, "original sin" does imply this, as it is the first of many. St. Augustine did not know Greek, and many of the Greek Fathers did not understand Latin. So already in the fifth century Western and Eastern Christianity were drifting apart. The earlier Fathers held that there is no such thing as a sin nature, in the sense of a nature that inherits the guilt of another's sinful act. In the Orthodox understanding, only persons sin, not human nature.

Yet the Scriptures and sayings of the church fathers contain statements indicating that we are born into sin. For example, "Behold, I was brought forth in iniquity, / And in sin my mother conceived me" (Psalm 51:5). Infants have always been baptized for the remission of sins, though they have obviously not committed any personal sins. The Orthodox view the sinful state into which we all are born as an *inclination* to sin personally, as well as a spiritual and physical brokenness, corruption, mortality, and genetic/biological deterioration. But being born into sin does not imply having committed personal sin or being personally guilty for the sins of those living before us.

Orthodox view the disobedience of Adam and Eve as *their* personal sin, not our personal sin. So neither original sin nor salvation can be realized in a person's life without involving *personal* and free responsibility. This view assumes that though we are born with a fallen nature, we are not *compelled* to sin. Each of us possesses sufficient freedom and grace to turn to God, be strengthened by

Him, and personally resist sin. So we are personally responsible for our sins. We can't just blame our forefathers.

I found the discovery of how Orthodox Christianity views original sin refreshing. Orthodox Judaism also rejects the Western Christian understanding of original sin. Judaism teaches that children are born innocent, and though our general condition reflects the results of the Fall, each person retains free will and is personally responsible for his/her sins. This view is based on such scriptures as, "Fathers shall not be put to death for *their* children, nor shall the children be put to death for *their* fathers; a person shall be put to death for his own sin" (Deuteronomy 24:16); and "The soul who sins shall die. The son shall not bear the *guilt* of the father, nor the father bear the *guilt* of the son. The righteousness of the righteous shall be upon himself, and the wickedness of the wicked shall be upon himself" (Ezekiel 18:20, emphasis mine).

Orthodox Judaism interpreted the scripture, "For I, the LORD your God, *am* a jealous God, visiting the iniquity of the fathers upon the children to the third and fourth *generations* of those who hate Me" (Deuteronomy 5:9), in the same way Orthodox Christians would interpret it—as referring to our general state of fallenness, not to specific sin or guilt. Both Orthodoxies view sins only as personal acts, and not at all as acts of nature. Neither would hold that man is inherently sinful, and both stress that though there is in man an inclination to sin, children are—using non-theological terminology—basically good, not bad.

Lasting Repercussions of Augustine's Theology ∾

ST. AUGUSTINE'S VIEW OF INHERITED SIN AND GUILT RESULTED IN lasting repercussions for the Roman Catholic Church and Western Christianity in general. The first of these repercussions concerns

Augustine's concept that all infants are born guilty of sin, not because they have personally sinned but because they have sinned "in Adam." Because of this, St. Augustine held that infants should be baptized as soon as possible, because if they should die without baptism, "they shall not have life, but the *wrath* of God abideth on them"[21] (emphasis mine). This view affects the practice of the Roman Catholic Church to the present day.

In wonderful and refreshing contrast, I learned that Orthodoxy in general views unbaptized infants who die as "holy innocents." Therefore, nothing prevents them from advancing in the afterlife and experiencing heaven. The Orthodox Church often waits to baptize infants until they are several months old.

Orthodox Judaism and Orthodox Christianity both have a more positive view of children than does non-Orthodox Christianity. To give an example: In viewing religious art in the wonderful New York City art museums, I noticed that paintings from the Puritan era often depict children as tiny adults, both in look and in dress. This seemed odd. I discovered that it was because the Puritans viewed childhood as undesirable, a necessary evil. The sooner children grew up the better. So they tried to ignore childhood, even in their art. This is in sharp contrast to Orthodoxy, in which children are adored. Orthodox theology teaches that Christ Himself sanctified childhood as He passed through every state of development, from embryo, to fetus, to infancy, to childhood and then young adulthood. Through the Incarnation each stage has been sanctified, making it holy and sacred and worthy of celebration.

A second lasting consequence of St. Augustine's view of inherited sin and guilt was the negative cloud placed over sexual intercourse and reproduction in the Western Church. Sexual intercourse was viewed as the means by which the guilt of original sin was passed from generation to generation. What a shock it was for me to hear that some even go so far as to view intercourse itself as the original sin!

Once again, Orthodox Judaism and Orthodox Christianity agree that sexual intercourse is neither sinful nor the transmitter of sin. As St. Paul says, "Marriage *is* honorable among all, and the bed undefiled" (Hebrews 13:4). In fact, the Orthodox liturgical cycle recognizes and commemorates holy days devoted to the conception of specific saints, including the Virgin Mary and St. John the Baptist.

The fourth-century Council of Gangra enacted two canons addressing those who disparage sexual intercourse between marriage partners; in fact, it excommunicates them.

> If any one shall condemn marriage, or abominate and condemn a woman who is a believer and devout, and sleeps with her own husband, as though she could not enter the Kingdom [of heaven] let him be anathema. (Canon 1)
>
> If any one shall maintain, concerning a married presbyter, that it is not lawful to partake of the oblation when he offers it, let him be anathema. (Canon 4)[22]

A third repercussion of St. Augustine's understanding of guilt and original sin is that it forced the Roman Catholic Church to attempt to solve a problem that did not exist for the Orthodox. The Roman Church was faced with having to explain how the taint of original sin and its guilt was kept from being present in the Virgin Mary when she miraculously conceived Christ. Their solution was to address the way the Virgin Mother herself was conceived. According to Roman Catholic teaching, God applied merits to Mary at the moment of her conception so that she would not inherit original sin. (This view, called the Immaculate

Conception, refers to the way Mary herself was conceived, not, as many mistakenly believe, to the way Jesus was conceived.) This teaching was officially made a dogma of the Roman Catholic Church at Vatican I in 1854.

The dogma of the Immaculate Conception became still another barrier dividing Orthodoxy from Roman Catholicism. Orthodox theology has no problem with Mary's conception to begin with: we believe her conception was as pure as it could be and did not need the application of any special "merits."

The fourth impact of St. Augustine's doctrine of inherited sin and guilt was that it became the basis on which a substantial segment of Protestantism developed its view of total depravity. The Protestant reformer John Calvin and those following him took Augustine's presuppositions to their logical conclusion, holding that man has fallen so deeply into an abyss that he no longer retains any ability to believe, to have faith, or to do any authentically good deed. This understanding developed into what is called double predestination, discussed in greater depth earlier in this chapter.

Our EOC Friends Become Orthodox ⌒◡

WHILE I WAS COMPLETING MY SEMINARY STUDIES, OUR OLD friends in the EOC were completing their journey into the Orthodox Church. On the weekend of February 6–8, 1987, Juliana Schmemann (the widow of Fr. Alexander Schmemann, former dean of St. Vladimir's Seminary), Lex and Julianna (Sheila) Hixon, and I flew from New York City to Los Angeles. We were going to witness the reception of the EOC into the Antiochian Orthodox Church by Metropolitan Philip, the head of the Antiochian Archdiocese.

Those being received included my old friends Jack Sparks, Jon

Braun, Peter Gillquist, Richard Ballew, Gordon Walker, Weldon Hardenbrook, my New York City buddy Charlie Lehman, and their wives. Over two hundred laity were also being received into the Church. I had the opportunity to spend a special time with Peter Gillquist and Gordon Walker the evening before their reception.

The service took place at St. Michael Antiochian Orthodox Church in Van Nuys. I felt strange as I watched, knowing that my family and I had become Orthodox over five years earlier and I was now in my second year of seminary as a layman, while they were in the process of being received and made archpriests. I was on the slow track, but I had no regrets at all. Of the EOC clergy leadership, I would be the only one with an Orthodox seminary degree.

The reality of our new unity within the Orthodox Church and receiving Communion together was an overwhelming experience for me. I was so glad for them and for myself. Upon returning to seminary, I discussed with Bonnie and several respected priests the idea of transferring from the OCA to the Antiochian Archdiocese, because I continued to share a common vision with the former EOC leadership. They were in the process of forming what was to be called the Antiochian Evangelical Orthodox Mission (AEOM), and I wanted to be part of that effort. I put in a request, and my transfer from the OCA to the Antiochian Archdiocese was approved. Now we were not only in the same Church, but also in the same jurisdiction.

My Ordinations ∾

AFTER BEING ORDAINED A DEACON BY BISHOP ANTOUN (KHOURI), I was ordained to the priesthood by Archbishop Michael (Shaheen) at the Antiochian East Coast Parish Life Conference held in

Parsippany, New Jersey, on July 10, 1988. At forty-two years of age, with a wife and four children, I was beginning a new adventure. My initial parish assignment, while I continued my studies at the seminary, was to assist at St. Anthony Antiochian Orthodox Church in Bergenfield, New Jersey. I was to serve there for two years under the tutelage of Fr. Joseph Allen, the vicar general of the archdiocese and a professor at the seminary.

During my seminary studies, Bonnie worked full-time as a nurse at St. John Riverside Hospital in Yonkers. The hospital fully covered her tuition, enabling her to pursue her Master's degree in nurse midwifery at Columbia University Medical Center. She eventually received her degree *summa cum laude* and did her delivery training at North Central Bronx Hospital and Harlem Hospital. We were both receiving Master's degrees and both gaining the opportunity to do what we most wanted to do—I as an Orthodox priest and Bonnie as a registered nurse midwife. We made a wonderful team: she could deliver babies and I could baptize them. I was so proud of her!

Chapter 15

What Salvation Is Not: Solutions to Problems That Don't Exist

In many ways, a problem's definition determines its solution. Because the problem of the Fall is understood differently in Western Christianity than in Orthodoxy, the solutions offered in both the Roman Catholic and Protestant churches differ from those of the Orthodox Church. In the West, a number of soteriological views (doctrines of salvation) have developed that seek to explain how man's fallen position, status, or relationship with God is repaired. The Orthodox Church of the East would for the most part reject these views, not only because some elements of them cannot be found in the Scriptures and writings of the church fathers, but because they distort the Christian understanding of God's Love and His salvation. Sometimes these views are called theories of atonement.

The concept of atonement and its place in salvation has played an important role in my life because of the emphasis placed on it in the Old Testament and Jewish history. Resolving my many questions about atonement and the sacrificial system was vital in my spiritual journey. As I delved into these issues, I became further convinced that Christian Orthodoxy fulfills Jewish Orthodoxy.

Will There Be the Devil to Pay? 〜

THE FIRST SIGNIFICANT THEORY OF ATONEMENT PRESENTED IN THE West was called the "ransom" or "bargain" theory. Its position is that in the Fall, Adam and Eve sold humanity to the devil. Because of this, we have all come under the devil's ownership, and justice demands he must be paid a ransom for our freedom. From this idea comes the expression, "There will be the devil to pay." The solution presented in this theory is that God tricks the devil into accepting Jesus' death as a ransom. Death and Hades could not maintain a hold on Jesus, but His sacrifice and death nevertheless satisfied the devil's claim for justice. In providing Himself as the sacrificial Lamb of God, Jesus has freed fallen humanity from the devil's claim over us.

This view dominated the West during the first thousand years of Christianity. In the eleventh century, Anselm, Archbishop of Canterbury, wrote, *Why Did God Become Man?* This critique of the ransom/bargain theory resulted in its virtual abandonment in the West. Anselm's critique held that the devil is an outlaw and has no claim on humanity. Thus God does not have to pay him anything in order to free us.

While it is true that some Fathers used imagery such as the fishhook, the mousetrap, and the ransom paid to Satan, that imagery did not express theological precision but was used simply for rhetorical effect. These were attempts to illustrate how the powers of darkness, by instigating Christ's crucifixion, actually disarmed themselves. The apostle Paul refers to the way spiritual and physical rulers were tricked when he says, "But we speak the wisdom of God in a mystery, the hidden *wisdom* which God ordained before the ages for our glory, which none of the rulers of this age knew; for had they known, they would not have crucified the Lord of glory" (1 Corinthians 2:7, 8).

St. Gregory the Theologian (also known as St. Gregory of Nazianzus, fourth century) addresses the issue from the Orthodox perspective as he refutes the ransom/bargain view. He writes:

> Now we are to examine another fact and dogma, neglected by most people, but in my judgment well worth enquiring into. To Whom was that Blood offered that was shed for us, and why was It shed? I mean the precious and famous Blood of our God and High Priest and Sacrifice. We were detained in bondage by the Evil One, sold under sin, and receiving pleasure in exchange for wickedness. Now, since a ransom belongs only to him who holds in bondage, I ask to whom was this offered, and for what cause? If to the Evil One, fie upon the outrage! [It is an outrage] if the robber receives ransom, not only from God, but a ransom which consists of God Himself, and has such an illustrious payment for his tyranny, a payment for whose sake it would have been right for him to have left us alone altogether.[23]

A Payment to Appease an Angry God?

WHILE LIVING IN BERKELEY, CALIFORNIA, DURING THE SEVENTIES, I sometimes manned the campus Christian book table in Sproul Plaza. It was always a challenge, as one never knew who would stop by or what discussions would arise. On one particular day, an Orthodox Jew from the Chabad Center stopped to discuss theology with me. He was a nice and very civil fellow.

As we talked, he asked me, "Why can't God simply forgive sins? Why does He need a sacrifice? In fact, why does He need anything?"

This was a subject I thought I knew well, and so I explained to the inquirer, "God cannot forgive our sins because He is just, and from the beginning has provided sacrifices to atone for our sins." I then spoke about how the Old Testament animal sacrifices were a type of Jesus, the Lamb of God, our true Sacrifice. Then I drew on a memorized text from Leviticus 17:11, which for me was always the clincher: "For the life of the flesh *is* in the blood, and I have given it to you upon the altar to make atonement for your souls; for it *is* the blood *that* makes atonement for the soul." I followed this verse with the challenge, "You have no sacrifice—how will God be able to forgive your sins?"

My interrogator explained that atonement can mean many things and that the Leviticus passage did not necessarily mean God could not forgive sins without blood. He referred to scriptures such as Jeremiah 7:22, 23: "For I did not speak to your fathers, or command them in the day that I brought them out of the land of Egypt, concerning burnt offerings or sacrifices. But this is what I commanded them, saying, 'Obey My voice, and I will be your God, and you shall be My people. And walk in all the ways that I have commanded you, that it may be well with you.'" He suggested I read Isaiah 1:11–20. His point was that living a holy life and praying was more important than having a sacrifice.

The Chasidic Jew concluded by stating two things that would stay with me for years to come. First, because God is Love, he didn't understand why God's love could not be unconditional. Second, he thought I had a very legalistic view of God and of His Love, because I believed that God was incapable of forgiving us or loving us without a sacrifice.

We parted peacefully, and I did not let him know that I was taken aback at being accused by an Orthodox Jew, of *all* people, of having a legalistic view of God and His Love! I had always thought of Orthodox Jews as being the pinnacle of legalism and juridicalism, and now, as a Christian "saved by grace," I was being accused of having a juridical view of salvation. I tucked what he said into the back of my mind. Only years later, after I became an Orthodox Christian, did his accusation make any sense. What I did not realize then, but do now, was that what I had told him reflected a view of atonement popularized in the eleventh century by Anselm, who is often considered to be the originator of the Scholastic school of theology.

Anselm's view of atonement became known as the second major theory of atonement in the West. This theory, which replaced the ransom/bargain theory, has come to be called the "debt" or "satisfaction" theory. It was based in part on the concept of total depravity, which posits that man's sin against God (which is total) must be punished by God absolutely. According to the debt/satisfaction theory, God's honor and justice demanded that to avoid punishment, the debt owed Him by the human race must be paid or satisfied. By ourselves we could not pay the debt owed God, because we are all fallen and sinful. Only Jesus Christ could pay what we owe to God, because He is sinless and perfect. In dying on the cross, Christ completely paid this debt for each of us. If we believe in Jesus' substitutionary atonement, then we are forgiven, and God is free to bestow on us His grace and mercy.

In the ransom/bargain theory of atonement, the debt was owed to the devil. In the debt/satisfaction theory of atonement, the debt was owed to God. In this understanding, even if we repent, God is unable to forgive us our sins outright because He is constrained by the demands of what is called divine justice. Divine justice and offended honor demand a payment, a sacrifice, and a punishment to meet the demands of justice before God can forgive us. It seemed to me that God was being presented as a prisoner of His own justice. Though God is Love, unless His fierce wrath was placated He had no choice in this view but to punish sinners.

The central assumption of this non-Orthodox legal and punitive view of God is that He was "under necessity" to pronounce the legal sentence of death on all humanity, because we have all inherited the guilt of original sin. This view expresses two assumptions about divine justice: first, it is essentially penal and punitive; and second, this penal and punitive justice is in some sense necessary. Therefore, being just, God *must* punish the impenitent and unbelieving by sentencing them to hell, where they spend eternity in torment separated from His Presence.

This concept of offended honor seemed to me to have more to do with the medieval code of chivalry than with the Gospel. By failing to punish impenitence with everlasting torment, God would be like a knight failing to punish an insult to his betrothed with death. God *must* reward evil with evil, or else He would be seen to take evil lightly. This theory presents God as the personification of inexorable, retributive, penal exactitude, like the "hanging judge" of the Old West. Central to the debt/satisfaction theory of atonement is the concept of "necessity." This necessity is akin to the impersonal Fate (Gr. *anangke*) that governed pagan gods. The problem with this concept of necessity is that it can create a God above God. If God is truly sovereign, then He is under no necessity whatsoever. He is what He is and will do what He will do without constraints.

An essentially legal view of sin leads inevitably to a legal view of salvation. If salvation is primarily about the Father punishing the Incarnate Son in our stead, then as a judicial necessity our failure to believe in Jesus compels God to punish us. Such theologies see the Cross as saving us from the punitive, legally determined wrath of God—God the Son saving us from God the Father. In this view, I wondered, is God really the obstacle that must be overcome, and must He overcome Himself for our salvation? Viewing God as vindictive can cause us great damage, particularly if we believe that the physical and spiritual harm we inflict on ourselves through sin comes from God. Confusing our guilt with God's anger can cause us to fear and flee from Him, which only weakens us further, continuing the vicious circle.

In the passage previously quoted from St. Gregory the Theologian, he clearly exposes the ransom/bargain theory of atonement, in which a debt is owed to the devil. The concluding portion of this passage directly addresses the debt/satisfaction theory, in which a debt is owed to God the Father.

> Now, since a ransom belongs only to him who holds in bondage, I ask to whom was this offered, and for what cause? . . . if to the Father, I ask first, how? For it was not by Him that we were being oppressed; and next, On what principle did the Blood of His Only begotten Son delight the Father, Who would not receive even Isaac, when he was being offered by his father, but changed the sacrifice, putting a ram in the place of the human victim? Is it not evident that the Father accepts Him, but neither asked for Him nor demanded Him; but on account of the Incarnation, and because Humanity must be sanctified by the Humanity of God, that He might deliver us Himself, and overcome the tyrant, and draw us to Himself by the mediation of His Son, Who also arranged this to the honour of the Father, Whom it is manifest that He obeys in all things? So much we have said of Christ; the greater part of what we might say shall be reverenced with silence.[24]

The debt/satisfaction theory became the dominant theory of atonement in virtually all Western churches. It is reflected in the words of many Western hymns, including the lyrics of a popular

Protestant hymn, "He paid a debt He did not owe; I owed a debt I could not pay."

Indulgences: Punitive or Remedial? ◆

A NOTEWORTHY OUTGROWTH OF THE DEBT/SATISFACTION THEORY of atonement was the development of indulgences in the Roman Catholic Church. Although the Catholics never took the concept of total depravity as far as the Calvinists, they had a tendency to view spirituality in legal terms. This is perhaps best exemplified through the practice of indulgences.

For years I had thought that indulgences were a medieval practice that was abused and eventually contributed to the sixteenth-century Protestant Reformation. I assumed the practice had been discontinued after the Reformation. I was wrong. What a surprise when some of my children, who were attending a Roman Catholic parochial school at the time, came home with cards that had a picture of a saint on one side and on the other side prayers for that saint's intercession. Below the prayers was written, "Indulgence, 300 days, each time. Plenary, once a month, on the usual conditions."

A number of years later, Pope John Paul II declared the year 2000 to be a jubilee year in which special indulgences would be granted. By doing certain acts and praying specific prayers, the faithful would have their sins pardoned, punishment lessened, and amount of time spent suffering in purgatory decreased by specific amounts.[25]

Certainly, it is good to encourage good deeds, special acts of love and kindness, and acts of personal denial. But the framework in which these good things were being encouraged consisted of detailed bookkeeping of spiritual merits, with its primary goal being the deterrence of God's punishment. This understanding could, it seemed to me, only develop within a culture that encouraged a juridical concept of virtue. Let me explain.

Expanding on the debt/satisfaction theory, the Roman Catholic Church created the concept of a "treasury of merits." They hold that the "extra merits" of Christ and the saints can be applied or deposited into this treasury. The Church then mediates these extra merits to the faithful in the form of indulgences. An indulgence is "the extra-sacramental remission of the temporal punishment due, in God's justice, to sin that has been forgiven, which remission is granted by the Church in the exercise of the power of the keys, through the application of the superabundant merits of Christ and of the saints, and for some just and reasonable motive."[26]

A plenary indulgence is a special type of indulgence providing a full pardon for sins committed. That is, though the sins themselves may already have been forgiven by God, a certain amount of punishment is still due for those sins and must be exacted, either in this life or in purgatory. The *Catholic Encyclopedia* defines plenary indulgence thus:

> By a plenary indulgence is meant the remission of the entire temporal punishment due to sin so that no further expiation is required in Purgatory. A partial indulgence commutes only a certain portion of the penalty; and this portion is determined in accordance with the penitential discipline of the early Church. To say that an indulgence of so many days or years is granted means that it cancels an amount of purgatorial punishment equivalent to that which would have been remitted, in the sight of God, by the performance of so many days or years of the ancient canonical penance. Here, evidently, the reckoning makes no claim to absolute exactness; it has only a relative value. God

alone knows what penalty remains to be paid and what its precise amount is in severity and duration.[27]

Here we see how the non-Orthodox Christian interpretation of the Fall combined with the debt/satisfaction theory of atonement to devise a complex legal system and a juridical view of spirituality and salvation.

It was revealing to me that Orthodox Christianity and Orthodox Judaism share a much more benevolent view of God and of judgment. How refreshing it was for me to discover in Orthodoxy a rejection of the debt/satisfaction theory of atonement that so pervades non-Orthodox churches.

The Penal Substitutionary Theory of Atonement ∽

THE PROTESTANT REFORMERS BUILT UPON THE SATISFACTION theory and developed a third theory of atonement called the "penal substitutionary" theory. Whereas the debt/satisfaction theory emphasizes that Christ paid the debt that we owe God, the penal theory emphasizes that Christ received the punishment we deserve. In this view, justice demands that our sins be punished. In suffering and dying on the Cross, Christ received God's punishment for us so that we no longer need to be punished. This view has gained great popularity and is perhaps the best known of the three theories of atonement.

On a popular level the ransom/bargain, debt/satisfaction, and penal substitutionary theories of atonement are combined, so that in Christ's death payment is seen to be made to both the devil and God the Father, and additionally the Son of God is punished for our sins.

An interesting modern variation of this penal theory of atonement which has gained prominence among some Protestant circles is the view that because Jesus suffered the punishment due us, we should not have to suffer in this life or in the next. This view, called the gospel of success, claims that if Christians in faith claim healing derived from Jesus' suffering on our behalf, we need not suffer and will be prosperous in every way. This extreme view is held by a narrow but growing segment of Protestants.

Sinners in the Hands of an Angry God ∾

IT IS DIFFICULT FOR ME, LIVING IN SUCH A SECULAR AND PROSPEROUS age, to fully comprehend the tremendous impact the juridical understanding of atonement has had on the West. The view of God as a fierce Judge, angry, vindictive, pouring out His divine wrath on His Son Jesus because of "love" for us sinners, appears ludicrous to many non-Christians. It explains in part why so many are repulsed by institutional churches and only admit to admiring Jesus on a strictly private and non-institutional level.

As I shared before, I have enjoyed a number of strongly Calvinistic Christian friends through the years, especially in my youth, some of whom I would consider to be far more spiritual than I. They greatly admire the American colonial leaders of what is called the Great Awakening, which took place in the early 1770s and included two prominent evangelists, Jonathan Edwards and George Whitefield, both fierce preachers and staunch defenders of the Calvinist and Puritan heritage. They had a tremendous impact on the American colonies of their time.

Following is a condensed version of Jonathan Edwards' most famous sermon, "Sinners in the Hands of an Angry God." It is a historically memorable sermon because it is representative of a view of God that permeated Western Christianity following the eleventh-century Great Schism between the Orthodox East and the Roman Catholic West. Note how often the word "wrath" is used.

They deserve to be cast into hell; so that divine justice never stands in the way, it makes no objection against God's using his power at any moment to destroy them. Yea, on the contrary, justice calls aloud for an infinite punishment of their sins. They are already under a sentence of condemnation to hell. . . . The wrath of God burns against them, their damnation does not slumber; the pit is prepared, the fire is made ready, the furnace is now hot, ready to receive them; the flames do now rage and glow. The glittering sword is whet, and held over them, and the pit hath opened its mouth under them. . . .

God has laid himself under no obligation, by any promise to keep any natural man out of hell one moment. . . . So that, thus it is that natural men are held in the hand of God, over the pit of hell; they have deserved the fiery pit, and are already sentenced to it; and God is dreadfully provoked, his anger is as great towards them as to those that are actually suffering the executions of the fierceness of his wrath in hell, and they have done nothing in the least to appease or abate that anger, neither is God in the least bound by any promise to hold them up one moment; the devil is waiting for them, hell is gaping for them, the flames gather and flash about them, and would fain lay hold on them, and swallow them up; the fire pent up in their own hearts is struggling to break out . . . all that preserves them every moment is the mere arbitrary will, and uncovenanted, unobliged forbearance of an incensed God. . . .

The wrath of God is like great waters that are dammed for the present; they increase more and more, and rise higher and higher, till an outlet is given; and the longer the stream is stopped, the more rapid and mighty is its course, when once it is let loose. It is true, that judgment against your evil works has not been executed hitherto; the floods of God's vengeance have been withheld; but your guilt in the mean time is constantly increasing, and you are every day treasuring up more wrath; the waters are constantly rising, and waxing more and more mighty; and there is nothing but the mere pleasure of God, that holds the waters back, that are unwilling to be stopped, and press hard to go forward. If God should only withdraw his hand from the flood-gate, it would immediately fly open, and the fiery floods of the fierceness and wrath of God, would rush forth with inconceivable fury, and would come upon you with omnipotent power. . . .

Thus all you that never passed under a great change of heart, by the mighty power of the Spirit of God upon your souls; all you that were never born again, and made new creatures, and raised from being dead in sin, to a state of new, and before altogether unexperienced light and life, are in the hands of an angry God. . . .

The God that holds you over the pit of hell, much as one holds a spider, or some loathsome insect over the fire, abhors you, and is dreadfully provoked: his wrath towards you burns like fire; he looks upon you as worthy of nothing else, but to be cast into the fire; he is of purer eyes than to bear to have you in his sight; you are ten thousand times more abominable in his eyes, than the most hateful venomous serpent is in ours. You have offended him infinitely more than ever a stubborn rebel did his prince; and yet it is nothing but his hand that holds you from falling into the fire every moment. . . .

Consider this, you that are here present, that yet remain in an unregenerate state. That God will execute the fierceness of his anger, implies, that he will inflict wrath without any pity. When God beholds the ineffable extremity of your case, and sees your torment to be so vastly disproportioned to your strength, and sees how your poor soul is crushed, and sinks down, as it were, into an infinite gloom; he will have no compassion upon you, he will not forbear the executions of his wrath, or in the least lighten his hand; there shall be no moderation or mercy, nor will God then at all stay his rough wind; he will have no regard to your welfare, nor be at all careful lest you should suffer too much in any other sense, than only that you shall not suffer beyond what strict justice requires. . . . God will have no other use to put you to, but to suffer misery; you shall be continued in being to no other end; for you will be a vessel of wrath fitted to destruction; and there will be no other use of this vessel, but to be filled full of wrath. . . .

When the great and angry God hath risen up and executed his awful vengeance on the poor sinner, and the wretch is actually suffering the infinite weight and power of his indignation, then will God call upon the whole universe to behold that awful majesty and mighty power that is to be seen in it. It is everlasting wrath. . . . For "who knows the power of God's anger?" . . . Therefore, let every one that is out of Christ, now awake and fly from the wrath to come. The wrath of Almighty God is now undoubtedly hanging over a great part of this congregation: Let every one fly out of Sodom: "Haste and escape for your lives, look not behind you, escape to the mountain, lest you be consumed."[28]

Certainly there is need to recognize that but for the grace of God we would all descend into the abyss of everlasting sorrow and pain. Focusing on the judgment we deserve can bring some to repentance. Yet I recoil at this presentation of God as vindictive, indeed ruthless. I cannot accept that this wrath somehow expresses a deeper love. Certainly the sermon does not present God as loving His enemies. It is no wonder that so many presented with this image of God recoil and pursue other religions, or become atheists and anti-Christian.

Too Hard to Bear: The Moral Exemplar Theory of Atonement ∾

I HAD NEVER BEEN DRAWN TO WHAT ARE CALLED LIBERAL CHURCHES. As an evangelical Protestant I had some degree of contempt for them, as I felt they so watered down the gospel that it became virtually unrecognizable. It was difficult for me to find positive qualities in churches that would deny or question the basic dogmas and doctrines of the Christian Faith, such as the inspiration of sacred Scripture, miracles, the Virgin Birth of Christ, His Resurrection and Second Coming. What I did begin to see and appreciate more after becoming Orthodox were the *reasons* that these Christians had drifted into their current theological camp.

A driving force was a deep-seated reaction against viewing God the way many conservative Christians did, as angry and vindictive. The liberals seemed to be recoiling from both traditional Protestant and Catholic views of God. On one hand, there was the wrathful God of the radical Puritan Protestants, who taught total depravity and the predestining of the lost to hellfire. And on the other hand, there was the juridical God of traditional Roman Catholics, who presented a legalistic view of spirituality. The nineteenth- and twentieth-century liberal Christian desire to discover a softer, gentler, and more approachable God led to their reinvigorating a fourth view of atonement, called the "moral exemplar" theory, first popularized in the eleventh century by the theologian Peter Abelard.

Shortly after Anselm presented his debt/satisfaction view of atonement, Peter Abelard reacted energetically against Anselm's teaching by asking why God demands satisfaction for sins that He can simply forgive. Abelard held that the Father does not *need* the sacrifice of His Son and that the primary purpose of Christ's life was to provide the perfect moral model and example of love for us to follow. Abelard deemphasized the crucifixion and emphasized Christ's life of love. Hundreds of years later, Abelard's views were taken up by liberal theologians who sought to emphasize a social gospel of softness, kindness, and love.

Though this view of Christ is to some degree true—Jesus says "Follow Me"—the Orthodox hold that the moral exemplar view is inadequate. It underemphasizes the uniqueness of Jesus' life, death, and Resurrection. Also, it ignores the spiritual, mystical, ontological, and eschatological—indeed the cosmic—dimension of Christ's life and instead confines His life to a strictly earthly, moral dimension.

The Purpose of the Sacrificial System ❧

SACRIFICES AND SACRIFICIAL SYSTEMS ARE PERPLEXING FOR MOST modern, civilized people; they are typically viewed as primitive and disgusting. Some even call Christianity "a bloody religion." Nevertheless, because sacrifice has traditionally been understood as indispensable for atonement and salvation, it seemed necessary to understand it better.

As I researched the subject, I discovered an essential aspect of the sacrificial system described in the Old Testament: the outer act of sacrifice should reflect the inner state of the offerer seeking personal reconciliation with God. The goal of the sacrifice was to gain interior cleansing and change of heart, *not to change God.* This contrasts with the pagan view, in which the efficacy of the sacrifice is not at all dependent on the state of the individual offering it. Its purpose is not to change the state of the offerer, but to appease and change the deity. This attitude is reflected in a proverb of the ancient Vedic civilization in India: "Here is the butter; where are thy gifts?"

The purpose of ancient pagan sacrifices was to gain the attention of and influence deities. The sacrifice was a form of magic, focused on gaining influence, control, or power over the elements, animals, people, and most importantly, the deities. Because magic involves the invisible realm, some think it encompasses some degree of spirituality. But in reality it has a materialistic and utilitarian motivation; its goal is not to gain interior change, healing, or love, but instead to gain control over other people and objects. Magic is concerned with gaining power over that which is exterior to the human heart rather than over that which is interior.

As the purpose of casting magic spells could be to control people, similarly the pagan sacrifice was a means of casting a spell on the deity so as to influence and even control it. This attitude is seen in another ancient Vedic proverb: "The sacrificer hunts Indra like game, and holds him fast as the fowler does the bird; the god is a wheel which the singer understands how to turn." Pagan sacrifices could be offered to appease, to seek general favor, to have a request fulfilled, or to change the course of nature, but they were *not* for the purpose of changing the sacrificer's own interior life or to gain love.

While researching how sacrifice was viewed in the Bible, I realized that it was quite different from what I had thought. I found at least three purposes of sacrifice.

First, sacrifice was viewed as a gift. It is returning to God what is already His, on the assumption that all we are and have were created by Him and are His. In addition to animal sacrifices, the ancient Hebrews made offerings of fruits, grain, wine, and incense. These offerings, mingled with an inner attitude of repentance, expressed dependence on God and His love. The emphasis was *not* on the destruction of that which was offered.

In examining the sacrificial system, I discovered many kinds of sacrifices. The slaughter of the animal prior to the actual offering was often carried out by the offerer, not by the priest. A verbal confession of specific sins often accompanied the sacrifice. For example, when a trespass offering was brought the Scriptures say, "And it shall be, when he is guilty in any of these matters, that *he shall confess that he has sinned in that thing;* and he shall bring his trespass offering to the LORD for his sin which he has committed. . . . The priest shall make atonement for him, for his sin that he has committed in any of these matters; and it shall be forgiven him" (Leviticus 5:5, 6, 13, emphasis mine).

For some reason, I had always assumed that the confession was nonverbal and private, not involving anyone else. I supposed that it was sort of like Protestant confession, secret, just me and God, no one else's business. Now I discovered confession as verbal, specific, and spoken to a priest. The confession was not optional; the sacrifice was not acceptable unless accompanied by an expression of sorrow for sins committed. Could this be viewed as an embryonic form of what developed into the Christian rite of confession?

Second, sacrifice was a form of communion. Sacrifice expressed a desire for communion with God. The portion of the sacrifice that was burned was thought to have been received or consumed by God. Remains were often eaten as a sacrificial meal by the offerer and the priest. The consumption of the same sacrifice by both God and the one presenting the sacrifice indicates the establishing of a covenant or communion between the two. In fact, the actual consumption by the worshiper and/or the priest was an essential reason most sacrificial animals were killed. It was a sharing by the offerer in the life of God. This aspect of sacrifice is also present in the Christian understanding of the Eucharist, as Christ the Lamb of God, the forever Sacrifice, is consumed in the eating of His Glorified Body and Blood.

I learned that the meaning of the word "sacrifice" is not "vicarious victim," but "holy gift." In Hebrew, "sacrifice" is *korban,* from the root *karov,* which means "[come] close [to God]" or communing with God. The Hebrew word *ola,* which is often translated as "holocaust," means "that which goes up." The Septuagint translated this into the Greek word *holokauston,* a combination of *holes,* "whole," and *kaustos,* "burnt." In some English translations *ola* is translated as "whole burnt offering," because the offering was unique among sacrifices in that it was entirely consumed by fire. Combining these word themes, a holocaust sacrifice is a holy gift, complete, whole, offered in its entirety to God and representing the totality of the penitent's life, enabling him to ascend to and approach God without destruction.

The Old Testament sacrifices were not essentially substitutionary, in which animals take the place of those desiring to be forgiven in order that they might appease an angry God. If some viewed them that way, this was in part due to the ongoing and pervasive influence of surrounding pagan cultures. Virtually all such cultures had a pantheon of deities that were angry, vindictive, capricious, even mischievous. In the effort to appease an angry deity, not only were animals ritually offered, but humans as well. The indigenous Canaanite culture was described in Scripture as offering infant sacrifices to the deity Molech. In contrast, the Jews strictly forbade human sacrifice. In fact, such sacrifices, along with other diabolical deeds, were given as the primary reason for upheavals among the pagans (see Leviticus 18:21–29; 20:2–5; Deuteronomy 12:30, 31).

Christians view the temple sacrifices as pedagogical, as types and shadows of the sacrifice of the true Lamb of God, Christ, who in His death takes away the sins of the world. His sacrifice is the offering back to God of a perfect portion of His creation as an acceptable gift and an act of perfect worship. In this understanding, man's consumption of the sacrifice of Christ with a repentant heart and desire to live a holy life at every level was not an afterthought; it was the goal of the entire process. Emphasis is not placed solely on the sacrificial act, but on each person's participation in that sacrifice, manifest in repentance and a changed life.

Many Scripture passages in the Old Testament indicate that sacrifices alone could not take away sins; a repentant heart was necessary. The prophet Micah said regarding the inadequacies of sacrifice:

> With what shall I come before the Lord,
> *And* bow myself before the High God?
> Shall I come before Him with burnt offerings,
> With calves a year old?
> Will the Lord be pleased with thousands of rams,
> Ten thousand rivers of oil?
> Shall I give my firstborn *for* my transgression,
> The fruit of my body *for* the sin of my soul?
> He has shown you, O man, what *is* good;
> And what does the Lord require of you
> But to do justly,
> To love mercy,
> And to walk humbly with your God?
> (Micah 6:6–8)

Likewise in the Psalms of David, God says to Israel:

> "If I were hungry, I would not tell you;
> For the world *is* Mine, and all its fullness.
> Will I eat the flesh of bulls,
> Or drink the blood of goats?
> Offer to God thanksgiving,
> And pay your vows to the Most High.
> Call upon Me in the day of trouble;
> I will deliver you, and you shall glorify Me."
> (Psalm 50:12–15)

> For You do not desire sacrifice, or else I would give *it*;
> You do not delight in burnt offering.
> The sacrifices of God *are* a broken spirit,
> A broken and a contrite heart—
> These, O God, You will not despise.
> (Psalm 51:16, 17)

> Sacrifice and offering You did not desire;
> My ears You have opened.
> Burnt offering and sin offering You did not require.
> Then I said, "Behold, I come;
> In the scroll of the book *it is* written of me.
> I delight to do Your will, O my God,
> And Your law *is* within my heart."
> (Psalm 40:6–8)

Propitiation or Expiation? ❧

THE THIRD PURPOSE OF THE SACRIFICIAL SYSTEM WAS TO PROVIDE expiation. Whereas propitiation implies that in the sacrifice God's anger is appeased, in expiation the emphasis is on the change that takes place in the offerer.

One amusing aspect of being of Jewish descent is that people assume I am an expert on the subject of sacrifices. The Old Testament describes in detail many types of sacrifices offered for different purposes. Most people have absolutely no interest in this subject but assume that I do. I can somewhat appreciate their assumption because my father was a Levite. Should I therefore have some natural affinity for sacrifices?

But one thing I did know about the Jewish view of sacrifices and offerings was that their purpose was expiatory rather than propitiatory. As a Protestant Christian, I had assumed that the rabbinic Jewish view distorted the Old Testament Scriptures in order not to accept the propitiatory sacrifice of Christ. As an Orthodox Christian, I have begun to understand that the biblical view of sacrifice is essentially expiatory rather than propitiatory, and in that regard Judaism has a commonality with Orthodox Christianity.

For the Jews, offering a sacrifice to God was an act of self-denial, an aspect of purification. Orthodoxy taught me a new view of sacrifice: The sacredness of the blood and its efficacy consists not in what the offering of the blood does to God (to influence or change God), but in what it does to the offerer (to influence and change him). When the offerer places his hands on the head of the animal to be offered, he indicates that the offering is being given in his name and for his benefit. It does not imply a magical transference of sins from the offerer to the animal being sacrificed. Discarding sin from one's heart and life should be so easy!

So when Orthodox read a verse like "Christ died for our sins according to the Scriptures" (1 Corinthians 15:3), it is understood to mean that Christ died *for us*—to heal us, to change us, to make us more godlike—not that He died *instead of us*. The ultimate purpose of His death is to *change us,* not to avert the wrath of God.

Scripture and the patristic teaching of the Church clearly and extensively present that Jesus, the Lamb of God, was sacrificed for us and is our atonement. It is helpful to understand the words used in the original languages, but I was disappointed to discover that due to theological bias, words are often translated so as to miscommunicate the sense of the original. For example, a most significant Greek word, *hilasmos,* is often translated as "propitiation," and also as "atonement," "expiation," "mercy," or "grace."

Though both propitiation and expiation include the concept of being made acceptable, enabling us to draw near to God, a significant difference exists between the two words. Expiation is *directed toward us*, or more specifically, toward something in us that prevents the offering of perfect worship. It changes man's actual condition or state, the same way that bleach changes a stain, as opposed to changing something outside of us, such as God's will. In contrast, propitiation seeks to change God's offended will and achieve a forgiveness that He cannot grant without that appeasement. Thus, while propitiation seeks to assuage divine wrath (assuming it exists), it does not claim to strengthen our condition.

St. Anthony the Great (fourth century) explains the difference between the concepts of propitiation and expiation most clearly:

> God is good, dispassionate, and immutable. Now someone who thinks it reasonable and true to affirm that God does not change, may well ask how, in that case, it is possible to speak of God as rejoicing over those who are good and showing mercy to those who honor Him, while turning away from the wicked and being angry with sinners. To this it must be answered that God neither rejoices nor

grows angry, for to rejoice and to be offended are passions; nor is He won over by the gifts of those who honor Him, for that would mean He is swayed by pleasure. It is not right to imagine that God feels pleasure or displeasure in a human way. He is good, and He only bestows blessings and never does harm, remaining always the same. We men, on the other hand, if we remain good through resembling God, are united to Him; but if we become evil through not resembling God, we are separated from Him. By living in holiness we cleave to God; but by becoming wicked we make Him our enemy. It is not that He grows angry with us in an arbitrary way, but it is our own sins that prevent God from shining within us, and expose us to demons who punish us. And if through prayer and acts of compassion we gain release from our sins, this does not mean that we have won God over and made Him change, but that through our actions and our turning to God, we have cured our wickedness and so once more have enjoyment of God's goodness. Thus to say that God turns away from the wicked is like saying that the sun hides itself from the blind.[29]

Chapter 16

What Is *Salvation?*

THE ORTHODOX CHRISTIAN UNDERSTANDING OF ATONEMENT is incarnational. It has as its basis not the law or the courtroom, but God's unconditional love and grace. We begin with the understanding that forgiveness and atonement are not essentially legal or juridical concepts. They are principally therapeutic, organic, synergistic, transformational, and ultimately ontological in nature. In fact, the Greek word translated as "salvation" is *soterias*, whose root meaning is "health." So being saved means more than being saved *from* something, such as death or hell; it also means being healed or made whole. When Jesus says, "Your faith has *saved* you" (Luke 7:50), He means, "Your faith has *healed* you," or "Your faith has *made you whole*." Forgiveness and atonement pertain to God's participation in His creation in order to renew His image and likeness in us, bringing us to wholeness and fulfillment.

The biblical and theological terminology I had been familiar with before becoming Orthodox dealt with justification and atonement as forensic categories pertaining to legal concepts. These included terms such as covenant, justification, judgment, judge, atonement, redemption, breaking and fulfillment of law and commandments, retribution, imputation, pardon, debt, payment, ransom, and propitiation. Such terms convey the sense that salvation is primarily a juridical issue that deals with morality. Faith in Christ's salvific work is viewed as the means by which sins can be canceled so that God will see us as if we had not sinned. Saving faith tends to be understood and applied juridically.

God as "The Lover of Mankind" ∾

NO DOUBT BOTH THE SCRIPTURES AND THE THEOLOGY OF THE Church are permeated by juridical language. I did not want to ignore this language or attempt to explain it away. My desire was to more fully understand and appreciate it. I found at least two reasons such terms are used. First, there *is* a sense in which our relationship with God and overcoming sin, death, and the devil can be understood in juridical terms. This is particularly true in the Old Testament. Salvation has many facets and aspects, and a distinctive understanding will develop depending on what perspective is stressed.

I was already familiar with the concept of *progressive revelation*, made clear by the postbiblical writings of the church fathers and the ecumenical councils, in which God is ever more manifest and truth ever more clearly seen. This process brought about a transformation of understanding in which juridical concepts and terminology were increasingly viewed not simply in a new, but in a more intense light.

Secondly, it became apparent that God often deals with people on the level at which they are living, and then moves them to a higher plane. The culture in which Israel was immersed tended to include strong influences that viewed God in juridical terms. This was natural to the times and the popular view of gods in general, and of the God of Israel in particular. The view of God as a Judge whose anger must be placated did help, and can in fact continue to help, people live more spiritually. But it has its limitations. It reminded me of the way fear of punishment inhibits children from being naughty. It does serve its purpose. But for the mature, love is a far greater and more enduring motivator than fear. No doubt the two synergize to some extent.

Orthodox Christians are invited to receive Holy Communion with the proclamation, "With fear of God and faith and love, draw near." The progression is fascinating. We begin with fear. King David said, "The *fear* of the LORD is the beginning of wisdom" (Psalm 111:10, emphasis mine). David's son King Solomon said, "Let us hear the conclusion of the whole matter: / *Fear* God and keep His commandments, / For this is man's all" (Ecclesiastes 12:13, emphasis mine). From fear we move on to faith, which acts as a bridge between fear and love, and we conclude with love. St. John, who is called the disciple of love, wrote, "And we have known and believed the love that God has for us. *God is love*, and he who abides in love abides in God, and God in him. . . . There is no fear in love; but *perfect love casts out fear*, because fear involves torment. But he who fears has not been made perfect in love" (1 John 4:16, 18, emphasis mine).

As I became more immersed in Orthodoxy, I began to experience God not only as Judge, but as He is referred to in Orthodox services: "the Lover of Mankind." In my transition I did not want to diminish the importance of "tough love." Rather, I wanted to provide a corrective to the horrendous popular notion that has developed in much of the West, in which the Christian God is viewed as vindictive, unsympathetic, distant, a tyrant who has no qualms about sending all humans except a very few chosen elect to everlasting hellfire.

Orthodox incarnational theology teaches that God Himself, the second Person of the Trinity, became incarnate not in order to pay a debt to the devil or to God the Father, nor to be a substitutionary offering to appease a just God, but in order to rescue us from our fallen condition and transform us, enabling us to become godlike. That is, the way God chose to deliver us from our condition—our illness, fallenness, mortality, corruption, and sin—was by taking upon Himself our human nature and participating with us in the limitations that creaturehood encompasses. Forgiving our sins is part and parcel of a much larger whole, as forgiveness in itself is not enough to ensure healing, purification, illumination, wholeness, and transfiguration. Actual organic participation in the life of the Incarnate God is required, in addition to being forgiven.

The Greek fathers speak of a triple barrier between God and man: the barrier between the uncreated and the created; the barrier of sin; and the barrier of death. God overcomes the barrier of nature in the Incarnation, which unites the divine and human natures (without confusing them) and thus raises human nature to divine fullness (John 1:12, 13). He overcomes the barrier of sin on the cross (Romans 8:2–4), and He overcomes the barrier of death in His glorious Resurrection on the third day (John 14:19). Salvation is not an end in itself, but the means to an end. We are saved *from* something (namely, death, sin, and the devil) in order to be saved *for* something else (union with God). Union with God is a journey that begins in this life, and because God is infinite, the journey continues forever.

Diagnosing the Disease of Sin ᘓ

To understand the cure, it was necessary to grasp the disease called sin. I knew that for the Orthodox, sin is more than breaking a rule, and forgiveness more than God's pardon for not keeping the Law. I discovered that Orthodoxy views sin as the denial of love, as the denial of life itself. Sin is turning away from God. It is a sickness, primarily spiritual, that has spread to our flesh. So for us, sin is more than "missing the mark," or a moral shortcoming, or the failure to live up to some external code of behavior. Sin is *the failure to realize life as love and communion*—the failure to be whole, healthy, complete. It is the rejection of personal communion with God. Sin is restricting ourselves, isolating ourselves in order to live autonomous, independent, and self-sufficient lives. In a sense, sin is an obsessive *self-love*. For the Orthodox, the absolute autonomy of the individual is sin, indeed *the* "original sin." Our offense against God is not that we have "offended His honor," but rather that we have turned from life itself. Sin is the denial of God's image in man and of God Himself. It is self-destructive. God hates sin, not because of what it does to Him, but because of what it does to us.

In non-Orthodox theology, sin, righteousness, heaven, and hell tend to be unrelated to our own essential being. In the Western understanding, sin is a stain on our record which the blood of Jesus can wash away. Righteousness is inclined to be viewed as a credit which God places in our account, or which in the life to come guarantees greater rewards and more elaborate crowns. In contrast, Orthodoxy views sin as a *state of being* in which we at a core level turn from and resist God's love. Therefore, when God forgives us, this is understood as being much more than an act of forgiving transgressions or specific immoral actions. For us, to be forgiven means to be embraced by God's love and brought into ever deeper union (without confusion) and communion with Him. It is to be purified, purged, illumined, and ultimately transfigured organically, within the very essence of our being. Forgiveness is therapeutic and includes the process of healing and removal of sin from our lives.

An example: If our spiritual heart is rotting, it gives off a foul odor, putrid and offensive to God and man alike. Viewing forgiveness of sins as strictly a legal enactment by which our status is now made "acceptable" to God is akin to pouring perfume on the putrid and rotting heart to remove the stench. For the Orthodox, forgiveness of sin is not a change in legal status concerning the exterior of our life, but a change in the very *condition and state* of our heart, inner being, and essence. Forgiveness of sin is the *actual removal* of sin, which includes our effort and participation. It replaces or heals our heart, removing its stench. Forgiveness of sin addresses not only the odor, but at an organic level, its cause.

The Language of Salvation in the New Testament ∾

ORTHODOXY INTRODUCED ME TO A WHOLE SPECTRUM OF terminology that spoke of salvation in a non-juridical manner. It was not that I hadn't read these expressions before; they simply did not enter my everyday understanding relating to atonement, justification, and redemption. The Orthodox understand that in Christ's death and Resurrection we are united with Him, not in a legal, positional, or virtual sense, but in a very real, literal sense. This is possible because in the Incarnation, Christ took upon Himself our human nature and united it to His Person. In His Passion, death, Resurrection, and Ascension, the common human nature He shares with us is now glorified.

The Scripture uses imagery that reinforces this concept of organic participation and unity with Christ in His human nature. For example, unity with Christ is presented as being like that between parts of a body. St. Paul often speaks about salvation as being included within the *Body of Christ*.

> For as the body is one and has many members, but all the members of that one body, being many, are one body, so also *is* Christ. For by one Spirit we were all baptized into one body—whether Jews or Greeks, whether slaves or free—and have all been made to drink into one Spirit. For in fact the body is not one member but many.

. . . Now you are the body of Christ, and members individually. (1 Corinthians 12:12–14, 27, emphasis mine)

He reaffirms the actuality of our unity with Christ's humanity by employing terms including "united with," "with," "together with," "in," "live in," "into," "share," "put on," and so forth. The use of this terminology demonstrates that we are able to be united with Christ in His Baptism and Resurrection, not figuratively but actually, as we die to sin in the flesh and share in His Resurrection. We die *with* Christ and we are raised *with* Christ as we participate in His life. In Holy Communion we partake in faith of His glorified humanity, and His humanity and our humanity become one. Our hope is that though we do not now fully experience glorification, in the life to come we will. St. Paul continues:

> Or do you not know that as many of us as were baptized *into* Christ Jesus were baptized *into* His death? Therefore we were buried *with* Him through baptism *into* death, that just as Christ was raised from the dead by the glory of the Father, even so we also should walk in newness of life. For if we have been *united* together in the likeness of His death, certainly we also shall be in the *likeness* of His resurrection, knowing this, that our old man was crucified *with* Him, that the body of sin might be done away with, that we should no longer be slaves of sin. For he who has died has been freed from sin. Now if we died *with* Christ, we believe that we shall also live *with* Him, knowing that Christ, having been raised from the dead, dies no more. Death no longer has dominion over Him. For the death that He died, He died to sin once for all; but the life that He lives, He lives to God. Likewise you also, reckon yourselves to be dead indeed to sin, but alive to God

in Christ Jesus our Lord. (Romans 6:3–11, emphasis mine)

He also says:

> I have been crucified *with* Christ; it is no longer I who live, but Christ lives *in me*; and the life which I now live in the flesh I live by faith in the Son of God, who loved me and gave Himself for me. (Galatians 2:20, emphasis mine)

> But God, who is rich in mercy, because of His great love with which He loved us, even when we were dead in trespasses, made us alive *together with* Christ (by grace you have been saved), and raised us up *together*, and made us sit *together* in the heavenly places *in* Christ Jesus. (Ephesians 2:4–6, emphasis mine)

> If then you were raised *with* Christ, seek those things which are above, where Christ is, sitting at the right hand of God. Set your mind on things above, not on things on the earth. For you died, and your life is hidden *with* Christ *in* God. When Christ who is our life appears, then you also will appear *with* Him in glory. (Colossians 3:1–4, emphasis mine)

During services that relate to baptism the Orthodox sing, "For as many of you as were baptized *into* Christ have *put on* Christ" (Galatians 3:27, emphasis mine).

In John 15 Jesus speaks to His disciples, telling them to "abide in Me," and promising that He will abide in them. He repeats these expressions numerous times. The example He gives is of a vine with branches sharing the same life, which flows from the vine into the branches. He refers to Himself in verse 5, saying, "I am the vine, you are the branches."

In John 17 Jesus prays to God the Father, asking that He be "in" His disciples and that they be "in" the Son and "in" the Father. The term "in" is a significantly more organic term than the popularly used Protestant phrase of having a "personal relationship with"; "being in" implies a union or, as this Scripture states, a "oneness" at the deepest level.

> "I do not pray for these alone, but also for those who will believe in Me through their word; that they all may *be one*, as You, Father, are in Me, and I in You; that they also may be *one in Us* . . . that they may be one just as We are one: *I in them*, and You in Me; that they may be made perfect in one . . . that the love with which You loved Me may be in them, and *I in them*." (John 17:20–26, emphasis mine)

Christ is often called the Bridegroom, and the Church the Bride of Christ. The Bridegroom leaves the Bride, but is to return at the Second Coming for what is called the marriage supper of the Lamb (see Matthew 22:1–14; Ephesians 5:25–32).

In the following passage, St. Paul presents marriage as reflecting the relationship of Christ to the Church, in which Christ is presented at the same time as both husband and head of His body the Church. He concludes by saying that in a mystery the expression that the "two will become one flesh" refers to "Christ and the church."

> Christ is head of the church; and He is the Savior of the body. Therefore, just as the church is subject to Christ,

so let the wives be to their own husbands in everything. Husbands, love your wives, just as Christ also loved the church. . . . *For we are members of His body*, of His flesh and of His bones. "For this reason a man shall leave his father and mother and be joined to his wife, and the two shall become one flesh." *This is a great mystery, but I speak concerning Christ and the church.* (Ephesians 5:23–25, 30–32, emphasis mine).

The terminology used in the above scriptures speaks of salvation as an organic experience that is preeminently non-juridical. The words and phrases used include: being crucified *with*, dying *with*, being buried, resurrected, and living *with* Christ and *in* Him, being *united with* and *together with* Him, as well as *putting on* Christ. They also include *abiding in* Him and He *in* us, being *one with, married to, members of His Body,* and of *one flesh with* Christ.

Placing the Fall, sin, and death into a legal framework leads to viewing the Person and work of Christ as part of that same framework. Accepting our inheritance of Adam's guilt leads to viewing judicial guilt for sin as our main problem, which results in the belief that once divine justice is satisfied on the Cross, redemption is complete. That is why many expressions of Christianity had seemed shallow and simplistic to me: sanctification, virtue, holiness, life in Christ, transfiguration, union and communion with God were held to be added on to redemption and salvation, not integral to their very essence.

It seems that for many non-Orthodox, the Crucifixion practically exhausts the entire dogma of redemption. Some Roman Catholic dogmaticians have even expressly said that the Resurrection of Christ is not a contributing cause of our salvation. Fr. Joseph Pohle, for example, has written, "From the distinctive viewpoint of Soteriology, the Resurrection of Christ was not, strictly speaking, the chief, or even a contributing cause of our redemption. . . . The Catholic Church regards the Resurrection as an integral, though not an essential, element of the atonement."[30]

The Resurrection tends to be seen as an appendix, serving to demonstrate Christ's divinity and His reward by the Father for His sacrifice. This helps to explain why the recent hit movie, *The Passion of the Christ*, devoted 125 minutes to His Passion, including His Crucifixion, and a total of 75 seconds to the Resurrection. I have been told that during the movie's production, a discussion took place about whether the Resurrection scene should even be included.

In contrast, St. Paul made it abundantly clear that there is no such thing as salvation apart from the Resurrection:

> Now if Christ is preached that He has been raised from the dead, how do some among you say that there is no resurrection of the dead? But if there is no resurrection of the dead, then Christ is not risen. And if Christ is not risen, then our preaching is empty and your faith is also empty. Yes, and we are found false witnesses of God, because we have testified of God that He raised up Christ, whom He did not raise up—if in fact the dead do not rise. For if the dead do not rise, then Christ is not risen. And if Christ is not risen, your faith is futile; *you are still in your sins!* Then also those who have fallen asleep in Christ have perished. If in this life only we have hope in Christ, we are of all men the most pitiable. But now Christ is risen from the dead, and has become the firstfruits of those who have fallen asleep. For since by man came death, by Man also came the resurrection of the dead. For as in Adam all die, even so in Christ all shall be made alive. (1 Corinthians 15:12–22, emphasis mine)

Chapter 16 ❧ What *Is* Salvation?

St. Paul says that if Christ is not raised from the dead, then "you are still in your sins." The crucifixion alone is not enough to redeem or save us.

Orthodoxy emphasizes that we tend to sin because we die. We die because we are born in a fallen state in which we have inherited mortality, death, and corruption (but not guilt). Although death is not from God, it is the inevitable result of turning from God. Sinful acts are the rotten fruit or stench given off by death. Our actual sins sprout from the root of death and corruption. The Epistle to the Hebrews speaks of this:

> Inasmuch then as the children have partaken of flesh and blood, He Himself likewise shared in the same, *that through death He might destroy him who had the power of death, that is, the devil, and release those who through fear of death were all their lifetime subject to bondage.* For indeed He does not give aid to angels, but He does give aid to the seed of Abraham. Therefore, in all things He had to be made like His brethren, that He might be a merciful and faithful High Priest in things pertaining to God, to make propitiation [expiation] for the sins of the people. For in that He Himself has suffered, being tempted, He is able to aid those who are tempted. (Hebrews 2:14–18, italics mine)

This *fear of death*, of being mortal, leads us to grasp at illusions such as power, fame, fortune, and self-indulgence in its various forms. The fear of death leads to sin. For the Orthodox, because being born fallen is essentially about *mortality*, salvation is essentially about Christ vanquishing sin, death, and the devil, enabling us to share His life. He destroys the power of the fear of death in our lives, as well as the fear of suffering, pain, sorrow, and abandonment. This is why the Resurrection of our Lord Jesus Christ is of paramount importance in Orthodoxy: sin, Satan, and death, not God's justice or wrath, are the obstacles Christ overcomes for our salvation.

The Language of Salvation in St. Athanasius ∿

AMONG THE POSTAPOSTOLIC CHURCH FATHERS I MOST ADMIRE is the early-fourth-century saint, Athanasius. He was the pivotal defender of the Orthodox Faith against the Arian heresy, which taught that Jesus is not divine but instead a creation of God.

In the early decades of the fourth century, Emperor Constantine had just accepted the Christian Faith and made it legal to be a Christian in the Roman Empire. To his chagrin, he found that because of the rise of the Arian heresy, the Christians were divided and the empire torn apart theologically. So to resolve the issue, in AD 325 Constantine convened a council of bishops and church leaders from throughout the empire. Athanasius attended the council as a deacon from Alexandria, Egypt, and became Arius's primary adversary.

The council promulgated the basic creed of the Christian Church, the Nicene Creed, and condemned Arius and his followers. In spite of the Orthodox effort, the Arians subsequently gained great influence, especially in the eastern provinces; in time a subsequent emperor and many bishops became Arians. During this conflict, St. Athanasius, who had by this time become bishop of Alexandria, was exiled about five times as the Arians took and then lost control of the Alexandrian Church. At one point St. Athanasius was so isolated in his defense of Orthodoxy that the famous expression arose concerning him, *Athanasius contra mundum*—"Athanasius against the world."

During his exiles he spent time with the desert fathers of Egypt and befriended St. Anthony the Great, who lived a life of extreme asceticism as a hermit and is considered to be a spiritual father of monasticism. St. Anthony so loved St. Athanasius that he left the depths of his wilderness isolation in order to help defend his friend in the great city of Alexandria. St. Athanasius in turn was so impressed with St. Anthony's life that he wrote a book entitled *The Life of St. Anthony.*

St. Athanasius was the first person to identify the twenty-seven books of the New Testament in use today. Among the books he wrote, the most famous, *On the Incarnation,* is believed to have been written when he was in his early twenties. C. S. Lewis, in his introduction to the St. Vladimir's Seminary Press edition of the book, writes, "When I first opened his *De Incarnatione [On the Incarnation]* I soon discovered I was reading a masterpiece . . . for only a master mind could have written so deeply on a subject with such classical simplicity."[31]

Because of St. Athanasius's own personal faith and courage, I could not imagine a better book to read to discover how the ancient Church viewed the Incarnation and its accomplishments in terms of atonement, redemption, and salvation. Throughout St. Athanasius's writing I discovered a reaffirmation of the Orthodox Christian understanding of the Incarnation as Jesus taking upon Himself our humanity in order to purify, heal, illumine, and transfigure it. I also found an absence of non-Orthodox views of sacrifice, including substitutionary atonement and satisfying the demands of punitive divine justice.

What Is Not Assumed Is Not Healed ∾

THE ORTHODOX UNDERSTANDING OF THE INCARNATION CENTERS on the concept that what is not assumed is not healed. By this is meant that therapeutic healing is the first stage of movement towards the ultimate goal of becoming transfigured and godlike. This interpretation is found not only in Scripture, but also extensively among the church fathers.

A sampling of St. Athanasius's reasons for the Incarnation follows (note that all emphases are mine). Note how great an emphasis he places on salvation as therapeutic healing, and how little on juridical justification. What St. Athanasius presents is representative of the views of the early fathers.

The Son of God took humanity upon Himself in order:

(1) To heal us

The Incarnation took place "in order *to heal* the existing evil. For that reason, therefore, He was made man, and used the body as His human instrument" (§44, p. 80).

(2) To renew the Image of God within us

". . . *renew His Image* in mankind."

"It was He [Christ] alone, the Image of the Father, Who could recreate man after the Image. In order to effect this re-creation, however, He had first to *do away with death and corruption*. Therefore He assumed a human body, in order that in it death might once for all be destroyed, and that man might be *renewed according to the Image*" (§13, p. 41).

". . . in order that He might *renew mankind made after Himself*" (§14, p. 42).

"Thus by His own power He *restored the whole nature* of man" (§10, p. 36).

St. Athanasius gives an example of a picture to demonstrate how the Image of God in us *can* be renewed. He assumes that we are not totally depraved:

"You know what happens when a portrait that has been painted on a panel becomes obliterated through external stains. The artist does not throw away the panel, but the subject of the portrait has to come and sit for it again, and then the likeness *is re-drawn* on the same material. Even so was it with the All-holy Son of God. He, the Image of the Father, came and dwelt in our midst, in order that He might *renew* mankind made after Himself, and *seek out* His lost sheep, even as He says in the Gospel: 'I came *to seek* and *save* that which is lost.' " (§14, p. 41, quoting Luke 19:10)

(3) To overcome death and give life

"For by the sacrifice of His own body He did two things: He put an end to the law of *death* which barred our way; and He made *a new beginning of life* for us, by giving us hope of *resurrection*" (§10, p. 37).

Many Christians consider the primary purpose for the Incarnation to be Christ's death, with His Resurrection simply vindicating His death. St. Athanasius says the exact opposite, and his statement is shocking. "The *supreme* object of His coming was to bring about *the resurrection* of the body" (§22, p. 52).

"Death had to precede resurrection, for there *could be no resurrection without it*. A secret and unwitnessed death would have left the resurrection without any proof or evidence to support it" (§23, p. 52). That is, Jesus died in order to be resurrected.

(4) To abolish death

". . . so that *in His death* all might die, and the law of *death* thereby be abolished" (§8, p. 34).

"But if death was within the body, woven into its very substance and dominating it as though completely one with it, the need was for *Life* to be woven into it instead."

"Had death been kept from it [the body] by a mere command, it would still have remained *mortal and corruptible, according to its nature*" (§44, p. 81). (That is, legal atonement cannot heal man's nature.)

"By the offering of His own body He abolished the *death* which they had incurred. . . . Now, therefore, when we die we no longer do so as men condemned to death, but as those who are even now *in process of rising*" (§10, p. 37).

It was revealing to find that in the Divine Liturgy, the priest does not say that Jesus' death was a ransom payment to the Father or to the devil, but that it was "a ransom to death." His death delivers us from the actual power, influence, and control the devil has over us—*not* from an imaginary legal "right" that he exercises.

Similarly, the most joyous proclamation repeated at Holy Pascha (Easter) is, "Christ is risen from the dead, trampling down death by death, and upon those in the tombs bestowing life." Jesus died in order to be resurrected. Thus we joyously celebrate not the debt payment to a vindictive Father or to the devil who owns us, but destruction of the power of death and the bestowing of new life. In the following quotation, we see that the adversaries Jesus' death and Resurrection have overcome are the power of death and of the devil. St. Athanasius employs terms that he rarely uses, such as "debt" and "paid" and "settle man's account." Note that though juridical terminology is used, the payment is not given to a person, but is spoken of as rescuing us from *our condition*—the payment is given to death.

After having spoken about Jesus' recreating the Image of God in us, St. Athanasius then says,

> But beyond all this, there was a *debt* owing which must needs be *paid*; for, as I said before, all men were due to *die*. Here, then, is the second reason why the Word dwelt among us, namely that having proved His Godhead by His works, He might *offer the sacrifice on behalf of all*, surrendering His own temple to death *in place of all*, *to settle man's account with death and free him* from the

primal transgression. In the same act also He showed Himself mightier than death, displaying His own body incorruptible as the first-fruits of the resurrection. . . . Thus it happened that two opposite marvels took place at once: the death of all was consummated in the Lord's body; yet, because the Word was in it, *death and corruption* were in the same act utterly abolished. Death there had to be, and death for all, so that *the due of all might be paid.* Wherefore, the Word, as I said, being Himself incapable of death, assumed a mortal body, that He might offer it as His own *in place of all,* and *suffering for the sake of all* through His *union* with it, "might bring to nought Him that had the *power of death,* that is, the *devil,* and might deliver them who all their lifetime were enslaved by the fear of death." (§20, p. 49)

So in the statements, "He died to ransom all" (§21, p. 51), and "Who was made the Ransom for the sins of all" (§40, p. 74), we see that the ransom is *not* paid to a person, either to God or to the devil, but is paid to deliver us from our fallen state, from "the power of death and corruption."

(5) To transfigure and deify us
". . . recognize the fact and marvel that things divine have been revealed to us by such humble means, that through death deathlessness has been made known to us, and through the Incarnation of the Word the Mind, whence all things proceed has been declared, and its Agent and Ordainer, the Word of God Himself. *He indeed, assumed humanity that we might become God* [godlike]" (§54, p. 93).

It was revealing to me that St. Athanasius hardly mentions forgiveness of sins! It seems that it did not hold a prominent place in his book *On the Incarnation*. For many this might be shocking, as Christians often view forgiveness as the main point of Christ's Incarnation and death. St. Athanasius no doubt assumes it is part and parcel of the gospel. He emphasizes that the Incarnation is about healing, giving life to our human nature and overcoming the power of death, sin, and the devil.

Chapter 17

God Became Man So That Man Might Become God

Our first parish assignment in which I would serve as pastor was a small mission of about thirty souls called St. Paul in Lynnwood, Washington, only fifteen miles north of downtown Seattle. Our family made the long cross-country trek from New York to Seattle in the fall of 1990. We were ecstatic about being assigned to the West Coast, near the ocean, in such a scenic area of the country. The church, which steadily grew in numbers, met at a Roman Catholic chapel. In a few years we expanded enough to build our own church temple in the neighboring town of Brier. Our family grew to love both the St. Paul parishioners and the Seattle area.

Returning to the Holy Land 〜

Following the model of St. Paul, my ministry was among Gentiles. Most of our membership was of Scandinavian/British Isles descent. Additionally, Washington had the dubious distinction of being the most unchurched state in the country. I had my work cut out for me. Though I knew few Jews, I still retained a hidden hope that someday Jews would have exposure to a friendly expression of Orthodox Christianity.

A unique aspect of the Antiochian Orthodox Christian

Archdiocese is that its patriarch is Arabic and resides in Damascus, Syria; most of its bishops in America are of Arabic descent. So of all the various Orthodox jurisdictions in America, including Russian, Greek, Romanian, and Serbian, I found myself in the one of Arabic origin. I viewed this as not accidental, but providential. How ironic that I, of Jewish descent and the son of a man born in the Old City of Jerusalem, was now in a church that had large numbers of Arabic Christians from Lebanon, Syria, and Palestine—the Holy Land. I must say that I did feel a kinship with them, as many had characteristics that strongly reminded me of my uncles Morris, Max, Jacob, and Abe, as well as my gregarious aunts.

My first bishop was American-born Bishop Basil (Essey), a very gifted and pastoral graduate of St. Vladimir's Seminary. My second was Bishop Joseph Al-Zehlaoui, who was born in 1950 in Damascus, Syria. He was educated in Syria, Lebanon, and Greece and served in Greece, Syria, England, and Cyprus. In 1991 he was consecrated a bishop, and in 1995 was assigned to the West Coast in the Antiochian Orthodox Christian Archdiocese of North America. I recall saying to myself when I first saw him at a convention, "This man will have a profound impact on my life," and time proved this to be true. I came to respect him dearly as one who has great pastoral insight, discernment, patience, and love.

I was acutely aware that many of the Orthodox Christian immigrants in our archdiocese were Palestinians from the Holy Land. I was reminded of my one-year stay there in 1967, while still a Protestant, and how I had taken note that the indigenous Christians were Orthodox. Now here I was, a priest in the same archdiocese as these Palestinian immigrants. I felt profound sorrow as I grew more aware of the disarray of the indigenous Christians in the Holy Land and the rapid disintegration of their church communities.

My friend, Fr. Peter Gillquist, encouraged me to make a

pilgrimage with a number of American Orthodox priests originally from the Holy Land to assess the state of the church communities there. So in December 1997 I traveled with Fr. Constantine Nasr, Fr. Nicholas Dahdal, some laymen, and another convert priest, Fr. Richard Ballew. During a two-week period we visited approximately fifty Arabic Orthodox communities in Jordan, Israel, and Palestine.

The most moving experience for me was our visit to the Arab Orthodox community in the Old City of Jerusalem. I was saddened to think that while various Christian sects seemed to be growing in the Holy Land, the Orthodox Church appeared to be dying. What Orthodox witness would there be if all the Arab Orthodox Christians emigrated? Rather than vibrant sites of worship, the Orthodox churches there were in danger of becoming museums. And the Greek Orthodox hierarchs in the Holy Land were in danger of becoming museum caretakers.

As we were traveling from Nazareth to another area in the north, we passed by some towns and the Arab Orthodox tour guide said to me, "Over there are many Orthodox Christians who have emigrated to Israel from Russia. They are Jews who are also Orthodox Christians." At the time I took his words to be an oddity and did not make much of them, thinking, "Wouldn't it be nice if there were more than just a handful?" Little did I know that our tour guide's words would open a new door of hope and opportunity in years to come.

Beyond Forgiveness ❧

MEANWHILE, MY UNDERSTANDING OF ORTHODOX THEOLOGY AS the fulfillment of Jewish belief continued to grow. As Jews, we were taught that we could not believe in Jesus because it is blasphemy to think that a man can be God. At sixteen, when I was seriously considering Christianity, I struggled with the questions, What if God *wanted* to manifest Himself in human nature? Who are we to say, "No, God, You are not allowed to nor can You be a man." Accepting the possibility that God can do whatever He wants, including manifesting Himself in human nature, was a major paradigm shift for me.

But there was a second aspect to this issue. Why would God want to become a man? It seemed to me that Protestants and Catholics tended to present the reason for the Incarnation in juridical terms that often came down to God not being able to forgive man's sins without Christ dying for us. In contrast, Jews believed that sacrifices were not necessary for God to forgive. We held that there are no constraints on God's forgiveness other than the repentant heart of the sinner. To view a payment to God as a necessary requirement for His forgiveness was for us akin to saying that God could not absolve sin unless He was bribed. That God had to become human in order to be able to forgive sins did not make sense. The belief that God the Father had to kill God the Son in the flesh (a form of God killing Himself) in order to forgive sin made even less sense.

As an Orthodox Christian, I came to understand that the focus of the Incarnation was not to enable God to forgive; the emphasis was on the healing, purification, and ultimate transfiguration of mankind. The goal of the Incarnation was to energize our fallen human nature and to make it godlike—a process variously referred to as *deification, divinization,* or *theosis.* The Orthodox teach that God in His wisdom chose to accomplish this by assuming our human nature and transforming it from within—not from without. Our human nature will be perfected by more than the Holy Spirit working on it. This perfection takes place from within, as God shares with us a common human nature. Because His humanity is perfect, ours can be also as we are united to Him.

I found the Orthodox Christian rationale for the Incarnation to be much more reasonable than the Western version.

"I said, 'You are gods'" (John 10:34) ⌒

THE POSTAPOSTOLIC CHURCH TAUGHT THAT THE PERFECTING OF human nature was a twofold process. The first of the two steps has already been discussed: the healing of our humanity by Christ's glorified human nature. This healing makes possible the achievement of an ideal, which is the second step.

To understand this one must ask, "What is the ultimate purpose of life?" For each of us this no doubt includes living forever in joy (eternal life), entrance into the glories of heaven, sanctification, and experiencing the beatific vision of God.

The ultimate goal of life does include these, but they are not enough. "Well," one might ask, "what can possibly provide a greater purpose in life than these?" The ultimate reason for our existence can be understood more clearly from the classic Orthodox statement, "God became man so that man might become god." Our aim is to forever become more like God—but without ever becoming God.

This understanding is in sharp contrast to what I knew non-Orthodox believed. Despite their many differences, I realized that all forms of non-Orthodox Christianity have far more in common with each other than with Orthodoxy. After all, what non-Orthodox church teaches that man's eternal goal is deification (Gr. *theosis*), meaning *to become by grace what God is by nature*? Because the process of becoming is everlasting, the redeemed are forever becoming more like God by grace, without ever becoming God.

From the beginning as a Protestant, I had been taught that Adam and Eve's original sin included the *desire to be like God*.

Indeed the Scripture says, "Then the serpent said to the woman, 'You will not surely die. For God knows that in the day you eat of it your eyes will be opened, and *you will be like God*, knowing good and evil'" (Genesis 3:4, 5, emphasis mine). Also, it is a universal Christian belief that Satan's great sin was seeking to be godlike through pride:

> "How you are fallen from heaven,
> O Lucifer, son of the morning!
> How you are cut down to the ground,
> You who weakened the nations!
> For you have said in your heart:
> 'I will ascend into heaven,
> I will exalt my throne above the stars of God;
> I will also sit on the mount of the congregation
> On the farthest sides of the north;
> I will ascend above the heights of the clouds,
> *I will be like the Most High.'*
> Yet you shall be brought down to Sheol,
> To the lowest depths of the Pit."
> (Isaiah 14:12–15, emphasis mine; see also Ezekiel 28:14–17)

The Orthodox agree that pride is the mother of all sins, and that to desire to be like God *without* God is fatal. But we believe that it is not sinful to desire to forever be more godlike, in love and humility, *with* His help. In fact, being created in God's image and likeness includes *forever becoming more like God!* Jesus directly addresses our being godlike in the Gospel of John. Speaking to the unbelieving, He said:

> "I and My Father are one." Then the Jews took up stones again to stone Him. . . . The Jews answered Him, saying,

"... for blasphemy, and because You, being a Man, make yourself God." Jesus answered them, "Is it not written in your law, '*I said, "You are gods"*'? [quoting Psalm 82:6] If He called them gods, to whom the word of God came (and the Scripture cannot be broken), do you say of Him whom the Father sanctified and sent into the world, 'You are blaspheming,' because I said, 'I am the Son of God'?" (John 10:30–36)

My conviction grew that non-Orthodox Christianity severely obscured the true teaching about man's destiny, which is to be a partaker of the Divine Nature. The apostle Peter wrote:

Grace and peace be multiplied to you in the knowledge of God and of Jesus our Lord, as His divine power has given to us all things that pertain to life and godliness, through the knowledge of Him who called us by glory and virtue, by which have been given to us exceedingly great and precious promises, that through these *you may be partakers of the divine nature*, having escaped the corruption that is in the world through lust. (2 Peter 1:2–4, emphasis mine)

St. Maximus the Confessor (seventh century) wrote:

A sure warrant for looking forward with hope to the *deification of human nature* is provided by *the incarnation of God, which makes man god to the same degree as God Himself became man.* For it is clear that He who became man without sin (cf. Heb. 4:15) *will divinize human nature without changing it into the divine nature,* and will raise it up for His own sake to the same degree as He lowered Himself for man's sake. This is what St. Paul teaches mystically when he says, ". . . that in the ages to come He might display the overflowing richness of His grace" (Eph. 2:7).[32]

St. Athanasius says of God, "He indeed, assumed humanity that we might become God." (By this is meant godlike/a god.)[33]

The ancient Church's understanding is that the goal of our salvation is, by grace, to become ever more what God is by nature. This is accomplished without annihilating the absolute ontological distinction between the Uncreated and the Created. Man never actually becomes God. Rather, he is forever becoming like God, a never-ending process or journey. In other words, in his deification man experiences real union with God, but he is not merged with the Divine Essence.

For St. Athanasius in particular and Orthodoxy in general, the answer to the question, "Why did God become a man?" is, "So that man can become god," or ever more godlike. A more theologically precise wording states: God, who is God by nature, became man in order that man might forever become more like God by grace, without ever becoming God by nature. So for the Orthodox, if the primary goal were merely to become morally better, there would have been no purpose or need for Christ's Incarnation, as God could improve on our character without it. The purpose of the Incarnation was to enable us to experience a metamorphosis that could happen only by our being actually united to the humanity of the Incarnate God.

Eucharist: Divine and Human ᴄᴠ

SOME ORTHODOX CONCEPTS HELPED ME TO UNDERSTAND deification, theosis, divinization, or what I liked to call transfiguration. Central to the Orthodox understanding is the concept of hypostatic union. "Hypostatic" comes from the Greek word *hypostasis,* which means "personal." So hypostatic union means personal union. In Jesus, divine nature and human nature are united. They are joined to the Person of Jesus Christ, the preexistent and eternal Son of God, the second Person of the Blessed Trinity, the eternal Word (Gr. *Logos*). The two natures being united to the Person of Christ results in union, but not confusion or mingling; both natures retain their uniqueness. These concepts were clarified during the ecumenical councils of the ancient Church.

It became clear to me that participation in Christ's glorified humanity as He was raised from the dead, ascended into heaven, and was seated at the right hand of God the Father is more than an imitation of Jesus and His life. It is not simply an issue of belief, faith, justification, sanctification, or a personal relationship with Jesus. It is more than what Protestants call positional truth; it includes these, but it is much more.

After His Resurrection, Jesus ascended into heaven with the same humanity He had when on earth, except that it was glorified. Being glorified, His humanity is not corruptible and mortal as our bodies are now. Not only His body ascended into heaven, but His entire human nature, which includes His human mind and will. This glorified humanity of Christ is *deified*, meaning that it is energized and interpenetrated by the divine nature of God. To participate in Christ's glorified human nature is to enter into union and communion with it: to take His glorified human nature into our own. The Orthodox understand that when we receive the sacrament of eucharistic Communion, the glorified humanity of Christ interpenetrated by His divine nature is consumed and assimilated into our being.

The early Christians used the imagery of iron in fire to explain deification: When an iron sword is thrust into a fire, it takes on fire's characteristics of heat and light, but does not become fire.

Iron represents the human nature of Christ; fire represents His divine nature. The divine nature interpenetrates Christ's human nature just as fire interpenetrates iron, energizing it. This is a good image of the relationship between Christ's two natures.

If our lives are thought of as a sword, and in most cases a very cold one, each of our swords is heated by being brought into contact with Christ's humanity. Christ then shares God's life and energy with us, warming our life so that in time it can blaze as does His. The Orthodox teach that this union and communion with His humanity takes place in two ways. The first is partaking of the sacramental life of the Orthodox Church, including Holy Baptism, confession, and Communion. We are taught that during Holy Communion we are not just receiving the Blessed Sacrament into our stomach. Rather, we receive the glorified humanity of Christ, interpenetrated by the divine energies, the grace and fire of God's Holy Spirit, into our very being, heart and soul.

To Be Filled One Must Be Emptied

THE SECOND WAY OF GAINING UNION AND COMMUNION WITH Christ's glorified humanity is through ascetic effort, which rids us over time of self-absorption, self-centeredness, self-gratification, corrupt passions, and sin, freeing us to truly love. This effort includes prayer, fasting, self-denial, acts of charity, struggle, enduring trial, pain, sorrow, abandonment, and humiliation, and most of all the sacrifice of love.

Asceticism is often called "works" in non-Orthodox churches, but for Orthodox it is more than works or good deeds. It includes the effort by which we empty ourselves of sinful desires, thoughts, passions, habits, attachments, addictions, and sins through ascetic effort, in order to more fully receive and be *filled* with God's Holy Spirit. Asceticism and participation in the sacramental life of the Church complement one another. There is also a sense in which asceticism is included in the sacramental life of the Church; the Sacrament of Confession assumes the pursuit of the ascetic life of struggle, as well as the martyric life of sacrificial love. A contemporary theologian, Metropolitan Hierotheos Vlachos, says:

> The cure and deification of man is achieved, on the one hand, by the sacramental life, and on the other hand, by the ascetic life which we live in the Church. I want to particularly emphasize that all the Holy Fathers of the Church teach that man's salvation is a combination of sacraments and asceticism. We cannot understand the sacraments without asceticism in Christ, and we cannot live a real ascetic life without the sacraments of the Church. . . . In our time a great deal is being said about the sacramental life, the eucharistological life is being much emphasized. This is very good. But, unfortunately, the ascetic tradition of the Church is being overlooked.[34]

Knowing God Is Progressive ᴖ

WHEN ORTHODOX SPEAK ABOUT PARTICIPATING IN THE DIVINE nature via the glorified humanity of Christ in the Holy Spirit, they refer to a fundamental change in our very being—a new creation, life, and heart. This is more than a change in relationship or position. It is a new state of being, living in Christ and partaking of His life.

The Bible often speaks of knowing God. St. Paul said, "I know whom I have believed" (2 Timothy 1:12). The word translated "know" is derived from the Greek word for communion, showing us that the biblical understanding of knowledge includes more than data, information, and facts. "To know" in the New Testament is to enter into communion at the deepest level, including but also transcending the mind. It is a communion of hearts. The Old Testament word translated "to know" is *yodayah*. This word is similar to the Greek in that it means knowledge at the deepest level. The Old Testament Book of Genesis says that Adam "knew" his wife Eve. The word is used elsewhere in the same sense, referring to sexual intercourse. In this context, knowing occurs at the most basic level.

I have often been asked, "Do you know God?" As a Protestant I usually answered, "Yes, I know Him and am saved." Now my answer is different, because for the Orthodox knowing someone is a process. So sometimes I respond, "I am *beginning* to know God. We Orthodox believe that knowing God and salvation are both a never-ending process."

In a sense we can never completely know God, because we are creatures and He is the Creator. This understanding is very Jewish, because we always understood salvation and knowing God as a lifelong process, never as an instantaneous event. Orthodox Christians are taught that the Son of God, Jesus Christ, can and does know the Father completely because He is the Son by nature, the second Person of the Blessed Trinity. In contrast, we only know God by the gift of grace, and only in a limited sense, as He chooses to reveal Himself to us. So on one hand the Orthodox hold that we do not now nor ever will completely and fully know God. On the other hand, we experience God through His Holy Spirit, His constant love, life, power, grace, attributes, light, energies, and actions as He reveals Himself. Forever beyond our experience is *God's essence*, which we will never know.

So in a sense we know God, or more accurately are beginning to know God; in another sense we don't know God, nor ever will. This phenomenon is understandable on a human level when we consider our loved ones—for instance, my wife Bonnie. I know her attributes, looks, speech, and actions, but I also know her at a deeper level, as a person. I know something of her very being. How? *Through* her love for me, her actions, speech, looks, and attributes. Yet there is much about her that I do not know, nor ever will.

This is helpful in terms of our life in God. We know God because He loves us and has revealed Himself to us, and yet on another level, we don't know Him. This Orthodox attitude helps us to gain humility and explains from a spiritual perspective why Orthodox don't tell people, "I know God—and you can know Him, too." Or worse, "If you don't know God you are going to hell."

This Orthodox reserve exists precisely because we are just *beginning* to know Him. And it explains why fundamentalist Christians often appear cocky and proud to the Orthodox. It is not because we don't believe that we can have an authentic relationship with, life in, union and communion with Christ, but because the expression "I know God" is presumptuous, assuming a depth of knowledge forever hidden from us. This expression tends to undermine the sense of mystery and transcendence of God.

Chapter 18

Is God Humble?

THE TEACHING THAT IS FOUNDATIONAL TO THE CHRISTIAN understanding of God is that "God is love" (1 John 4:8, 16). Monotheistic religions such as Judaism and Islam also teach that God loves. Judaism would answer the question of whom or what God loves by saying that He loves His creation. But Orthodox Christianity, I discovered, holds that God *is* love, meaning that love is more than an attribute or created grace of God; love somehow reveals in a mystery who God is before He created the universe and time. God *is* love *before* He creates; His love is not just an expression of His will towards creation, but rather He loves by nature because of who He is.

Love is rooted in God the Father. The Scripture says, "For God [the Father] so loved the world that He gave His only begotten Son, that whoever believes in Him should not perish but have everlasting life" (John 3:16). During the Divine Liturgy the priest proclaims to the people, "The grace of our Lord Jesus Christ and *the love of God the Father* and the communion of the Holy Spirit be with you all" (emphasis mine). With regard to the unique love of God the Father, Fr. Lev Gillet writes:

> We are accustomed to thinking of the Father in terms of power. Yes, the Father is omnipotent, but the Father's heart is meek and humble like the Saviour's. It is meek for in Him there is nothing brusque or abrupt, no violence, no fury, but only kindliness, goodness, and affection. His

heart is also humble—not that the Father bows before one greater, as the Son becoming man bows before His Father, but He attaches no importance to display or appearances. He prefers the poor means and is united to the voluntary abasement of His Son who took on our nature and suffering. We must learn to see the Father in this light.[35]

But how can one God, who is perfect and lacks nothing, *be* love when love necessitates a relation to another? It has been said that a monad God who has not yet created would have nothing to love except Himself. Some even speculate that such self-love is monstrous.

The issue of *whom* God loves before the creation of the universe is resolved in Orthodoxy; God is understood to be not an absolute unity or monad, but a composite unity, a Trinity of Father, Son, and Holy Spirit. Each Person of the Blessed Trinity is fully divine and for eternity loves the other two. The Trinity is a union of love. None of the Persons of the Blessed Trinity exists in terms of Himself alone; each exists relative to the other two Persons. Each fully loves the others as only God can love. Love then defines who God is in a way in which nothing else does. As Fr. Lev Gillet says, "Yet we must not forget that the one and only definition of God in the New Testament is in the words 'God is love.'"[36]

God: Composite Unity or Absolute Unity? ❧

THE PROCLAMATION THAT MOST IDENTIFIES JUDAISM IS CALLED IN Hebrew the *Shema:* "Hear, O Israel: The LORD our God, the LORD *is* one" (Deuteronomy 6:4). As a Jew I had always been taught that God is One, an *absolute unity*, not two, three, or more gods.

What I discovered on pursuing Christianity is that two different Hebrew words can be translated "one," although their meanings are significantly different.

The Hebrew word in the *Shema* passage is *echad*. In examining how this word is used in Scripture, I discovered that it does not mean *absolute* "one"; rather it means a *composite* or *compound* "one." For example, Genesis 1:5 speaks of evening and morning as comprising one (*echad*) day. Genesis 2:24 refers to the coming together in marriage of a man and a woman and their becoming one (*echad*) flesh. Ezra 2:64 says that the whole multitudinous assembly of people were "together" (*echad*). Ezekiel 37:17 speaks of two sticks being united in order to be one (*echad*). These references indicate that the word translated as "one" in Israel's great confession of faith means a composite or compound unity.

In contrast, the word often used in Scripture to signify "one" in an absolute sense is *yachid*. The reason *echad* was used in the *Shema* instead of *yachid* is that God is a composite unity, not an absolute, monad unity. The second of Rabbi Maimonides' "Thirteen Articles of Faith" says that the Creator is "a Unity" or One. It is revealing that the Hebrew word he uses to stress the *absolute* oneness of God is *yachid, not* the Hebrew word *echad* used in the biblical *Shema*.

Additionally, the Hebrew word in the proclamation translated as "our God" is from the Hebrew *Elohim*, which is plural. The actual meaning of the word is "our Gods." So the *Shema* could be translated, "Hear, O Israel: The LORD our Gods, the LORD *is* One Composite Unity."

God's Condescension: In His Incarnation ∾

WITHIN JUDAISM I ALREADY HAD AN UNDERSTANDING OF GOD'S condescension in creating a universe outside of Himself. In both the Jewish and Christian understandings, God is not identified with His creation, although He is omnipresent within it. The act of creating beings who have free will and can even choose to resist Him is truly profound. The creation is an object of God's love. It is also an expression of His condescension and humility, because it is brought into being separately from Him and is not fully under His control. To create a universe that is capable of resisting His will, God had to some degree to withdraw His omnipotence. This kind of distancing provides room in which His creatures can respond to His love without being forced. God's condescension in the act of creating is a supreme act of love. But is condescension in love the same as humility?

While attending the Eagle River Institute in Alaska in August of 2003, I privately asked the renowned bishop, author, and lecturer Kallistos (Timothy) Ware, "Is God humble?"

We discussed this, and he then also chose to answer my question publicly as part of his recorded lecture. His answer was, "It is as natural for God to be humble as it is to be almighty." Another way I heard him say it was, "God is as humble as He is almighty." That is, God is *both* almighty and humble.

The bishop's answer shocked me because I immediately realized that its implications were beyond human grasp. A God who is humble is incomprehensible and inexplicable. The concept is mind-numbing. A paradox in Orthodoxy is sometimes called an *antinomy*. An antinomy exists when two apparently correct statements do not agree, and therefore seem to produce a contradictory and illogical conclusion. On one hand, God is the omnipotent, omniscient, omnipresent Creator of the universe, eternal and in need of nothing. On the other hand, God is humble! Not only God in Christ but also the other Persons of the Trinity. For me, this was the ultimate antinomy.

The Scriptures speak of God's humility:

Let this mind be in you which was also in Christ Jesus, who, being in the form of God, did not consider it robbery [or something to be held onto] to be equal with God, but made Himself of no reputation, taking the form of a bondservant, and coming in the likeness of men. And being found in appearance as a man, *He humbled Himself* and became obedient to the point of death, even the death of the cross. (Philippians 2:5–8, emphasis mine)

Also, Jesus said, "Come to Me, all you who labor and are heavy laden, and I will give you rest. Take My yoke upon you and learn from Me, for I am gentle and lowly [or *humble*] in heart, and you will find rest for your souls" (Matthew 11:28, 29, emphasis mine).

For some reason, I had always thought that Jesus' humanity or human nature was saying, "I am humble," as if His human nature could speak independently of His Person. Now, being Orthodox and having the Christological tools with which to understand more fully who Christ is, I realized that human nature cannot speak as an independent agent; rather, persons speak in and through their human nature. Clearly, it was not Jesus' created human nature that said, "I am gentle and humble in heart"; rather, the very Person of Christ said this *in and through* His human nature. It is the preexistent and eternal Word of God, the Second Person of the Blessed Trinity, who says, "I am gentle and humble in heart."

One of the Trinity Suffered in the Flesh ❧

THAT IT WAS SPECIFICALLY THE SECOND PERSON OF THE TRINITY who said this was reaffirmed in the Fifth Ecumenical Council's acceptance of what is called the Theopaschite formula, based on

St. Cyril of Alexandria's teachings. The formula, *Ilnus ex Trinitate passus est* (meaning "One of the Trinity suffered in the flesh"), declared that the Second Person of the Blessed Trinity, the eternal Logos, is the unifying principle linking the divine nature of God and the human nature of man. And it is this Person who is the acting subject not only in Christ's miracles, but also in His suffering. The Person of Christ, who *is* divine, indeed God, enfleshed love by condescending and being humbled in His human nature. The tenth anathema of the Fifth Ecumenical Council held in Constantinople (AD 553) affirms, "If anyone does not confess that our Lord Jesus Christ who was crucified in the flesh is true God and the Lord of Glory and one of the Holy Trinity, let him be anathema."[37]

A previous formula, proclaimed at the Third Ecumenical Council at Ephesus (AD 431), stated that God was born in the flesh and Mary therefore is the Theotokos (the Mother of God). Building on this, the Fifth Council, in order to reaffirm that it was a divine Person who became incarnate and not simply a nature, unambiguously stated that *God Himself was crucified in the flesh!*

The Fifth Council's anathema was a paraphrase of 1 Corinthians 2:8, which refers to the evil powers that be: "none of the rulers of this age knew; for had they known, they would not have crucified the Lord of glory." In order to enshrine this understanding in the Orthodox Christian Divine Liturgy, a hymn attributed to the emperor Justinian was added. Called the "Only Begotten Son," it is sung at the second antiphon:

Only begotten Son and Word of God, although immortal You humbled Yourself for our salvation, taking flesh from the holy Theotokos and ever virgin Mary and, without change, becoming man. Christ, our God, You were crucified but conquered death by death. You are one of the Holy Trinity, glorified with the Father and the Holy Spirit—save us.[38]

A leading Orthodox theologian, Fr. John Meyendorff, has written, "The preexistent Word is the *subject* of the death of Christ, for in Christ there is no other personal subject apart from the Word; only *someone* can die, not something, or a nature, or the flesh."[39]

The Second Person of the Blessed Trinity, the eternal Word of God, in love became incarnate, taking to Himself humanity (human nature), then permitted Himself to suffer and die *in* His humanity. It was not His humanity that suffered and died in place of His Personhood; it was His Personhood that suffered and died in His humanity. (Of course, when we speak of God "dying," we are not saying that He ceased to exist; rather, a three-day separation took place between the preexistent Person of Christ and His flesh.)

Two Greek words used in the New Testament convey what transpired in the Incarnation. The phrase "made Himself of no reputation," from Philippians 2:7, is based on the Greek word *kenosis*, which means "emptying." It has also been translated, "made Himself nothing," or "emptied Himself." Similarly, the Greek word *sugkatabasis* means literally, "to go down together with," signifying condescension or abasement. That in this act of condescension God the Son is born into His creation as a vulnerable man is incomprehensible. And in doing so He submits Himself to all the pain, sorrow, and temptations common to man, even to suffering and dying on a cross.

The Passion of Christ during Holy Week is called by Orthodox Christians "the extreme humility of Christ." Jesus' entry into Jerusalem on Palm Sunday set the pattern for Holy Week:

All this was done that it might be fulfilled which was spoken by the prophet, saying:

"Tell the daughter of Zion,
'Behold, your King is coming to you,
Lowly, and sitting on a donkey,
A colt, the foal of a donkey.'" (Matthew 21:4, 5)

Christ's humility is viewed by Christians not as moral weakness but as moral strength. God's humility is not an expression of fault or inadequacy, but a manifestation of perfection. God does not cease being humble after the Resurrection, as if humility had no eternal reality—as if it were merely a created, utilitarian, temporary quality needed to save man. Christ, when seen by the apostles following the Resurrection, continued to bear His wounds—the apostle "doubting" Thomas even touched their imprint. The Orthodox Christian understanding is that Christ has ascended into heaven *with* His glorified humanity, but *retains* His wounds forever. Why? Because His wounds provide an everlasting witness and confirmation of God's love, expressed to us in extreme humility. His Incarnation is not just a temporary event; it is everlasting, because it has been brought into eternity. God never ceases to be humble because He loves, nurtures, and sustains us without end. This understanding is unique to the Christian Faith and is most clearly presented and understood within Orthodoxy.

Humility: Strength or Weakness? ❧

MANY VIEW HUMILITY AS A WEAKNESS RATHER THAN A STRENGTH. Some think it reflects a soft, weak, even wimpy or cowardly character. This comes in part from the belief that being humble is the result of a poor self-image, often accompanied by serious depression and self-destructive behavior. Humility is also believed by some to excuse inaction in the face of abuse, and even to justify slavery and servitude. Yet when we consider the life of Christ, we see that He was anything but weak. His humility was tough, and His life is respected as exemplary even by those who do not believe in Him.

It was certainly incalculably easier for me to view humility as a desirable characteristic for created beings than for God. Nevertheless, I accepted Orthodoxy's teaching that the Second Person of the Blessed Trinity says of Himself, "I am humble of heart," and that both the Father and the Holy Spirit share solidarity with the Son. It is evident that humility is truly a divine quality. And because humans are created in the image and likeness of God, we should reflect not only His love, but also His humility.

Among all earthly creatures, man alone displays the ability to acquire these divine qualities. What animal has within it the divine spark that can enable it to love its enemies and be authentically humble? These traits distinguish man as uniquely created in God's image and likeness. Because of this, I realized that I would need to acquire a greater respect for all of God's creation, including other forms of life. If the Creator God descended the virtually infinite distance between Himself and humanity in order to manifest divine love, should not I be willing to descend the comparatively short distance between myself and God's other creatures to express love?

For the Orthodox, humility is the first step on the path leading to purification, enlightenment, and transfiguration. The word "humility" is derived from the Latin *humus*, which means "fertile ground." The soil of humility is the fertile ground in which our spiritual life grows. It is the foundation on which everything else is built, because without humility one cannot repent. And without repentance one cannot be saved.

The Ladder of Divine Ascent, written by St. John Climacus (seventh century), presents an individual's spiritual ascent to God in terms of thirty steps on a ladder stretching from earth to heaven. This ascent is solidly grounded on the *humus* of humility. St. John so emphasized humility that he said, "Pride and nothing else caused an angel [Lucifer] to fall from heaven. And one may reasonably ask whether one may reach heaven by humility alone without the help of any other virtue."[40]

Humility is not just one of many spiritual qualities; Jesus says it enables one to reach the summit of spirituality: "Therefore whoever humbles himself as this little child is the greatest in the kingdom of heaven" (Matthew 18:4). Similarly: "For whoever exalts himself will be humbled, and he who humbles himself will be exalted" (Luke 14:11).

The apostle Paul tells us it is through the weakness of humility that God's strength is manifest:

And He said to me, "My grace is sufficient for you, for My strength is made perfect in weakness." Therefore most gladly I will rather boast in my infirmities, that the power of Christ may rest upon me. Therefore I take pleasure in infirmities, in reproaches, in needs, in persecutions, in distresses, for Christ's sake. For when I am weak, then I am strong. (2 Corinthians 12:9, 10)

Peter, considered to be chief of the apostles, says:

Likewise you younger people, submit yourselves to your elders. Yes, all of you be submissive to one another, and be clothed with humility, for

"God resists the proud,

But gives grace to the humble."

Therefore humble yourselves under the mighty hand of God, that He may exalt you in due time, casting all your care upon Him, for He cares for you. (1 Peter 5:5–7)

Humility is the soil in which repentance, faith, and trust grow. Next comes the struggle against passions resulting from the Fall, in order to be purified. This involves great effort; the Scriptures speak of forcing our way into the heavenly state by asceticism as an extreme act of spiritual violence: "And from the days of John the Baptist until now the kingdom of heaven suffers violence, and the violent take it by force" (Matthew 11:12). The church fathers speak of this martyric life of spiritual sacrifice in the bluntest of terms: "Give blood and receive Spirit."

As we are purified through struggle, we gain virtues, the greatest of which is love. So the spiritual journey begins with humility and ends with love. How much humility is needed in order to experience salvation? The more the better; the further down we descend, the higher we will ascend. Christ's threefold condescension is our model: first He descended to be incarnate in a manger; then He descended further to suffer and die on the Cross; and finally He descended further still into Hades to free the captives there.

We cannot be too humble. This characteristic is basic to the understanding of Orthodoxy, and is emphasized to a degree I have not seen in other monotheistic faiths or Christian denominations. A unique aspect of Orthodoxy is the set of tools it provides by which to acquire humility.

Tools with Which to Gain Humility ⌐

A NUMBER OF YEARS AGO, I READ ON THE FRONT PAGE OF A NATIONAL newspaper that the divorce rate among Orthodox Christians was among the lowest of all Christian denominations. A local Protestant counselor asked me to come to a session of Protestant pastors to explain what I thought contributed to the low divorce rate. In researching the issue, I realized that the Orthodox Christian emphasis on humility has a significant influence on the preservation of marriages. All marriage relationships require daily expressions of love and humility. This includes a willingness to defer, to ask forgiveness and to forgive, to examine weaknesses honestly and to confront them. Humility is a call to repentance and change, without which it is difficult for any marriage or relationship to survive.

Among the tools Orthodoxy provides to encourage humility are:

(1) *Praying "Lord, have mercy" during services and personal prayers.* In the course of the Divine Liturgy the choir sings "Lord, have mercy" about fifty-five times. This is an exceptional number of repetitions for any one phrase. The prayer is said not because we doubt God's desire to love and forgive us, or because we feel He won't do it unless we persuade Him. It is prayed so often primarily because it reminds us that even as Orthodox Christians, we continue to sin and are constantly in need of God's help to change, to be healed, and to be purified. It is a cry of admission of our continued weakness and dependence on God. Praying "Lord, have mercy" encourages humility.

In contrast, a view prevalent among many Christians questions why we should pray for mercy for something already forgiven. Why ask forgiveness when our sins—past, present, and future—have already been once and for all time forgiven? Amazing as it may sound, many non-Orthodox Christians would refuse to say this prayer. For them it expresses a lack of faith in God's unconditional forgiveness and makes our salvation appear tenuous.

In explaining this prayer to the Protestant pastors, I pointed out a serious flaw with this way of thinking. If we no longer need to ask forgiveness from God after becoming a Christian because we have already been forgiven, then what is to prevent a person from thinking the same about an offended spouse? How would we feel if we offended our spouse and asked forgiveness, then heard in response, "I've already told you I love you the day I married you and have already forgiven you; do I have to tell you I love and forgive you every day?" The Orthodox response would be, "Yes."

(2) *The Jesus Prayer.* Closely associated with the prayer "Lord, have mercy" is the Orthodox practice of saying the Jesus Prayer throughout the day. This prayer, "Lord, Jesus Christ, Son of God, have mercy on me a sinner," is often prayed using a small prayer rope made of many knots tied in a row. As the individual places his thumb and forefinger on a knot, he says the prayer, then moves on to the next knot and says the prayer again, and so on. The idea is to move this prayer from the lips and mind into the heart, gaining a sense of God's continuous presence. The words of the prayer remind us of our unworthiness and need for ongoing forgiveness. This penitential prayer helps instill a sense of humility and ideally carries over into our relationships with others, especially our spouse.

(3) *The pre-Communion prayer.* Just prior to receiving Communion, the congregation says a special prayer in unison, aloud. This prayer in part states, "I believe, O Lord, and I confess that Thou art truly the Christ, the Son of the living God, who didst come into the world to save sinners, of whom I am first." Each of us is to consider himself or herself to be the worst of sinners. This means that though others may in actuality have sinned more than we, nevertheless, because we know and are primarily accountable before God only for our own sins, we can in full honesty say, "to save sinners, of whom I am first." It is evident that saying this prayer is an antidote to our fallen tendency to minimize our ongoing sins. It also instills in us the realization

that we need constant help and healing, and that none of us is ultimately worthy to receive Holy Communion. This attitude further softens the heart, enabling an attitude of humility that affects all our relationships.

(4) *Exchanging forgiveness.* Expressing forgiveness is an essential aspect of preparing for Communion and of developing humility. In Orthodoxy, the Sunday before Great Lent is called Forgiveness Sunday. The theme of this day is dramatically expressed in a special Rite of Forgiveness often performed following the Forgiveness Vespers service on Sunday evening. During this rite, everyone present, ideally everyone in the parish, literally forgives and asks forgiveness from everyone else. It is a most tearful and yet joyous occasion of reconciliation. It is also most humbling.

Similarly, during every Divine Liturgy, the kiss of peace takes place. This rite of exchanging greetings before receiving Communion is not just an opportunity to greet one's neighbors. It was originally an expression that paralleled the Rite of Forgiveness described above, providing individuals an opportunity to express in a special exchange that they are at peace with those within the church before receiving Holy Communion. This is in accord with Jesus' saying, "Therefore if you bring your gift to the altar, and there remember that your brother has something against you, leave your gift there before the altar, and go your way. First be reconciled to your brother, and then come and offer your gift" (Matthew 5:23, 24).

The kiss of peace assumes that individuals are working on their differences during the days between services, and that kissing each other on the cheek, hugging, or shaking hands expresses the reality of reconciliation and forgiveness, which encourages humility. As a daily personal effort to incorporate forgiveness and humility into our lives, Orthodox family members will often ask forgiveness of one another at the conclusion of their corporate evening prayers at home. This practice concludes each day with the need to be forgiving and humble.

(5) *The Sacrament of Confession.* Perhaps most significantly, the Orthodox Church offers the sacrament of Holy Confession. In this sacrament, the penitent bares his heart before God and his father confessor. Confession is made to God, with the priest as witness. The effort of preparing for confession involves self-examination and honesty in confronting one's sins, shortcomings, and weaknesses. The goal is not to conceal or hide them, but to reveal and expose them. This can be an intensely therapeutic experience that further instills a sense of humility.

An interrelationship exists between Confession (including receiving absolution from the priest) and subsequently receiving Communion. Therefore, within this rite is an expression of accountability for one's life and commitment to dealing with one's sin issues. If taken seriously, Holy Confession cannot but deeply affect one's relationship with others, including one's spouse.

These five aspects of Orthodox piety, in addition to the grace provided within the Orthodox sacrament of marriage and the ascetic efforts of fasting and self-denial, all assist in developing spirituality, whereby true love, humility, and repentance can be gained.

I was asked many questions following my presentation to the Protestant pastors, and all of them agreed that Orthodoxy in fact provides tools to gain humility and to deepen the bonds of love within marriage relationships. The therapist who had invited me to make the presentation subsequently decided to further examine the Orthodox Faith. Not long afterwards, he and his entire family were received into the Orthodox Church.

Chapter 19

The Divine Fire of God's Love

Light and fire are interconnected. Light radiates heat, and when focused produces fire; fire emanates light. Both also have a wide spectrum of electromagnetic rays and energy, such as radiate from stars. Light illumines, is life-giving, but also burns.

Orthodoxy teaches that on a supernatural level, uncreated light, fire, energy, and grace eternally emanate from God's divine nature. Like God's love, they existed before the creation of the universe and time, and are called "uncreated." We can see created light with our physical eyes, but uncreated light can only be seen with the eyes of the heart. The Orthodox prayer, "In Thy light, we shall see light," refers to the reality that when we walk and live in God's light we experience the uncreated light that is beyond visible light. God's divine essence is forever unknowable; yet God reveals Himself to us in His divine energies and grace, in which He *is* knowable. For simplicity's sake, this is like saying we cannot have a direct experience of the surface of the sun without being immediately destroyed, but it is possible to encounter the sun by means of its heat and light. In receiving its heat and light we actually do encounter the sun, but in a form we can survive.

The divine light, fire, energy, and grace of God pervade and sustain the universe. This light/fire was present in the burning bush from which God spoke to Moses on Mt. Sinai. It burned the bush, but did not consume or destroy it. During Jesus' Transfiguration on Mt. Tabor, the uncreated divine light of God's presence revealed Jesus' divine nature to His three closest disciples. They were enabled by God's grace to see this light, but had others been present, they might not have seen it. The Orthodox hymn for the Feast of the Transfiguration says the disciples experienced this "inasmuch as they could bear it."

Similarly, halos depicted in Orthodox icons are not rings or crowns as often represented in non-Orthodox religious art. They are rather spheres of light, like the sphere of light around a candle in a dark room. The light radiated by Christ and the saints in iconic halos represents the uncreated light of God, which can only be seen with the eyes of the heart.

As I immersed myself in the study of Orthodoxy, I discovered a truth that resolved a great problem I had always had as a Protestant. It also made clearer why Judaism in some regards seemed closer to Christian Orthodoxy than did other forms of Christianity. The Orthodox say that whether the divine light of God illumines or burns is determined not by the condition of the light or the action of God, but by the condition, nature, and perception of the person receiving the light. To the one who gladly receives the light, it illumines. To the one who resists the light, it burns. This holds true for both this life and the life to come.

This astounding personal epiphany deeply affected me, because it explains how God can love man unconditionally forever, and yet be experienced as the source of anguish and suffering by those who seek to flee Him.

Is Hellfire Physical or Spiritual? ❧

JUDAISM DOESN'T HAVE MUCH TO SAY ABOUT THE AFTERLIFE, OTHER than that it exists, and that the way we live now determines our ultimate state. The mainstream view is that in the world to come (Hebrew, *Olam-Ha-Ba*) Gan Eden, that is, the Garden of Eden, awaits those who reach a state of spiritual perfection. Most of the dead go to Gehenna or She'ol for up to twelve months before going on to Gan Eden. Gehenna is like a spiritual forge where the soul is purified. It is also seen as an entryway or waiting room for what is to follow.

Two views exist of what happens to those who are utterly wicked. One is that they continue to experience punishment forever after they leave Gehenna, and the other is that they are annihilated. Some Hasidic Jewish sects believe in a form of reincarnation, in which we go through many cycles with many opportunities to be perfected. Clearly, the Jewish views are wide in scope and not well defined.

In my youth I was never taught that God is vindictive and has to send the wicked to a place such as hell, where they are subject to literal fire forever in the worst torment imaginable. This is surprising to Christians, as they often assume that the God of the Jews is harsher, more judgmental, and more vindictive than the Christian God, and therefore the Jewish hellfire should be "hotter." We didn't believe the wicked would go unpunished, but that their suffering would be mitigated by God's love and thus not as severe as many Christians hold.

So when I first considered becoming a Christian and had read the Jehovah's Witness translation of the Scripture, I was attracted to their teaching that the utterly evil are annihilated. This seemed much more reasonable than the idea that a loving God would preserve their existence only to torment them forever, without ultimate purpose or hope of redemption. Also, because some Jews believe in the annihilation of the wicked, the Jehovah's Witness view seemed more compatible with Judaism.

As I learned more, I discovered that the Jehovah's Witnesses were totally outside the mainstream of traditional Trinitarian Christianity. This undercut my confidence in their view of the annihilation of the lost, but on the other hand it was difficult for me to accept the conservative Christian view of a vindictive God of hellfire. I didn't know how to resolve the issue other than by doing what many Christians do: either view hell as a place of everlasting gloom rather than active torment, or just refuse to think about it. The latter was difficult to do, as Protestant evangelists like Billy Graham emphasized that Jesus spoke far more about the terrors of hell than He did about the glories of heaven. And the hellfire-and-brimstone preachers I listened to never ceased reminding us of where the lost were going. The question of hell became one of those significant theological issues that I was not able to resolve for many years, until I encountered Orthodox Christianity.

The Christian Faith holds that at the general resurrection of the dead at the end of time, the souls of the lost will be re-united with their raised incorruptible bodies. Because the non-Orthodox view death as God's legal punishment for sin, their view of the afterlife is that God actively continues and intensifies this punishment forever. In their resurrected bodies, the lost will suffer forever—physically as well as spiritually. In this concept, the bodies of the damned are specially designed by God to endure all the suffering and physical pain imaginable with no destruction or deterioration. This torment has no hope of ceasing or producing reconciliation. It serves no purpose other than the satisfaction of the "necessity of divine justice." Therefore, those judged receive an infinite amount of punishment for a finite number of sins committed in a relatively short lifetime.

This is the traditional Catholic view of hellfire, the concept presented in Dante's *Inferno*. It is also the view of hell that Protestants inherited from the Roman Catholic Church when they broke from Catholicism during the Reformation. Many Protestants continued to believe, as did Roman Catholics, that hellfire is literal, created, physical fire.

In contrast to both Roman Catholics and Protestants, the Orthodox teach that hellfire is the presence of God. This fire is not physical but spiritual, because it is uncreated. For those who love God and desire Him, His divine light and presence make heaven. For those who want to escape God's presence, His light, purifying fire, and omnipotence make existence hell because the lost are unable to escape Him.

St. Basil the Great wrote, "The evils in Hell do not have God as their cause, but we cause them."[41] The oldest known creed of the Church, the Apostles' Creed, does not state that God created hell. It states, "I believe in one God, the Father Almighty, Maker of heaven and earth," not, "Maker of heaven, hell, and earth." God is not the creator of hell. We humans are the cause of our own suffering and death.

What Makes Heaven, Heaven and Hell, Hell? ～

IN TYPICAL NON-ORTHODOX TEACHING, HELL IS A *PLACE* CREATED by God for the express purpose of banishing the wicked for everlasting punishment. The damned are spatially cut off from God, His Kingdom, His people, and His love. But in the Orthodox Christian understanding, both heaven and hell are essentially not spatial, but relational. Hence, the goal of the Christian is not to "get to heaven" as to a locale, but rather to grow into deepening communion with God by acquiring the Holy Spirit, beginning in this life and continuing forever. Similarly, the Church does not see herself as sending people to heaven or hell, any more than God sends people there. Rather, the Church is the hospital for sinners, preparing people for the experience that all will have—being in the presence of God. The only real question is what effect seeing God will have on us.

The Orthodox understanding is that heaven and hell are primarily *states* of the human soul. What makes them what they are is our individual response to God's love, whereby God is either included or excluded from our being. In this present life we can experience a foretaste of heaven as we live in communion with God, regardless of our physical circumstances. Jesus says, "For indeed, the kingdom of God is within you" (Luke 17:21). We can also experience a foretaste of hell by excluding Him from our lives: "but he who does not believe is condemned already" (John 3:18). In either case, it is neither a change in our physical location nor a change in God's attitude that determines our soul's state; it is our own choice.

As the Kingdom of God is brought forth in our hearts in this life, we partake of the blessings of heaven. This is why many saints who underwent the worst of tortures nevertheless rejoiced and experienced the life-giving warmth and comfort only God can give. They were, in a sense, in the "wrong" place, but their souls were in the right state. The opposite is also true. In this life we can experience the material comforts that come from wealth, power, and fame, yet be internally confused, desolate, angry, and tormented.

Jesus says that the unrighteous are to be cast into outer darkness (see Matthew 8:12; 22:13; 25:30, which refer to She'ol). Orthodox Christianity speaks of hell as darkness; its fire is a dark fire. Though the fire itself is light and spiritually illuminating, it is not perceived as such by the lost because they are spiritually blind. St. Irenaeus (second century) said:

> But on as many as, according to their own choice, depart from God, He inflicts that separation from Himself which

they have chosen of their own accord. But separation from God is death, and separation from light is darkness. . . . It is in this matter just as occurs in the case of a flood of light: those who have blinded themselves, or have been blinded by others, are for ever deprived of the enjoyment of light. It is not, [however,] that the light has inflicted upon them the penalty of blindness, but it is that the blindness itself has brought calamity upon them.[42]

Thus, because of the willful blindness of the lost, the light appears as darkness. This provides insight into our Lord's saying, "If therefore the light that is in you is darkness, how great *is* that darkness!" (Matthew 6:23). Likewise, St. Anthony the Great of Egypt, often called the father of monasticism, said, "Thus to say that God turns away from the wicked is like saying that the sun hides itself from the blind."[43]

It was with great comfort that I discovered that the Orthodox believe God never withdraws His love or ceases loving the lost. In resisting God, we do not change Him; we only change ourselves. Resisting the divine light of God's love does not change God, but it has everlasting consequences for those in opposition.

In their shame, Adam and Eve tried to hide from God (Genesis 3:8–10). Their effort was irrational, because God is omnipresent and omniscient. Also, God is love, and there is no reason to hide from Him even if it were possible to do so. Similarly, when we sin but remain unrepentant, we begin to experience God's love as fear and wrath. This is not because God has changed and become vindictive and wrathful, but because we have changed our relation to, and therefore our experience of God (John 1:5, 9–11; 3:19–21; 1 John 1:5–7). Jesus never turned away anyone who came to Him seeking forgiveness, healing, and life.

The River of Fire ∾

An example of this divine fire is presented in the Orthodox icon of the Last Judgment, which depicts the river of divine fire proceeding from the throne of God. This river is presented as heaven for those on one side, and as hell for those on the opposite side. Saint Mark of Ephesus (fifteenth century), in his first of four homilies refuting the Roman Catholic view of created purgatorial and hell fire, quotes the ancient church father Saint Basil the Great (fourth century):

> Basil the Great also speaks of this in the "Morals," in interpreting the passage of Scripture, *the voice of the Lord Who divideth the flame of fire* (Psalm 28:7): "The fire prepared for the torment of the devil and his angels, is divided by the voice of the Lord, so that after this there might be two powers in it: one that burns, and another that illumines; the tormenting and punishing power of that fire is reserved for those worthy of torment; while the illumining and enlightening power is intended for the shining of those who rejoice. Therefore the voice of the Lord Who divides and separates the flame of fire is for this: that the dark part might be a fire of torment and the unburning part a light of enjoyment."[44]

Consider Shadrach, Meshach, and Abednego, who refused to worship the idol in Babylon (Daniel 3). King Nebuchadnezzar threw them into a fiery furnace, which was heated "seven times more." The significance of seven is that it can symbolize the furnace of heaven, the place where God dwells. The three Jewish youths were unharmed by the fire, where one "like the Son of God" was among them. An Orthodox hymn says they were "united by a fire that did not consume them." However, the heat of the same fire killed the king's mightiest soldiers. This is analogous to the way the presence of God is light and warmth to those who love Him, and pain and destruction to those who oppose Him; *yet it is the same fire.*

In the Orthodox Christian understanding, the degree of material rewards or punishments does not make heaven and hell. Neither does the amount of sensual pleasure or suffering experienced. Nor are heaven and hell defined by location (heaven is up and hell is down) or physical distance from God. Rather, the light of God's presence, which is everywhere, makes heaven, heaven and hell, hell. The uncreated light of God, emanating from Him before the creation of the universe, pervades and sustains all things. How the individual receives and experiences this "river of fire that proceeds from the throne of God" determines his state in the afterlife.

Hearts of Wax or of Clay? ∽

Every year at Passover, Jews read how God hardened Pharaoh's heart prior to the Exodus so that he would not let the Jewish people go. Scripture contains numerous references to this (for example, Exodus 4:21; 6:12; 10:1, 20, 27; 11:10; 14:4, 8, 17). For years I wrestled with why God would purposely cause Pharaoh to rebel against Him by hardening his heart. Now, understanding the twofold aspects of God's light, I began to understand. It was not that God wanted Pharaoh to be evil; rather, Pharaoh responded to God's light by hardening instead of softening his own heart. It was Pharaoh's choice, not God's.

The church fathers' use of the metaphor of wax and clay illustrates this dynamic. St. Maximus the Confessor (seventh century) wrote:

God, it is said, is the Sun of Righteousness (cf. Mal. 4:2), and the rays of His supernal goodness shine down on all men alike. The soul is wax if it cleaves to God, but clay if it cleaves to matter. Which it does depends upon its own will and purpose. Clay hardens in the sun, while wax grows soft. Similarly, every soul that, despite God's admonitions, deliberately cleaves to the material world, hardens like clay and drives itself to destruction, just as Pharaoh did (cf. Exod. 7:13). But every soul that cleaves to God is softened like wax and, receiving the impress and stamp of divine realities, it becomes "in spirit the dwelling-place of God" (Eph. 2:22).[45]

Likewise, St. Peter of Damascus (twelfth century) wrote:

We do not all receive blessings in the same way. Some, on receiving the fire of the Lord, that is, His word, put it into practice and so become softer of heart, like wax, while others through laziness become harder than clay and altogether stone like. And no one compels us to receive these blessings in different ways. It is as with the sun whose rays illumine all the world: the person who wants to see it can do so, while the person who does not want to see it is not forced to, so that he alone is to blame for his lightless condition. For God made both the sun and man's eyes, but how man uses them depends on himself.[46]

So the Scriptures and the Orthodox Church understand that it is not the absence or exclusion of God that makes hell; rather, because He is everywhere present, it is the impossibility of completely excluding God that makes life hellish for the lost. Human freedom permits a certain degree of exclusion of God from one's will and life, but total exclusion is impossible—even the continued existence of the lost is the result of His grace and love.

The constant, futile attempt to exclude God from one's heart and life results in ongoing suffering. Stated another way, the unwanted inclusion of God results in hell for those who do not desire Him. As St. Paul says, "Now when all things are made subject to Him, then the Son Himself will also be subject to Him who put all things under Him, *that God may be all in all*" (1 Corinthians 15:28, italics mine).

So to say, "I want to sin but not suffer its consequence," is to state the impossible. It is like saying, "I want to live in darkness, but experience the warmth and brightness of light," or, "I want to live apart from God, My Creator, but receive the blessings and benefits of being in union and communion with Him." Sin is not breaking a law; it is the attempt to exclude God. Holiness and life are not found in keeping the law; they are found in welcoming God's presence. Both paths contain within themselves their own reward or punishment; their consequences are not imposed from without.

Viewing the divine fire of God as an instrument not of torture but of divine love was a paradigm shift for me. Saint Isaac the Syrian (seventh century) said:

> I also maintain that those in Gehenna, are scourged by the scourge of love. Nay, what is so bitter and vehement as the torment of love? . . . It would be improper for a man to think that sinners in Gehenna are deprived of the love of God. . . . The power of love works in two ways: it torments sinners. . . . Thus I say that this is the torment of Gehenna: bitter regret. But love inebriates the souls of the sons of Heaven by its delectability.[47]

In another homily he said:

> I say that those who are suffering in Hell, are suffering in
> being scourged by love. . . . It is totally false to think that
> the sinners in Hell are deprived of God's love. Love is a
> child of the knowledge of truth, and is unquestionably
> given commonly to all. But love's power acts in two ways:
> it torments sinners, while at the same time it delights those
> who have lived in accord with it."[48]

Divine Fire Purifies ᏫᏍᎣ

IT IS A PARADOX THAT THE SAME FIRE THAT PURIFIES GOLD ALSO
burns and consumes wood. It is "like a refiner's fire . . . a refiner
and a purifier of silver" (Malachi 3:2, 3). Previously we discussed
the metaphor of the sword in the fire, where the sword represents
Jesus' glorified human nature and the fire the energy of God's
divine nature. The heated sword represents the indwelling and
energizing of Christ's human nature by His divine nature. When
we bring the sword of our life or nature into contact with the
energized sword of Jesus' human nature by receiving His Body
and Blood and living holy lives, our lives take on similar qualities,
radiating spiritual energy, light, fire, and love.

Extending this metaphor, we can view God as the furnace
a craftsman uses to temper a sword. When a properly prepared
sword is placed within a fire, it is purified and strengthened, and
takes on the properties of the fire by radiating heat and light. If
the metal is properly forged and wrought, it will not be destroyed.
However, this same fire will melt and destroy a sword that is not
properly prepared. This metaphor illustrates how those who desire
God and His light/fire are purified, energized, and transformed,
while those who abhor His light/fire experience destruction.

St. Symeon the New Theologian (tenth century) said:

God heard my cries and from unimaginable heights stooped down and looked upon me . . . uniting himself to me inexpressibly, joining himself to me ineffably, suffusing himself in me unconfusedly, in the way that fire permeates iron or light shines through crystal, so he made me become like fire itself, revealing himself to me as Light.[49]

The fire of God's furnace is a loving fire, for God is love and the divine fire of His presence is love. In discussing love, St. John of the Ladder (seventh century), abbot of St. Katherine Monastery at Mt. Sinai, says of the saints, "for just as subterranean waters nourish the roots of a plant, the fires of Heaven are there to sustain their souls."[50]

The divine light of God is also a two-edged sword. The surgeon's sharp scalpel of healing can also be used as a dagger of death. For the one who permits the master surgeon to wield the knife, it removes the sinful spiritual tumor. In contrast, for the one who distrusts the master surgeon and struggles and resists, the potentially healing and life-giving scalpel can be deadly.

St. John Climacus contrasts those in the process of being purified with the saints:

When heaven's holy fire lays hold of the former, it burns them because they still lack purification. This is what one of those endowed with the title of Theologian tells us [St. Gregory the Theologian of Nazianzus: cf. Or. 21, 2 (PG 35, 1084D)]. But as for the latter, it enlightens them in proportion to the perfection they have achieved. It is one and the same fire that is called that which consumes (cf. Heb. 12:29) and that which illuminates (cf. John 1:9).[51]

This purging or burning of the Holy Spirit is a purification for our good as we receive it in faith and love. I was surprised to find how many Orthodox prayers contain this theme of being tried and cleansed by God's divine fire. As I pray these prayers, I recall St. Paul's imagery of a living sacrifice: "I beseech you therefore, brethren, by the mercies of God, that you present your bodies a living sacrifice, holy, acceptable to God, *which is* your reasonable service" (Romans 12:1).

A few of the prayers Orthodox Christians pray in preparation for Holy Communion follow:

Thou who art a fire consuming the unworthy, consume me not, O my Creator, but rather pass through all my body parts, into all my joints, my reins, my heart. Burn Thou the thorns of all my transgressions. Cleanse my soul and hallow Thou my thoughts . . . that from me . . . every evil deed and every passion may flee as from fire.[52]

With love hast Thou drawn me, O Christ, and with Thy divine love hast Thou changed me. Burn away my sins with a spiritual fire and satisfy me with joy in Thee. (p. 159)[53]

A prayer of St. John Chrysostom:

But let the fiery coal of Thy most pure Body and Thy most precious Blood bring me sanctification, enlightenment and strengthening of my lowly soul and body. (p. 142)

A prayer of St. Simeon the New Theologian:

I who am grass partake of fire. O strange wonder! I am sprinkled with dew and am not burned [consumed], as the bush burned of old without being consumed. (p. 152)

This uncreated fire is both a spiritual and a loving fire, for God is Love and the divine fire of His presence is Love. St. Symeon the New Theologian (tenth century) said:

> God is fire and when He came into the world, and became man, He sent fire on the earth, as He Himself says; this fire turns about searching to find material—that is a disposition and an intention that is good—to fall into and to kindle; and for those in whom this fire will ignite, it becomes a great flame, which reaches heaven . . . this flame at first purifies us from the pollution of passions and then it becomes in us food and drink and light and joy, and renders us light ourselves because we participate in His Light.[54]

I discovered a most fascinating account of Abba Joseph of the Egyptian desert (fourth century), who was kindled by God's divine fire:

> Abba Lot went to see Abba Joseph and said to him, "Abba, as far as I can I say my little office, I fast a little, I pray and meditate, I live in peace and as far as I can, I purify my thoughts. What else can I do?" Then the old man stood up and stretched his hands towards heaven. His fingers became like ten lamps of fire and he said to him, "If you will, you can become all flame."[55]

God Never Stops Loving All ❧

GOD COMMANDS CHRISTIANS TO LOVE EVERYONE, EVEN OUR enemies. This passage from the Sermon on the Mount could not possibly be clearer:

"You have heard that it was said, 'You shall love your neighbor and hate your enemy.' But I say to you, love your enemies, bless those who curse you, do good to those who hate you, and pray for those who spitefully use you and persecute you, that you may be sons of your Father in heaven; for He makes His sun rise on the evil and on the good, and sends rain on the just and on the unjust." (Matthew 5:43–45; see also Romans 12:14, 17–21)

Christ manifested this love most forcefully as He pleaded with His Father from the Cross, "Father, forgive them, for they do not know what they do" (Luke 23:34).

In my earlier years I never felt obligated to follow Christ's directive to love one's enemies, because I never understood it to be a tenet of Judaism or taught in the Jewish Scriptures. Additionally, being raised in the shadow of the Holocaust and during the time of the State of Israel's establishment, my generation of Jews were in no frame of mind to be passively slaughtered as millions had been during World War II. The teaching of Christian pacifism was not popular among the Jews I knew. The idea of loving one's enemies was viewed as excessively idealistic and virtually impossible.

We took some delight in talking about Christian hypocrisy and the ridiculousness of trying to uphold such an impossible standard. Certainly the Christian treatment of Jews throughout history had proven to us that the command to love one's enemies had fallen on deaf ears. Also, it was not lost on us that the most horrific wars, including two world wars, had been fought between historically Christian nations. If Christians "love" other Christians this way, we thought, imagine how they "love" their enemies.

Looking back on my earlier views, I now have no doubt that the progressive revelation of God's love in Scripture culminates in the life of Christ. Discovering God *as* Love and His manifesting

Love in humility had the most profound impact on me. If man is truly created in the image and likeness of God, then we are created to reflect within us His love and humility.

There is perhaps no clearer indication of becoming like Him than loving our enemies. In this we show ourselves to be His children, because we manifest His nature in our lives. God's love for His enemies is the very basis of our salvation, because Christ became incarnate and suffered and died for the ungodly. While we were sinners and His enemies, God saved us (see Romans 5:6–11). That God in humility loves His enemies and tells us to do the same has unfathomable implications.

Additionally, it did not make sense to me for God to tell us to love *our* enemies, while He Himself planned everlasting vengeance on *His* enemies. It seemed much more reasonable that the very changelessness and inescapability of God's love causes pain to those who oppose that love. The fact that He does not annihilate them has also traditionally been considered an act of love because, being created in God's image and likeness, man reflects the Divinity and as such is intrinsically sacred.

Understanding Scripture on the Judgment

SEVERAL PLACES IN THE SCRIPTURES APPEAR TO SAY THAT GOD IS the one who punishes and casts the sinners out of His presence. Examples include the parables of the unforgiving servant (Matthew 18:21–35); the wedding feast (Matthew 22:1–14); the wise and foolish virgins (Matthew 25:1–13); and the great supper (Luke 14:15–24). These all imply that people were punished and cast out at the Master's command. However, these passages should be taken metaphorically; in every case the cause of the suffering is the people's own actions. In general, their suffering is caused by being in the presence of the Master unprepared.

In the parable of the wise and foolish virgins, the poor choices of the foolish ones cause them to be shut out. The doors are closed because the bridegroom is present and they are not prepared. They are excluded from the feast (heaven) as a result of the bridegroom's presence, but they are not closed off from the *effects* of the bridegroom's presence. In the parable of the sower (Luke 8:4–8), the sun causes some seeds to grow and others to dry up. In both cases it is the same sun and seeds.

Moreover, in this life, chastisements are fatherly corrections or, as in the destruction of the Flood and that of Sodom and Gomorrah, necessary to put an end to evil. This is similar to a surgeon amputating a gangrenous limb to save the patient's life. However, such chastisements have reference only to this temporal life; their purpose is to correct what can still be corrected.

I knew that the Scriptures do represent God as a judge and the judged as suffering torment, but I came to understand that such passages should be interpreted in harmony with the whole biblical teaching on the subject. The Fathers taught that such language communicates truth to those who are able to understand only at the most simple and basic level, which includes most of us. St. Basil the Great wrote that such representations of God are given because "fear . . . edifies simple people."[56]

Likewise, St. Isaac said:

> This is the aim of Love. Love's chastisement is for correction, but it does not aim at retribution. . . . But the man who considers God an avenger, presuming that he bears witness to His justice, the same accuses Him of being bereft of goodness. Far be it that vengeance could ever be found in that Fountain of love and Ocean brimming with goodness! The aim of His design is the correction of men.[57]

And St. Theognostos said:

Only through repentance shall we receive God's mercy, and not its opposite, His passionate anger. Not that God is angry with us: He is angry with evil. Indeed, the divine is beyond passion and vengefulness, though we speak of it as reflecting, like a mirror, our actions and dispositions, giving to each of us whatever we deserve.[58]

The Lord's Prayer, the only prayer recorded in which Jesus explicitly teaches His disciples to pray, includes the phrase, "And forgive us our debts, as we forgive our debtors" (Matthew 6:12). Some Christians I have known say this phrase should be understood as meaning that God as a Judge will only be *willing* to forgive us as much as we forgive others. That is, He measures how much we forgive and then responds proportionally.

In Orthodoxy I came to understand this differently. As we are able and willing to love others, we are empowered to experience and integrate the love and forgiveness of God. It is not a legal issue in which a "spiritual scale" is used to weigh debts. When we remove the filthy glasses that prevent us from truly seeing and loving others in spite of their sins, at the same time we see the light of the sun—God's love and forgiveness—more clearly. There is an interrelationship between forgiveness and love: God's forgiveness of our sins is not in accordance with His justice, but in accordance with His love. As St. Isaac of Syria wrote:

Do not call God just, for His justice is not manifest in the things concerning you. And if David calls Him just and upright, His Son revealed to us that He is good and kind. "He is good," He says "to the evil and to the impious." How can you call God just when you come across the

Scriptural passage on the wage given to the workers? . . . How can a man call God just when he comes across the passage on the prodigal son who wasted his wealth with riotous living, how for the compunction alone which he showed, the father ran and fell upon his neck and gave him authority over all his wealth? . . . Where, then, is God's justice, for while we are sinners Christ died for us![59]

The Doors of Hell Are Locked on the Inside ◔

BEHOLD WHAT MANNER OF LOVE THE FATHER HAS BE-stowed on us, that we should be called children of God! Therefore the world does not know us, because it did not know Him. Beloved, now we are children of God; and it has not yet been revealed what we shall be, but we know that when He is revealed, *we shall be like Him*, for we shall see Him as He is. And everyone who has this hope in Him *purifies himself*, just as He is *pure*. (1 John 3:1–3, emphasis mine)

This life is either a foretaste of heaven or a foretaste of hell. Those who go to hell do not *want* to go to heaven; "going to heaven" is not a change of location, but drawing ever closer to the God who is repulsive and abhorrent to them. Some say that there are no doors in heaven—there is nothing preventing the lost from entering, other than their refusal. To "come in" means to commune with God forever. "Ultimately," states C. S. Lewis, "there are only two kinds of people . . . those who say to God, 'Thy will be done,' and those to whom God says, in the end, '*Thy* will be done.' All that are in Hell, choose it. Without that self-choice there could be no Hell. . . . The doors of Hell are locked on the *inside*."[60]

Such is the nature of a loving God. God really *is* Love, rather than merely *having* love. Thus, St. John Chrysostom (fourth century) challenges us to experience the healing and life-giving fire of God's love and presence:

> Let us clothe ourselves with spiritual fire, let us gird ourselves with its flame. No man who bears flame fears those who meet him; be it wild beast, be it man, be it snares innumerable, so long as he is armed with fire, all things stand out of his way, all things retire. The flame is intolerable, the fire cannot be endured, it consumes all. With this fire, let us clothe ourselves, offering up glory to our Lord Jesus Christ, with whom the Father, together with the Holy Spirit, be glory, might, honor, now and ever and world without end. Amen.[61]

We are told that on Judgment Day, as we stand naked before God, the penetrating divine light of His presence will open the "books" of our hearts. His light will reveal what these books contain. They will show whether our hearts are drawn to God or repulsed by Him, either foretasting heaven or foretasting hell. St. Symeon the New Theologian says that it is not so much what we believe or what we do, but what we *are* that will determine our future state. We have either a similitude with God or a dissimilitude with Him:

> In the future life the Christian is not examined if he renounced the whole world for Christ's love, or if he has distributed his riches to the poor or if he fasted or kept vigil or prayed, or if he wept and lamented for his sins, or if he has done any other good in this life, but he is examined attentively *if he has any similitude* with Christ, as a son does with his father.[62]

Chapter 19 ❧ The Divine Fire of God's Love

St. Irenaeus said:

> For as those who see the light are within the light, and partake of its brilliancy; even so, those who see God are in God, and receive of His splendour.[63]

From Glory to Glory: Perfection that Grows ◡

BECAUSE HEAVEN IS PRIMARILY A STATE OF BEING IN WHICH THE redeemed are moving into an ever-deepening life in God, the experience of heaven is not static, but ever intensifying. Yet we are told that not all advance at the same rate. The greater our desire, love, and inclusion of God in our life, the greater is our capacity to receive the divine light and the fuller is our experience of heaven. St. Gregory the Theologian (fourth century) wrote:

> Receive besides this the Resurrection, the Judgment and the Reward according to the righteous scales of God; and believe that this will be Light to those whose mind is purified (that is, God—seen and known) *proportionate* to their degree of purity, which we call the Kingdom of Heaven; but to those who suffer from blindness of their ruling faculty, darkness, that is estrangement from God, *proportionate* to their blindness here (emphasis mine).[64]

An everlasting rejection parallels an everlasting acceptance of God. Just as there exists the possibility of going from glory to glory, of drawing ever closer to God, going deeper and deeper into heaven, there exists the possibility of spiraling down into deeper degrees of hell. That is what the Scriptures mean when they speak of different levels of reward and punishment in the afterlife.

So the Orthodox understanding is that heaven is more than

a place with an inside and an outside. Similarly, it is more than an achieved condition that is static, never deepening or changing. Rather, it is a dynamic, living condition, moving from one degree or level of bliss to a deeper degree or level of bliss. It is an everlasting journey in which the redeemed go, as the Scripture says, from glory to glory (2 Corinthians 3:18).

As we consider the heavenly inheritors, we might ask, will each experience maximum joy and fulfillment, though all differ? The Orthodox answer is that each will experience maximum joy, bliss, and fulfillment, yet it will not be the same for each person. The redeemed will have different capacities to experience bliss, based on the life they have lived and the extent to which they love and desire God. Each will have his cup filled to overflowing, filled beyond his capacity to experience. However, each person will have a different-sized cup. The experience of heaven varies because it is not merely based on forgiveness, but on our degree of sanctity and desire for and love of God.

Another example I like to give is that of a light bulb. One light bulb is fifteen watts and shines to its maximum capacity. Does it shine perfectly? Yes, for it shines as much as a fifteen-watt bulb is able. On the other hand, a hundred-watt light bulb also shines perfectly, but gives off more light. *Both* bulbs shine perfectly, given their different capacities to shine. Here we have the concept of relative, different levels of perfection. In this view, as the transfigured advance in the life to come in heaven, they continue to change and progress from "glory to glory," or from one state of perfection to a deeper state of perfection. How long does this process continue? Forever, because they are forever becoming like God without ever being God.

Of course, mere words are inadequate to describe judgment and salvation. Human language uses words based on our common understanding and experience. The saints and the prophets received glimpses or foretastes of being in God's presence, then resorted to words and allegory to share these experiences in the Scriptures and their writings. St. Paul quotes from the prophet Isaiah: "Eye has not seen, nor ear heard, / Nor have entered into the heart of man / The things which God has prepared for those who love Him" (1 Corinthians 2:9).

Within the Divine Fire of God's Love ∾

SAHDONA (MARTYRIUS) THE SYRIAN (seventh century) wrote:

> Let us embrace the burning fire
> of God's love within our hearts,
> for the heart's purity is born from our closeness to him.
> It is only by unfailing and focused gazing
> that the spirit gravitates to God,
> but when the luminous ray
> of the simple eye of the soul
> is flooded with those intense rays of light
> that flash down on us from on high,
> then it is that the fire of God flares up
> in a great blaze within our hearts.[65]

Being "a living sacrifice," as St. Paul challenges us to be, is not seen as a desirable goal by many. Fewer still would want to be a holocaust, offered up in totality to God.

I think back to my childhood experience of that brick crashing through our window and am reminded of how I was raised in the shadow of the Holocaust. The Jews are a tormented people—not only from without, but also from within. As part of this people, I had to work through my own nightmares and confusion. How to make sense of it all—the centuries of suffering and persecution culminating in the Nazi attempt at genocide and the systematic slaughter of six million Jews during my parents' lifetime. Did these trials serve any purpose?

Only through beginning to understand who God is, and in what sense Jesus Christ presents for us the ultimate victory of life over death, could I deal with my own misery. This is why it was crucial for me to understand what God's love looks like, both in a broken world and in the afterlife. Only in seeing how God loves could I come to understand how *I* should love, and discover in what way love triumphs over death.

We all to some degree suffer trial, disaster, tragedy, pain, sorrow, loneliness, abandonment, despair, confusion, and even dread, horror, and terror. Most view these as abhorrent, destructive, and ultimately of no redeeming value. Yet as human suffering becomes sanctified and illumined with divine light and love, we understand differently. In His Incarnation, God the Word sanctifies not only our fallen human nature, but suffering as well. When in faith we share in Christ's sufferings, we are closer to fulfillment and godlikeness than when we do not.

This is why early Christians considered that the highest calling was to be martyred for the faith. Not the Islamic sort of "martyrdom" of death, in which the goal is to destroy others. Theirs was the true martyrdom of love, in which one is tortured and put to death because of one's unswerving love for God and others, including one's enemies. The true martyr seeks to save life, not destroy it.

Power is popularly understood as gaining increased control and mastery over the world, over others, or even over death itself. In contrast, for the Orthodox Christian, ultimate power is to be godlike, to love as He does, to be humble, to serve, to suffer, even to be smashed, like Christ on the Cross, yet through it all to maintain love and faith as did the Incarnate God.

St. Makarios the Great of Egypt (fourth century) said:

When a soul is full of expectant longing,
and full of faith and love,
God considers it worthy to receive
"the power from on high,"
which is the heavenly love of the spirit of God
and the heavenly fire of immortal life;
and when this happens, the soul truly enters
into the beauty of all love
and is liberated from its last bonds of evil.[66]

Archimandrite Sophrony said:

Unless we go through this fire that consumes the de-
caying passions of our nature, we shall not see the fire
transformed into light . . . in our fallen state burning
precedes enlightenment. Let us, therefore, bless God for
this consuming fire.[67]

For the Christian, authentic ultimate power is to be a human
burning bush, burning with divine love, light, and fire yet not
being consumed or destroyed. It is to be a living holocaust—an
offering to God—knowing that though we lose everything in this
life, we are not defeated if we have God, who *is* Life and Love.
While burning with the fire of God's love, true power is to be
thankful for all things at all times, yet simultaneously willing to
relinquish all things at all times, save God.

My life's sojourn and struggle within the divine fire of God's
Love has led me to discover that the true Jew is a martyr of love.
And true Judaism is fulfilled in the perfect Jew, Jesus Christ, the
ultimate Burning Bush and Living Holocaust.

Endnotes

1   *The Fifty-Third Chapter of Isaiah According to the Jewish Interpreters* (New York: Ktav Publishing House, 1969), pp. 374–375.

2   Op. cit., p. 11.

3   This sermon was delivered by Bishop Kallistos (Ware) on July 13, 1996, during the annual pilgrimage of the community of St. John of Kronstadt at Bath to the Saxon Church of St. Laurence at Bradford-on-Avon.

4   Dix, Dom Gregory, *The Shape of the Liturgy* (London, New York: Continuum, 1945), p. 546.

5   St. Ignatius of Antioch, *Epistle of Ignatius to the Ephesians*, ch. XX, in *Ante-Nicene Fathers*, Vol. 1 (Christian Classics Ethereal Library, http://www.ccel.org/fathers2/).

6   St. Justin Martyr, *First Apology*, ch. LXV, Administration of the Sacraments, in *Ante-Nicene Fathers*, Vol. 1.

7   Op. cit., ch. LXVI, Of the Eucharist.

8   St. Cyril of Jerusalem, *On the Body and Blood of Christ,* Lecture XXII, *Ante-Nicene Fathers*, Series II, Vol. VII (Christian Classics Ethereal Library, http://www.ccel.org/fathers2/).

9   St. Ambrose, Bishop of Milan, *The Book Concerning the Mysteries*, §54, 55, *Ante-Nicene Fathers*, Series II, Vol. X.

10   St. Leo I the Great of Rome, Sermon XCI, §III, *Ante-Nicene Fathers*, Series II, Vol. XII.

11   Ware, Timothy, *The Orthodox Church* (London: Penguin Books, 1997), p. 43.

12   *Ignatius to the Trallians*, 3 (Christian Classics Ethereal Library, http://www.ccel.org/ccel/schaff/anf01.v.iv.iii.html).

13   Irenaeus, *Against Heresies*, Book 3, ch. 3 (Christian Classics Ethereal Library, http://www.ccel.org/ccel/schaff/anf01.ix.iv.iv.html).

14   St. Gregory Palamas, *Natural, Theological, Moral, and Practical Chapters,* 150.

15   St. Basil the Great, *On the Human Condition* (Crestwood, NY: St. Vladimir's Seminary Press, 2005), p. 75. Homily: That God Is Not the Cause of Evil, P.G. 31, 345. (Note that in the concluding sentence St. Basil essentially says that it was the mercy of God that permitted us to be mortal and to die. That is, it was not an act of judgment but of mercy. And this is how Orthodox understand our mortality.)

16   First Canon, Fifth Session (http://history.hanover.edu/texts/trent/ct05. html).

17   Romanides, Fr. John, *The Ancestral Sin* (Ridgewood, NJ: Zephyr, 1998), pp. 32–33.

18   Ware, Timothy, *The Orthodox Church,* p. 223. (Note the first quotation is from *On the Perfection of Man's Righteousness,* iv, 9, and the concluding quote is from St. Dositheus, *Confession,* Decree iii. See also Decree xiv.)

19   *Against Heresies, Why Man Was Not Made Perfect from the Beginning,* Bk. 4, ch. 38, §3.

20   Meyendorff, John, *Byzantine Theology* (New York: Fordham University Press, 1974), ch. 11, §3—"On Original Sin."

21   The Nicene & Post-Nicene Fathers, St. Augustine, Series I, Vol. V, *On Forgiveness of Sins and Baptism,* ch. 28, p. 25 (Christian Classics Ethereal Library, http://www.ccel.org/ccel/schaff/npnf105.doc).

22   See http://www.newadvent.org/fathers/3804.htm

23   Nicene and Post-Nicene Fathers, Series II, Vol. VII, Gregory Nazianzen, Oration 45, §22, the 2nd Oration on Easter.

24   Ibid.

25   For details about the Jubilee Indulgences see the bottom of: *Incarnationis Mysterium,* Bull of Indiction of the Great Jubilee of the Year 2000, Conditions for Gaining the Jubilee Indulgence (http://www.vatican. va/jubilee_2000/docs/documents/hf_jp-ii_doc_30111998_bolla-jubilee_ en.html).

26   *The Catholic Encyclopedia* (http://www.newadvent.org/cathen/07783a. htm.)

27   Ibid.

28   http://www.jonathanedwards.com/sermons/Warnings/sinners.htm

29   St. Anthony the Great, *The Philokalia* (London & Boston: Faber and Faber, 1979), "On the Character of Men," ch. 150, p. 352.

30   *Soteriology* (St. Louis-London, 1946), pp. 101-102; or *Dogmatic Theology*, Vol. 5, referred to in the introduction to Romanides, John, *The Ancestral Sin*, p. 26 (italics mine).

31   St. Athanasius, *On the Incarnation* (Crestwood, NY: St. Vladimir's Seminary Press, 2003), p. 9 (or http://www.monachos.net/patristics/athanasius/di_plain_1-26.shtml).

32   St. Maximus the Confessor, *The Philokalia*, Vol. 2, "First Century of Various Texts," §62, p. 177 (italics mine).

33   St. Athanasius, *On the Incarnation*, §54, p. 93.

34   Metropolitan of Nafpaktos Hierotheos, *The Mind of the Orthodox Church* (Greece: Birth of the Theotokos Monastery, 1998), pp. 147, 148.

35   Gillet, Lev (a monk of the Eastern Church), *Jesus, a Dialogue with the Saviour* (New York: Desclee, 1962), pp. 134–135.

36   Gillet, Lev, *The Burning Bush* (Springfield, IL: Templegate Publishers, 1976), p. 12.

37   Meyendorff, John, *Byzantine Theology* (New York: Fordham University Press, 1979), p. 155. Also see: *Nicene and Post-Nicene Fathers*, Series II, Vol. XIV, *The Seven Ecumenical Councils*.

38   http://www.ocf.org/OrthodoxPage/liturgy/liturgy.html

39   Meyendorff, John, *Christ in Eastern Christian Thought* (Crestwood, NY: St. Vladimir's Seminary Press, 1975), p. 72.

40   St. John Climacus, *The Ladder of Divine Ascent* (Mahwah, NJ: Paulist Press, 1982), Step 23, "On Pride," p. 208.

41   St. Basil the Great, *On the Human Condition* (Crestwood, NY: St.

Vladimir's Seminary Press, 2005), p. 67.

42   *Against Heresies,* 5.27.2 (Christian Classics Ethereal Library, http://www.ccel.org/fathers2/ANF-01/anf01-63.htm#P8900_2545577).

43   *The Philokalia* (London & Boston: Faber & Faber, 1979), Vol. 1, p. 352.

44   Saint Mark of Ephesus quoting Saint Basil the Great, Homily on Psalm 28. Rose, Seraphim, *The Soul After Death* (Platina, California: Saint Herman of Alaska Brotherhood, 1993), p. 209.

45   *The Philokalia,* Vol. 2, p. 116 ("First Century on Theology," 1:12).

46   *The Philokalia,* Vol. 3, p. 78, "A Treasury of Divine Knowledge," Book 1.

47   *The Ascetical Homilies of Saint Isaac the Syrian* (Boston, Mass.: The Holy Transfiguration Monastery, 1984), Homily #28, p. 141.

48   St. Isaac the Syrian, Homily 84.

49   McGuckin, John, *The Book of Mystical Chapters,* pp. 166, 167; quoting St. Symeon the New Theologian, *Hymns of Divine Love,* 30. Koder, SC 174: 366-70.

50   St. John Climacus, *The Ladder of Divine Ascent,* p. 288.

51   Op. cit., Step 28, p. 280.

52   A prayer of St. Simeon the Translator, in *The Liturgikon* (New York: Antakya Press, 1989), Prayers of Thanksgiving after Holy Communion, p. 328.

53   This prayer and the two following are from *Orthodox Daily Prayers* (South Canaan, PA: St. Tikhon's Seminary Press, 1982).

54   St. Symeon the New Theologian, *Discourse 78,* http://catholica.pontifications.net/?p=573.

55   Ward, Benedicta, *The Desert Christian* (New York: Macmillan Publishing Co., 1975), p. 103, on Joseph of Panephysis.

56   St. Basil the Great, *On the Human Condition* (Crestwood, NY: St. Vladimir's Seminary Press, 2005), Homily: That God Is Not the Cause of Evil, P.G. 7.98.

57 *The Ascetical Homilies of St. Isaac the Syrian* (Boston, MA: The Holy Transfiguration Monastery, 1984), Homily #48.

58 *The Philokalia*, Vol. II, "On the Practice of the Virtues," §47, p. 370.

59 *The Ascetical Homilies of St. Isaac the Syrian* (Boston, MA: The Holy Transfiguration Monastery, 1984), homily #51.

60 Lewis, C. S., *The Great Divorce: A Dream* (London: Geoffrey Bles, 1945), pp. 66–67; *The Problem of Pain*, p. 115. Cited in Bp. Kallistos Ware, *The Inner Kingdom* (Crestwood, NY: St. Vladimir's Seminary Press, 2000), p. 208.

61 St. John Chrysostom, Homily LXXVI.

62 St. Symeon the New Theologian, *The River of Fire:* Homily 2, ch. 3 (Seattle, WA: St. Nectarios Press, 1980), p. 119. (The Homily (*logos*) is from the edition of Zagoraios, year 1886, actual page 33–34. Note that this homily is not included in *The Discourses of St Symeon* in The Classics of Western Spirituality, 1980, so it is different from the "Discourse 2" of that edition.)

63 St. Irenaeus of Lyons, *Against the Heresies*, Book IV, ch. 20:5 (http://www.newadvent.org/fathers/0103420.htm)

64 St. Gregory the Theologian, *Oration 40 on Holy Baptism*, 45 (http://www.newadvent.org/fathers/310240.htm).

65 McGuckin, John, *The Book of Mystical Chapters*, p. 76, quoting Sahdona (Martyrius) the Syrian, *The Book of Perfection*, part 2, 4.14. De Halleux 2:36.

66 Op. cit., p. 138, quoting St. Makarios the Great, *Fifty Spiritual Homilies*, 4.13. Dorries, 37.

67 Archimandrite Sophrony, *His Life Is Mine* (Crestwood, NY: St. Vladimir's Seminary Press, 1997), p. 65.